When Americans Came To Korea

by
ADA E. LEEKE with Evelyn Shaw

8211 Paseo del Ocaso
La Jolla, California 92037

Copyright © 1991 by
Evelyn Hanlin Shaw

Library of Congress
Catalog Card Number 91-90508

All rights reserved, including the right to reproduce this book
or portions of it in any form.

NOT TO BE SOLD.
Printed for gift distribution to selected public and school libraries
in the United States of America.

Printed in United States of America

PINE HILL PRESS, INC.
Freeman, S. Dak. 57029

Dedication

*To our neighbor across the street,
well-loved writing colleague
and friend Julie Thieme Olfe*

*And to our world's belovèd friend
Margaret Chase Smith,
educator
and former Senior Senator
from Maine*

Table of Contents

Introduction	ix
Ada E. Leeke—Military Record	xii
Reluctant Feet	1
Military Government personnel in Korea. Why they came and why stayed. The problems of their assignment to a country for which they were not prepared.	
Fish and Guests	6
The native counterpart of RELUCTANT FEET. How they received us in Korea.	
Epitaph to an Empire	12
Repatriation of Japanese in Korea following World War II. Treatment of their property by our Army.	
Woman Without a Country	17
The MacFarlane story.	
The Traitors and the Patriots	21
Koreans attempt to pin down "pro-Japanese collaborators and national traitors" after Japanese surrender.	
Nationalism Versus Communism	26
The conflict between communist influence and nationalist patriots in Korea after World War II.	
A Day In the Field	31
What was done directly by MG officers in the provinces to bring democracy to Korea.	
Assassination of the People, By the People, For the People	33
Korea's leaders. How they voted one another out with bullets.	
Syngman Rhee—Dictator or Democrat?	38
An interview with Doctor and Mrs. Rhee.	
I Meet the Russians	43
A visit north of the 38th parallel during our joint US-USSR occupation.	
United States Military Government in Korea and Economic Cooperation Administration	49
Picture section.	
Man Trouble—Korean Style	94
A WAC officer "leads" a staff of Korean men reporters and interpreters.	
Propaganda is a Two-Edged Sword	98
Our propaganda and Russia's. How each was received by the Korean people.	
You Can't Print That—Unless You Get the Paper	103
The difficulty of writing and printing our Department of Public Information publications. Shortage of materials. The language barrier.	
Life Is a Bowl of Rice	107
What rice means to Korea. Our efforts to direct its price and distribution.	

How Black Was the Black Market? 113
   The causes of the black market in Korea. Cures that did not "take." Why it was patronized and by whom.

Everybody Hates a Cop 117
   Is Korea a police state? Korean police methods, their source and reason for being.

Is There Any Justice? 120
   The Korean judiciary. Its origin, and the circumstances which perpetuated the system.

Youth Springs Eternal 124
   Education—the hope of the new Korea.

One Pace to the Left and Three Behind 129
   Korean women: past, present and future. What Korean men think of our women's place.

Ladies' Night In a House of Repute 134
   A visit to a Geisha house, with commentary on the background of these establishments.

Old Korea 136
   Picture section.

Kilroy's Father Was Here.. 165
   The "old days" in Korea. My father's first arrival. Brief history of America's previous relations with Korea. A few of the personalities involved.

I Meet the Russians Again 169
   Second US-USSR Joint Commission. First official US delegation goes north of 38°.

The United Nations in Korea 173
   Korea becomes a focus of world attention. MG steps down.

Korean Elder Statesman 176
   Interview with Doctor Philip Jaisohn. His thoughts on the new Korea.

First Election in 4,000 Years 179
   The election: Was it really "free"? What its results meant.

Ashes of an Era 183
   Why the Russians shut off South Korea's power supply. I go to the funeral of the "old Korea hand."

MacArthur's Korea 186
   Commentary on MacArthur. The Korea *he* failed.

Paved with Good Intentions... 190
   Where Military Government succeeded, where it failed, and what was left to be done. Some conclusions about the United States on the international policy level, and some lessons to be learned from our stay in Korea.

Introduction

by Evelyn Shaw

I am a novelist whose only work of nonfiction is SPHERES OF INFLUENCE (Pine Hill Press, 1984) a volume of essays on national and international affairs edited by Ada E. Leeke.

Our first collaboration was in 1936, the year we graduated from Stanford. One of our country's leading advertising agencies had invited university journalism directors to choose a most promising student for a nationwide competition. This student would select a name-brand company, review its advertising and merchandising policy and practice, and design a campaign to enhance its already acknowledged national standing. Chilton Bush, at that time head of Stanford's school of journalism, chose Ada Leeke.

Ada in her turn chose Hills Brothers Coffee, a San Francisco-based firm whose factory and offices she visited in preparation for the Bay Area marketing survey that would be the focal point of her campaign. She did all the legwork and the thinking and asked me to do the artwork and copy writing for the ads she wanted, because I drew more easily and she liked my style. I'll never forget the fun we had idea-dreaming — how hard we worked, and how thoroughly: we even revamped their coffee can art, which we agreed was Victorian clutter in a coming age of simplicity.

It was almost a year before our submission was judged: we placed among the top three contestants in the whole country! Ada was then invited via a daunting assignment sheet and questionnaire to enter a play-off by taking what amounted to an examination in advanced advertising and merchandising theory and technique.

By that time she had spent nearly a year as research assistant and writer at the San Francisco CHRONICLE and was a contributing editor on the regular staff of PENINSULAN magazine. This experience had shown her that her true vocation was academic: she did not want to go on as a working journalist only.

She suggested that I continue in the finals for the advertising contest, whose first prize was a job with the sponsoring agency. I was almighty interested in the writing end but utterly without qualification in her side of the endeavor, which was of course basis for The Whole Thing; so we were obliged to bow out of the adventure.

Ada left for Claremont Graduate School, and we did not work together again until after she returned in 1948 from her World War II tour of duty in Korea. Almost immediately she began writing WHEN AMERICANS CAME TO KOREA. When in 1950 she was selected to teach journalism at San Diego City College and advise their student newspaper THE FORTKNIGHTLY, she again asked me to help her. She was working from early morning until late at night in the newspaper office at the college, and because of the Korean War publishers were asking to see her manuscript. If she was to make a timely response to them, she would need assistance.

Here again my services to her were strictly those of a writer and not a doer or thinker in her major fields of history and political science. We worked closely together on the first two-thirds of the book.

But by the end of 1951 she decided it was a story without a market. After many submissions she accepted as a consensus this report by Virginia B. Carrick, then Associate Editor with Appleton-Century-Crofts, Inc.:

> ... We have had several conferences about it and regretfully have come to the decision that events are moving far too fast in Korea to make even a fine background book a good publishing risk ... (9/13/51)

One of the wonders I celebrate in SPHERES OF INFLUENCE is the services of Ada's family to this beautiful little country. They began when in 1910 her father Dana Winston Leeke graduated from the Colorado School of Mines and chose to go by slow steamer, pioneer rail, pack mule and foot to his very first mine near the north Korean border. They extended with brief interruptions until 1950, when his military government assignment as advisor to South Korea's mining industry was completed and he and his wife Mabel Brown Leeke (musician, scientist, teacher) followed their equally distinguished daughter back to the United States.

Ada was born in the northern mining country at Holkol, Hwang Hai Do, Chosen on August 9, 1914. For all of her life she loved Korea as a homeland. Added to this love was a profound talent for thought and scholarship that has made WHEN AMERICANS CAME TO KOREA the moving story of exactly, in everyday human terms, what the United States did and what we just naturally had to fail to do during our post-World War II years of military government.

After she died in the summer of 1988, I found this manuscript—which I didn't even realize she had finished.

I am the first woman graduate of our United States Naval War College, having during my last active years in the Coast Guard Reserve suspended the writing of fiction to complete two fully accredited years of graduate work in naval warfare and national/international affairs. I did this by correspondence, and it took me eight and a half years in which time I read classic papers and tomes on all these subjects. Virtually all of the writing suffers by comparison with Ada Leeke's living-everyday-color approach, the only notable exceptions being works by Harvard's John King Fairbank, by Bernard B. Fall who so unfortunately died young in Vietnam, and by old China hand Kenneth B. Landon—all three dedicated to an understanding of the Far East and all Doctors as well as true masters of the art of straight thinking.

I have rarely had as good a time as I did in Ada's book; and as I laid it aside at last with awe, my first reaction was outrage that no publisher had been big enough to lay this feast before our overfed and yet starving American people who so generally had been subsisting on journalistic junk food.

Then I had to think back as my lady-professor housemate herself no doubt had done in 1951, and understand that so little had ever been known in our country about Korea. When Ada after graduating from high school by correspondence came back home to finish her education at Chaffey College and Stanford, even at supposedly worldly-wise Stanford our peers looked at her blankly and said: "Korea? Where's that?" And as late as the close of World War II when she was in Civil Affairs Training School (which happened also to be at Stanford) the only information on the country of her birth was a single lecture—which she was invited to give.

So in our entrepreneurial world of trade publishing no editor or publisher had the background to appreciate her written history of our relationship with this particular country, at the time she submitted it. In considering what I should do now with the manuscript, once I came up with this thought another even more important realization immediately followed: WHEN AMERICANS CAME TO KOREA—like its author—belongs in the academic rather than in the working-mostly-for-money world. I chose the University of Hawaii for first offering because the professor herself considered it the western center for the study of eastern culture. Their response (February 28, 1990) through Stanley Schab, publications specialist at Center for Korean Studies, University of Hawaii at Manoa:

"All of the evaluators agreed that the manuscript provides a unique perspective on important and little studied events. However, that uniqueness in itself proves a major stumbling block to publication. The work lacks the critical apparatus and methodology of a scholarly analysis; yet as a personal memoir, the limited market precludes publication."

Mr. Schab expressed the hope

". . . voiced by two reviewers . . . that the materials eventually would be deposited in an archival collection; for while the work may be difficult to publish as a separate work, it would provide a valuable and unique resource for scholars in a variety of fields."

Our limited gift edition for public and university/school libraries and major national archives is a response to this suggestion.

The author was a remarkable professional with a uniquely versatile mind. Her relatively short career has been recognized by the WHO'S WHO volumes of American Biographical Institute, Marquis Publications and the International Biographical Centre in Cambridge England who cite her work as a journalist and political analyst as well as her college teaching of creative writing and world literatures. These often-conflicting disciplines are normally entered very separately by widely differing individualists who then find difficulty in getting along together. Professor Leeke's singular gift for bridging such differences is a hallmark of this invaluable history.

The manuscript is unaltered. In the two-year period immediately following her return from Korea she wrote it just as it stands, four-square upon past history as well as on the conditions and questions of its own time. Her story ends at the outbreak of the Korean War in June of 1950.

Evelyn Hanlin Shaw
La Jolla, California
March 1990

ADA E. LEEKE

August 9, 1914 – July 9, 1988

Military Record

1943	Joined WAC, trained at Ford Oglethorpe, Georgia. Commissioned Second Lieutenant
1944	Served as Assistant Public Relations Officer, Fort Oglethorpe
July 1944	Accepted as one of first four WACs by School of Military Government, University of Virginia
Sept. 1944-April 1945	Attended Civil Affairs Training School, Stanford University
April-Oct. 1945	Presidio of Monterey, Civil Affairs Staging Area, Assistant Editor, Post Newspaper
Oct. 1945-Feb. 1946	Ordered overseas, arrived in Korea Oct. 27, 1945. Political Analyst, Department of Public Information, U.S. Military Government in Korea
Feb.-June 1946	Liaison Officer to General Archer L. Lerch, Military Government of Korea
June 1946-March 1947	Editor of Chukan (Weekly) Digest, official Military Government publication (circulation 600,000) for all South Korea
**Nov. 4 1946	Accepted civilian appointment (CAF-11) after separation from WAC
March-August 1947	Editor of Farmers' Weekly, official Military Government newspaper for farmers in South Korea (circulation 600,000)
August 1947-August 1948	Chief of Publications Section (CAF-12) supervising all newspapers, magazines, pamphlets and leaflets issued by the Department of Public Information, U.S. Military Government. Held this position until Korean elections, when Military Government dissolved.

**The separation was necessary because she could not as a captain (promotion was pending) be appointed to the position Military Government wanted her to accept: she was being assigned to a billet which in the military called for a lieutenant colonel.

Reluctant Feet

COMMANDING GENERAL BOOED AT PRESIDIO OF MONTEREY!

This was the headline that burst upon us one morning in September 1945 as we sat down to breakfast in the Military Government officers mess at Monterey and shook out the *San Francisco Chronicle*.

The story told how the Commanding General had berated the Military Government officers who were requesting release from the Army under the new point system.

In a closed meeting the day before, the General had stated his intention to hold us to a contract: We had all promised in writing when we applied for Military Government and Civil Affairs Training schools that we would serve for the duration of the emergency and six months. The point system, he roared, did not apply to us. Our specialized training was all directed to Army administration of occupied areas—and we should have *known* our most important tour of duty would be after the war.

The General then made an award: "To those asking for release, the diaper citation with the safety-pin cluster!"

It was at this point that the booing started—a breach of military law for which any one officer would be courtmartialed. But there were 1,000 in the meeting.

The next morning when we came into the mess hall we found a crowd around the central bulletin board. Somebody had tacked a miniature cellophane diaper, with safety pin, on the General's Order of the Day. Then we opened the newspaper...

No doubt the pin-up was the work of the same officers who went to San Francisco after our meeting, to tell their side of the story to the press. It was incidentally, the only side the public ever heard. And to this day the identity of the officers in the unofficial delegation to the *Chronicle* has never been disclosed.

As a matter of fact the Commanding General, who walked stiff and whitefaced from that unhappy meeting, was technically quite right. But the officers had their reasons too. Personal reasons.

There was a major from Iowa, for instance—a postmaster in civilian life, with a wife and four kids and a little farm. The Army wanted to send him to Korea to help rehabilitate the postal system.

"But I want to see my kids before they're grown up," he said. "And my wife is having a dickens of a time finding extra help on the farm... Anyway, I spent two years in Africa organizing a postal unit at the beginning of the war. I think I've *had* it!"

And I talked to a young lieutenant in the Transportation Corps, a railroad man who was to be shipped over to ride herd on the rolling stock of the new Korea:

"I got married the same time I joined the Army," he said, "and was sent to Europe right after I got out of O.C.S. Sure, Military Government school at Harvard gave me one good year with my wife. But now we have a baby. And they can give me all the Stuff they want about making a decent democratic life for the children of the new Korea. I'm interested in *mine*!"

Perhaps most forlorn of all was the Navy lieutenant, a small-craft expert destined for the Korean Coast Guard or port authority.

"I had twenty months combat in the South Pacific," he told me, "on an LST. Sure, I applied for Military Government school to get out of it, just as the Commanding General says. I couldn't stand it any longer—and Military Government sounded like a good deal... But now we hear the Army's going to be running the show. In the first place," he said, jabbing at my WAC necktie with an emphatic forefinger, "the Army hasn't told us a thing about Korea. The only thing I ever heard in my life about the country is that lecture you gave in Civil Affairs Training at Stanford. But that's the Army for you; and damned if I want to be a dry-land sailor for an outfit like that! And besides: we don't like your Presidio Commanding General! Now in the Navy, we'd have handled that situation *this* way..."

The Army, no doubt to prove that it could, did ship these three officers and many others to Korea regardless of points. But after a rehearing the final decision was that Military Government officers with more than seventy-five points could be released without prejudice.

Others who still lacked a few points of being eligible for discharge went to Korea, added on the resulting "overseas" points, and came right back home again. All this cost the American taxpayers hundreds of thousands of dollars in wasted training and transportation. And the money was not the greatest loss. If the Koreans had been given an opportunity to know our officers as individuals, the burdens of the occupation would have seemed lighter on both sides. As it was, the ridiculously high turnover in Military Government personnel made impossible any continuity in our personal contacts with the Korean officials.

There were certain shining exceptions—American Army officers and civilians whose sympathy and attention to their jobs won loyal support among the Koreans they worked with. But so many officers who came, and even stayed, were there under protest. Not only did they come with no interest whatever in Korea; they stayed under conditions that offered them little or no chance to develop an interest.

The major who had been sent to "liberate" the Imperial Japanese Postal System in Korea burst into my office one day—to get, as he put it, "some lowdown on this goddam country."

The first question he asked, almost pathetic in its earnestness was: "Are the Koreans really as stupid as they act?" He was referring, he said, to the way the men in his department never understood what he wanted—and would smile and bow and look sheepish when he became impatient.

"They're not at all stupid," I said as gently as I could. "There are two things you must remember. One, the language handicap. Two, in our country it is not customary to meet this smiling politeness you speak of. In the States, if you get angry at an employee he gets angry at you. But the real trouble between you and the Koreans in your office is the language difference. And I'm afraid that from their side of that barrier, we must look just as stupid as they do from ours."

He gestured helplessly. "But we have interpreters. What good are they, if they can't keep things straight?"

"Nearly all of them are dictionary interpreters," I said. "And when there is anything at stake, I've never known two peoples to reach an understanding through that medium alone."

"But you use interpreters," he objected, "and you get along with the Koreans."

The Korean I spoke was a kitchen variety I had learned from our servants, entirely unsuitable for speech with Korean officials; so I did employ interpreters. "But I don't always get along with everybody," I told the major. "Who does, anywhere? Knowing Korean customs helps me avoid offending them; but actually I have to be even more careful than you. It is very difficult for these men to work for a woman, and I must see that they understand they are not losing face by doing so." Unconsciously I was choosing my words almost the way the Korean would choose them in English—as I always chose them now unless I was sure my Korean listener spoke idiomatic English.

"The more I hear, the more I want to go home," the major said. "If you get me to thinking of the Koreans as people, then I will be lost. With chessmen, I might eventually bring some order out of the chaos in the post office. But if I have to start worrying about the human side of it—"

"I know," I said. I wanted to go home as much as he did. Or perhaps I wanted to go back to the Korea I had known.

"I still don't understand why everything is in such disorder," he grumbled. "The postal system was good under the Japanese, wasn't it?"

"The best," I said.

"Well, it's still intact, supposedly. The facilities are the same, and except for the Japanese overseers even the personnel hasn't changed... But remember that letter I asked you to mail me?"

I nodded. The letter had been one of several he asked various people to send him as part of a spot check on postal deliveries.

"It took two weeks to get just half way across Seoul to my house. Two *weeks*! And when I tried to find out who was responsible for the delay, what did I get? Smiles and bows!"

The lieutenant in Transportation, the railroad man who had so reluctantly left his wife and baby in the States, was faring no better.

"My god, I've never seen such people! In the first place, you can't believe a word they tell you. I had a man come in the other day and tell me he was an engineer. I was frantic trying to get the yard clear for a shipment of chemical fertilizer to Cholla Pukto. I'd had to unload an incoming string, we're so short of rolling stock. The Koreans destroyed so much of it, you know. Some they just broke up out of spite for the Japanese—and some of the cars were burned when Korean squatters moved in and set up housekeeping after the surrender. They built fires on the plank flooring!"

He was almost shouting with exasperation, and had apparently forgotten what he started out to tell me. "What about the engineer?" I asked.

"Oh. Well, this jerk was sent to my office just as I was about to go out and get the empties up to the loading platform myself. So I practically kissed him on both cheeks. I hired him on the spot, and told him which engine to use, and he went off grinning like a kid. Ten minutes later I heard a locomotive tearing across the yard; and I got outside shouting what-the-hell just in time to see a tremendous grinding splintering crash—my 'engineer,' ploughing into those empty cars. It took two days to fix the engine, and the first car was a total wreck. The shipment didn't get out till the following week. And all because this Korean, who had been an oiler, thought he'd watched engineers long enough to handle a locomotive himself! He knew how to start one, but not how to stop it. Why, that's kid stuff! What's the matter with these people, anyway?"

"They're very proud," I said feebly. "And under the Japanese, they were treated like kids."

One evening at the officers club I met the Navy lieutenant, the small-craft and port authority man.

"How do you like working for the Army by this time?" I asked him. "I understand that at least they didn't beach you—make you a dry land sailor the way you were afraid they would." He was assigned to Chinhai, with the Korean Coast Guard.

"Boy, that's one worry I'd prefer right now, to the worries I've got," he said. "Say, there's something I've been wanting to ask you. Did the Koreans really build the first ironclad vessel?"

"Yes. About 270 years before the Monitor and the Merrimac. They called it a turtle boat. And it was used, incidentally, to beat off Admiral Hideyoshi—in Japan's first invasion of Korea."

"Hmmm," said the lieutenant. "But it isn't so, is it, that Koreans rather than Chinese invented the compass and discovered gunpowder?"

"Yes, that's what Korean historians claim. And no one I know of has been able to prove it's wrong."

"Then I'm afraid I've offended our Korean Coast Guard commander," the lieutenant said sadly, "but I just didn't believe those things could possibly be true. Honest—" and he waved his arms in the hysterical gesture of helplessness that by now was characteristic of most MG officers, "you should see these Koreans aboard ship! We have two little boats, and already one of them is up for repairs because they ran it on the rocks. And as for gunnery exercises—the way they handled the first lesson, I'm afraid to teach them how to load and fire!"

The Koreans, like all Orientals, are a sensitive people. While I know they seldom heard what my colleagues were saying, they knew how they felt about their assignment to Korea. And actually the Korean people are as intelligent as they are sensitive. By the end of our three-year Military Government most of my fellow officers would agree that nearly all Koreans responded well to effective instruction. The trouble was that we did not have the personnel to offer the start-from-scratch type of training the whole country so sorely needed.

Under the Japanese, so few Koreans were given any degree of responsibility in the postal system, for instance, that it did not matter that the system we inherited was theoretically intact. Only a handful of Koreans knew how it should operate; and their numbers, like our own, were insufficient to permit training and supervision of the rest. The result: incredibly poor postal service—and smiles, and bows.

In the Japanese regime, I never saw a Korean locomotive engineer. Undoubtedly many Korean boys, even as our own, dreamed of driving the big iron ox some day. But none ever had a chance, until the liberation. Before that, they were roundhouse coolies. I imagine an oiler was a gentleman of considerable prestige in the old Korea.

Afloat, the Japanese policy was the same as ashore. I never saw a Korean officer or petty officer aboard any of the vessels which served the ports of the peninsula before the war. And one could learn very little about the handling of a vessel from swabbing its decks and cleaning out the cabins and trotting with refreshments for the passengers.

The only thing Military Government could have done to compensate the Koreans' lack of experience in all branches of industry and administration was to retain the Japanese overseers until Korean replacements were qualified, as the Russians did in the North. But we listened to the loud "patriotic" outcry that was raised when we proposed this policy to the Koreans. We wanted to be "democratic."

So we repatriated all the Japanese executives and technicians and replaced them with—well, in many cases, with "oilers" who claimed to be "engineers." It was one of our first and worst mistakes.

And our people made other mistakes daily—without even knowing it. For one thing, we are a very impatient race. The pressure of our everyday lives is a thing of wonder and insanity, to the Koreans. They don't want to get upset. And they figure that time spent hurrying is time wasted, because all you see is a blur when you look back. They love looking back.

Learning itself is with them a gentle, leisurely process. You can imagine, then, the plight of a Korean working in a motor pool for an American tech sergeant. I once talked confidentially with such a Korean.

In the first place, he was insulted at having to work under an enlisted man. In the Japanese regime he would have worked cheerfully for an Imperial overseer with even less authority than the sergeant—because that overseer would have born some impressive title, such as Chief of the Gasoline Section of the Motor Bureau; and because the Japanese would have been overbearing in the Oriental manner, which the Korean understood. At the "democratic" impatience of the tech sergeant, he was bewildered and offended.

"You know I spill gasoline yesterday," the Korean said to me, "and Sergeant use much bad words very loud. All the time he use god words. Only other thing he say is okay, or hubba-hubba. But very seldom say okay!"

Hubba-hubba to the G.I. is Oriental for "hurry"—and to the Koreans, a horrid word.

I had been present at the motor pool the day before and seen—and heard—what happened. The Korean, because he knew me, was now saving face by reliving the incident from his own point of view.

In trying to fill his cigaret lighter, he had tipped over a five gallon tin of gasoline. He righted the tin, dabbed at the pools of gas with a handful of waste—and then stepped aside barely four paces to light a cigaret. The tech sergeant swung a long arm, knocked the cigaret lighter clear across the area—and let loose an almost inexhaustible list of "god words."

After first soothing my young Korean friend, treating him for "shock" with a few polite murmurs, I said: "But gasoline very dangerous around fire." I was speaking kitchen Korean. "If the sergeant had not acted so, you would have lighted your lighter and blown us all up. It acts just like a bomb, when you bring fire near the vapor of gasoline. Did no one tell you, when you took this job?"

He looked sad. "Maybe tell. I not understand English; only pretend understand. Want keep job."

All over Seoul this sort of incident was being repeated, with variations and often without the timely intervention of a tech sergeant. In all, at least four American billets and part of the Capitol building were burned to the ground because of this deadly Korean innocence, or just plain carelessness. For it was also true that many who could understand English did not bother to follow directions if they thought they knew better.

Outbursts of impatience soon became frequent on both sides, as the atmosphere of un-understanding thickened. You saw GI's swaggering four abreast along the sidewalks, shouldering aside Koreans. They were the same GI's who at first said Korean kids looked like little dolls, and gave them candy. The same who got a kick out of having a cigaret to offer a Korean man. You saw, finally, a Korean spit deliberately on an American, and bow and smile. Accident, so sorry! Or a Korean urchin would snatch a parcel from a jeep, and run. And yet these were the very same Koreans who had lined the streets to welcome the GIs as liberators.

Even I was ill at ease—and even among the Koreans I worked with, people who in the old days would have been my friends in spite of dictionary English and kitchen Korean. Their graciousness now made me uncomfortable; for nowhere in the world is business traditionally such a social affair as in Korea—and American personnel, GI's and officers alike, were forbidden to associate with the Koreans socially.

We were forbidden, by order of the Commanding General, to accept gifts from Koreans, even though they proffered them in the gracious Oriental custom which on a simple personal scale carries no implication of bribery. We were forbidden to present gifts to them, though we had so much and they so little. In consequence, Americans were insulting, Koreans began stealing—and everybody was very unhappy indeed with everybody else.

Granted the General's order forbidding us to eat at Korean restaurants was for the very good reasons of native food conservation and possible sanitary hazards; but we were forbidden even to eat in a Korean home. For some of us who had lived there before and had Korean friends, this was impossible. For others who had not lived in

Korea and did not know any of her people, it guaranteed continued separation from and ignorance of the Korean and his ways. In Japan, the occupation was not conducted under this type of restriction; and our greater degree of success in Japan was largely due to the fact that Americans and Japanese were permitted to know each other.

The Koreans themselves, however, must take some responsibility for the way our Commanding General decided the occupation there must be conducted. They are a different people from the Japanese. They are less tractible, more volatile, and not nearly so well trained in the modern necessities—such as sanitation—that would make it possible for an army of occupation to associate with the people in a normal manner.

The Japanese regime is also accountable for the strained conditions under which we occupied Korea. After all, they had forty years to teach the Koreans what Japan knew; but the Japanese imperial policy was to push, rather than lead—and the Korean who feels pushed will stubbornly close his mind.

In our three years as a Military Government, we did very little better than the Japanese had done as teachers in Korea. The time was too short for anything but a beginning; but we did not make a very good beginning.

Perhaps the biggest reason for this failure was a complete lack of official preparation—which may even have accounted in large part for the way our officers felt in the first place about being sent to Korea. Apparently no plans whatever had been drawn for the occupation. But of course until July of 1945—when the secret Potsdam agreement divided the country at the 38th parallel for joint occupation with Russia—no one in Washington or anywhere else seemed to think we would even enter Korea. We did not, after all, occupy Formosa—and that too was part of the fallen Japanese Empire.

So no one drew up a plan like that which helped the occupation of Japan to such a successful working agreement between the two peoples. No Military Government officer assigned to Korea had the sustaining help of a written guide, or even any oral briefing well thought out in advance. Unless he had been there before, he was like a tourist dumped at random without his guide book. Or worse still, like some poor soul who is not a very sharp hand at bridge and lets himself in for a "sociable" game which turns out to be deadly serious. In such a circumstance one is at first shocked by the complications, then roused to anger—principally at his own clumsiness—and finally resigned.

We stayed in Korea then, as we had come—reluctantly. Even I, who knew and loved the spiny little country; for I was listening daily to both sides of a very sad story.

Fish and Guests

*Fish and guests
smell after three days.*
        —an old Spanish proverb

When I returned to Korea, although I had not been in touch with any of her people for nearly seven years, the news soon reached the families who had known of us or been our friends in the old mining days. I am not quite sure how the grapevine operates in Korea, but whatever the way it is swifter than the Korean telegraph system and much more accurate than the society pages of any land.

Certain people then sent word that they wished to entertain me. Two such invitations stand out with special clarity in my memory. One because it was so atypical, the other because it was so Korean—and so American.

On the first occasion, a long shiny-black chauffeur-driven limousine called at my billet. I had no transportation of my own—and certainly could never have threaded my way through the devious streets and alleys of Seoul to an unfamiliar address. The chauffeur shot expertly through the tunnel-like byways, scattering frightened pedestrians to the walls. We went through slums more primitive than any this country has ever seen. But actually they were not slums. They were the ordinary homes of the average Korean.

Stray dogs and grimy children romped among the garbage and litter, and pattered about in the slops in front of mud huts or flimsy wooden dwellings. The smell as we whisked past was of decayed vegetables, unwashed people, urine and human excreta, dead water and sour earth.

Here, in each of these two- or three-room shacks would live two or three Korean families. In normal times, if a man owned his home, he might have it to himself. But now, with so many refugees pouring down from north of 38, he must share his shelter with those of his family who had no other. Even a fifth cousin with two wives and ten children must be housed without question, should he come seeking help . . .

At last, still in the midst of the filth and the noise and the fantastic crowding of the mud or weathered-wood hovels, we drew up to a towering gate in a high tile-topped wall.

Two dusky servants all in white swung open the massive double doors, then closed them after us. Slowly we rolled to the entrance of a magnificent building which I took to be the main establishment.

It was the "waiting room"—from which sprang several bright nervous young men in Western dress, to open the car door. They led us inside to sit on stiff-backed chairs and chat politely until some prearranged signal, discreet as the supersonic whistle, would announce to them that the master of the house was ready to receive his guests.

We left this building, and crossed a courtyard in which green grasses grew and the lotus blossomed and tall cranes stood on one leg by a shining blue-green pool in the manner of picture book prints.

The second building. This would be the one.

But we passed on through, for this housed the living quarters of the family.

Through another courtyard even more fabulous than the first, with brightly painted curved-roofed buildings, and moon gates opening into inner courtyards. From the air the estate must have looked like a string of colored boxes, with green excelsior packed between.

At last we stopped, entering a dining hall with tables set in the Western culture, and chairs. Here, after we were seated, our host joined us.

He was a huge man, in an even more huge white-starched Korean robe—and he made a large, dramatic entrance. He was a high potentate out of Marco Polo's journal—an Oriental prince, in Hollywood technicolor. And he wore great big shell-rimmed glasses. His name was Mr. Yun, and he belonged to a famous and wealthy old Korean family.

The dinner, consisting of numerous courses, was delicious if something of an oddity. In deference to our American tastes, it had been prepared according to the Korean idea of Western cuisine!

Servants moved like the shadows of our elbows, anxious to anticipate our smallest wish and springing to attention at the least gesture. If by chance these white hovering ones overlooked some small desire or difficulty, by a lift of one eyebrow Mr. Yun would indicate the need . . . Here, the eyebrow pointed out, is an American lady who is having trouble with her chopsticks—and in a matter of seconds a discreet brown hand had laid knife and fork under the rim of the lady's plate . . . And there, the eyebrow announced, is a plate but half full—and three men with three wide platters bore down . . .

It was an evening of full Oriental splendor—to most Occidentals the stuff of which dreams are made, for it is the splendor of another world. But I was depressed. The wall was not high enough, for me. I sat at the table thinking ungrateful sad thoughts—such as that no one can help inheriting money and influence, but if ever in our attempt to help the Orient we should ally ourselves or even seem to ally ourselves with the men who were known for their wealth and power, then all of the people of the East would turn and even rise up against us . . .

After dinner we retired to a handsome Korean-style room where we sat cross-legged on silk cushions and sewed a very fine seam of small talk.

The room was large—with sliding panels for walls, against which sat tall Korean chests of polished reddish-brown wood fitted with brass locks and butterfly hinges. And there were low red-lacquered tables bearing cigaret boxes of black lacquer inlaid with mother of pearl. The stone floor, covered with a tawny yellow Korean oil paper, concealed the heating system—a "modern" type in this country, but thousands of years old in Korea. The *kang* or flue was laid under the floor, a device American architects have recently discovered is the best for keeping a room at an even temperature.

"Yes, we are glad the Japanese have left." My host's raised voice came to me in a sudden hush after the usual confusion of after-dinner murmuring. "But the Japanese did a great deal for our country. They improved the roads, put in the rail system. They introduced modern industry. So after all, the Koreans who worked with them in doing these things were in their way working for the good of Korea."

It was a strange remark, to me, for I had not heard anyone introduce a question which led to it; and I was reminded of something the Military Governor had told me not long before, about a certain Mr. Pak. Mr. Pak, it seemed, had been a collaborator. Or at least that was what his countrymen were saying; and now his life was in constant danger. In seeking to establish whether the charges were true, and determine whether Military Government should offer him protection, Lt. Gen. Arnold, the Military Governor, had talked with Pak.

"Yes," said Pak, "it is true that I did own an aircraft factory which was supposed to produce planes for the Japanese war effort. But I did not finish a single plane. So actually do you not consider that I was doing my country a service, in tying up and wasting so much Japanese money?"

But, said the Koreans, a substantial part of this Japanese money had been "tied up and wasted" by Mr. Pak himself—in his mansion, that was big enough for one hundred families—and in his huge department store, itself a gold mine throughout the regime of the Japanese.

It is always so difficult to find the truth about anyone. But this evening I was uneasy and a little suspicious—partly because my host was an acquaintance of an acquaintance, rather than a friend. I sat cross-legged on a rust-colored cushion, politely answering his questions and trying to stifle the thought that I had been invited because of my father's recent appointment to Military Government's Division of Mining in the Department of Commerce.

My nasty little thought did not fit what I knew about this family. Yun Chi Ho, uncle to my host, had been one of the four leaders of the Progressive Party—a party whose members at the turn of the century had risked death and loss of fortune in their efforts to reform the Lee Dynasty and rid Korea of feudalism and political corruption so that she could take a place in the modern world.

Some of the Progressive Party leaders, including top man Soh Jai Pil, finally concluded that Japan's eagerness to help poor backward little Korea was a false promise—that Japan's intent was to subjugate and exploit. The Korean Progressive leaders who voiced this opinion eventually left their country in disillusionment, even disrepute; for no one would listen to their warning . . . But what of the fourth leader, Yun Chi Ho? I could not remember, try as I would, what had happened to him.

Many months later I learned that Yun Chi Ho had been considered such a close collaborator with the Japanese during World War II that after they surrendered he felt it necessary to commit suicide. Either he had not believed with the other three Progressive Party leaders, that Japan was an enemy, or he decided the enemy was more powerful and collaboration the greater part of discretion.

In any event, Yun the nephew carried on, displaying equal adaptability—or opportunism, as the case may be. Obviously he continued to interest himself in the Department of Commerce, for he ultimately became its Minister in the South Korean Government.

My second invitation came of friendship—from the nephew and son by adoption of K. I. Yun. Yun the father was a graduate of the Royal School of Mines in London. He had operated his own mines in Korea as subsidiaries to British and American enterprises, selling the gold to our companies. More than that, his professional skill and his friendship actually helped these early British and American mining engineers to success in a strange little country where they would literally have been lost—or have found nothing—without a native colleague.

Yun the son was now living in Seoul—in the Gold Coast area, where most of our high-ranking Army and Military Government officers were assigned to luxurious quarters commandeered from former Japanese officials. This Yun family, incidentally, was no relation to Yun Chi Ho and his nephew. There are very few surnames in Korea—so Yuns, Paks and Kims are very common. That is why each person is called by all three of his names; and I am told that actually you do not find in Korea nearly so many duplications as in a Manhattan telephone book!

On the appointed evening the car of Yun the younger called for me. It was a well worn 1939 Ford—a charcoal burner under wartime fuel shortages, now reconverted to gas. Only a few of the scars were showing.

This time we rattled cautiously through the teeming streets—and our courtesy was rewarded with the stares and the lethargy of pedestrians who realized there was no danger.

Mr. Yun's home was spacious and beautiful in its simplicity. Its architecture was the functional type, traditionally Japanese—again a development Americans call "modern," which has made famous our more daring architects. Its floor-to-ceiling windows looked out on a Japanese garden. And there was one Western-style room, where my friends awaited me in a polite circle.

Teddy Pak was there, who had been office manager at the Oriental Consolidated Mining Company where my father spent several years. Mr. Pak wore a grey pepper-and-salt business suit, cut from an approximation of wool which the Japanese had dumped on the Korean market. He was an older man, kindly, solemn and judicious in appearance, who always considered well before speaking and then chose his words with careful regard for their effect.

Also present was Huh Wha Kun, who because of his ability to get along with people had been selected to work with the Japanese liaison officer the Oriental Consolidated Mining Company hired to keep peace with the Empire. Huh was a very unusual Korean—a big jolly one who shook like a pudding when he laughed, and whose moon face, solid good humor and Santa Claus physique had earned him at the mine the nickname of Fat Huh. This evening as always, Huh wore Korean clothes. White of course.

White in Korea was originally the color of mourning, worn by all the people for three years after the death of a king. At one point in the country's history monarchs died off so fast that white became literally the national habit. Otherwise Mr. Huh's costume was exactly like that of his ancestors who brought the latest styles from China at the time of the Mings—short collarless jacket crossed and tied in a bow at one side (buttons are a Western innovation), loose floppy trousers with low-slung seat and ankle ties. A pair of unpolished broken-down Western oxfords were the only modern touch.

The dinner, after my prolonged digestive bouts with C-rations, was a rare adventure. There was delicately flavored soup, with tiny noodles cut all by hand, and little meat balls of the kind that in the Orient are a painstaking delicacy rather than a leftover. Following this we ate of twenty dishes, a little from each, that would correspond to Western entrees.

In Korea, when the host sees that you have room for something more on your plate, it is good manners for him to choose special morsels for you with his own chopsticks. Frequently during the meal Mr. Yun showed me this courtesy. I remember particularly how tender the meat was; for in Korea the cattle are used as beasts of burden and their flesh extremely well exercised before it ever reaches the table.

These "main" dishes were accompanied by an endless line of extras such as pickles and little shrimp—and by the fundamental sounds of appreciation which most Koreans still consider it is only polite to make over good food: smackings, slurpings—and then, as terminal punctuation, one loud belch. All my friends were eating in the Korean manner this evening—all, that is, but Teddy Pak, who was a graduate of a Los Angeles high school and extremely proud of his American table manners and idiomatic English.

At last the meal was ended with "dessert"—a huge bowl of rice—and tea.

I had come bearing a carton of cigarets—the only thing I had to offer—and now we smoked, and talked. Koreans do not talk much during a meal. First comes the food, then afterward the conversation—each equally important in its place.

We talked this evening about the new Korea and its problems. How wonderful it was to be liberated—and how confusing. There were so many political parties, my friends said, and so many opportunists making capital of the disrupted economy.

The true Korean is a much more sensible and enterprising person than Military Government ever gave him credit for. But then not one MG officer in a hundred ever talked as man to man with a Korean who was a success in a private business or professional field. As a matter of fact men like my host Mr. Yun, who would have been successful anywhere in the world with even half a chance, were likely to meet with prejudice from American officers by now infected with the general idea that only collaborators managed to accomplish anything during the Japanese regime. We as well as the Koreans too often failed to distinguish between competent energetic men who worked in the open, like this Mr. Yun, and ambitious politicians who finagled behind the scenes, like my first host.

Young Mr. Yun was twice suspect, for he had married a Japanese woman.

Mrs. Yun ate at the table with us, the only time in my life in Korea that I was ever permitted the pleasure of my hostess' company. After days and days of preparing the meal, most Korean women merely come to the door—if asked by their husbands to do so or if the guests insist—and smile, and bow. Mrs. Yun exchanged ideas with us, in better English than any of the men. She was a wife who would have been rare even in Japan, for she was a college graduate.

She was petite and vivacious, as most Japanese women are. And assertive, which most of them are not. This evening she was dressed in Korean costume, a long flowing white silk skirt topped by a short powder blue jacket. Her thick lacquer-black hair was drawn back in a knot held in place by crossed straight pins of ornamental silver, extremely heavy as they are greater in thickness than a knitting needle. A few officers I knew bought these pins for mixing drinks. They made excellent muddlers.

Mr. Yun, unlike most Korean men, was tall and light skinned—and unlike most of the Korean men in Military Government, a little hesitant. But his was the hesitancy of thought, not of apology; not of fear, but of wanting to make sure.

It was Mr. Yun the father who had said to my father: "You cannot give Koreans democracy in packages." And Yun the son was still eying the package our government had shipped to his people.

"That's just the trouble," Fat Huh said to me. Without any perceptible gesture, he indicated the young Mr. Yun. "All our best people are holding back. They are waiting to see what is going to happen."

"Opportunists," Mr. Pak, the office manager, nodded and looked at me solemnly over his spectacles, "that's what your Military Government is getting now. Not the ones who say to themselves, this is the new Korea and I want to help. You are getting the politicians, the ones who see every new order as a chance to help themselves!"

It was true and I knew it. But so few of our officers could tell who was who in this strange land. They knew only that there was a job to be done. If a Korean appeared who could speak and write English, they hired him as a translator—almost without question, even though the position of translator was at that time the most powerful in the new Korea!

"The thing for both sides to do," Mr. Yun was saying, "is to go slowly. There is so much for both sides to learn. Our people must learn to work. They do not know how. They must learn how to be independent. That too is a matter of work; it is a matter of not thinking that merely because there is no hard master, there will be no more hard work."

Mrs. Yun sighed, and as the men began to engage in further talk about work, turned to me.

"Most of us must spend so much time at serving without knowing—at laboring without being informed what it is we are working on," she said. "Our people are in this position, because there is no one who can explain what is going to happen. We must simply wait. And I feel so sorry for your boys, for it is the same with them. How they must hate it here!"

"I'm afraid they do," I said ruefully. GI's, unlike most of the officers, had been sent with absolutely no choice in the matter. And the difficulties of supply and quarters in the early days of Military Government did nothing to soften their discomfort or their disdain for a little country which, they were fond of saying, smelled a lot older than its 4,000 years. "But you understand they're a restless lot, as most Americans are," I said to my hostess. "They think there's nothing for them to do here—in their spare time, I mean."

"I know," she said. "And there isn't!"

"It's not the fault of your people," I said. "They tried."

She looked at me, and a sad little smile tracked the corners of her eyes.

In the beginning of our occupation, along the street that led to the Capitol building—Kwand Ha Mung, but called Pennsylvania Avenue because no American could ever remember its Korean name—there had sprung up dozens of cafes and entertainment places. These were part of an effort by enterprising Koreans to please the American soldier and to exploit him, the two motives being amiably mixed in equal parts.

The typical Korean cafe is a black hole lighted by one uncovered forty-watt globe, and furnished with stiff-looking round tables and wood or wicker chairs reminiscent of the American ice cream parlor of the gay nineties. There ends the resemblance to anything we have ever seen or smelled. The building itself is flush with the sidewalk, which is "washed" with the dishwater and the slops of every day. A gaudy sign—blinding blue, perhaps, with "yaller" letters—announces that here is the Tradewinds Bar, or the Hollywood Grill—or the Rapid Realization Bar and Grill, named no doubt for the Korean Society for the Rapid Realization of Independence. Inside, the smell's the thing—a combination of dead fish and soured cabbage.

In their haste to have "rare old" Korean brandy to offer the GI guest, these Korean innkeepers fell to using methyl alcohol to fill the rare old empty bottles in the back room. Knowing the Koreans, I am quite sure they did not realize that their guests would sicken and die, or go blind.

Other places catering to GI's were located on top floors of bank or department store buildings—dance halls, they announced themselves. From somewhere had sprung "new Korean" girls, svelte and sophisticated. They could rhumba and tango, the GI's said, better than most girls in the States. But the Commanding General seemed to question what these girls' other accomplishments might be, for he soon put off limits all the dance halls as well as the bars where our men had been poisoned.

This, then, was the "recreation" situation for American soldiers.

"Isn't it awful," Mrs. Yun said, and her eyes shone with regret, "the pathetic effort we made. Now some of those proprietors were good business men. The Moon Palace, for example, was a legitimate dance hall. And the American Bar and Grill—no one was poisoned there, and it is a respectable place in spite of the sign."

We laughed together. The sign was misspelled: American Bar and Girll.

"But," Mrs. Yun continued, "a few hasty, careless people have spoiled the whole situation for both sides. You understand?"

I smiled mirthlessly. "I wish I could say that I didn't," I said. "I wish it didn't sound so much like home!"

My next meeting with Mr. and Mrs. Yun was on the steps of the Capitol building. I was just returning to my office. And they looked as if they did not know where they were going.

"We have been waiting all day to see the Military Governor," Mrs. Yun told me, "but he will see no one. We did not even get past the Korean receptionist in his outer hall."

"He sees very few people," I said soothingly, and quite truthfully. "Perhaps I could do something to help?"

"An American Army colonel is going to move into our home," she said. "He will not believe that it is our home, that we bought it from a Japanese before he left. We did not move in as squatters, as your colonel thinks. See—we have the bill of sale. But no one will look at our bill of sale."

It turned out that I knew the colonel, Executive Officer to the Military Governor. He was a very amiable colonel, who had no idea he was encroaching on the private rights of a Korean citizen. Most of the Koreans now living in the Gold Coast *had* moved in as squatters after the repatriation of the Japanese. And the colonel, even if he had looked at it, would not have been able to tell the bill of sale from an Oriental laundry slip.

"I know someone who can help," I told the Yuns. "Let me make an appointment for you with Major Weems."

It is to Military Government's credit that whenever it could find officers who knew the country, it sent for them. But they were so pitifully few. Major Weems was the son of a missionary, who did understand Korea and its people and who spoke the language like a native. He helped the Yuns present their bill of sale to the Executive Officer and convince him of its validity. But the incident left me wondering what would have happened to the Yuns if they had not chanced to run into an old friend on the Capitol steps that day—and what might be happening day in and day out to the thousands of Koreans who would not know anyone to appeal to when trouble came.

It was due to misunderstandings exactly like this I am sure, if varying in degree or scope, that the Koreans and the Americans drew apart. We will never know how many of the deserving we mistreated—or how many of the undeserving got fat government jobs. We do know that gradually the day of rejoicing kept fading—the day we liberated the Koreans and they welcomed us. Gradually the walls rose higher, the barriers of incident being added to the barrier of language. Gradually our hosts wearied and sickened of our presence, and began to wish we would go home.

Epitaph to an Empire

My first Army billet was the former home of a Japanese banker named Mr. Tanaka, who had evidently hustled out of Korea at the first sign of the surrender. As the Japanese departed, MG was gradually taking over their residences in Seoul.

The southern capital of Korea is a city in a cup, its rim formed by seven high hills. In the days of the Mongol invasions, this offered a natural protection; but snaking over the hills are still to be seen the crumbling remnants of a twenty-foot wall the Koreans built around 1400 A.D., when they were first discovering that "natural" protection is not enough.

Now the seven hills of the city were blanketed with the estates of Imperial Japan's officialdom—homes palatial even by our standards, with dozens of foreign and Japanese-style rooms, long glass-enclosed verandas, and exquisitely landscaped gardens.

From these heights, for forty years the builders of empire had looked down on the natives of Seoul—who pushed noisily through narrow muddy streets, or crowded together in squalid slum dwellings, grubbing the years away to keep the conqueror housed in his eminence. For forty years hatred had burned in every one of the silent, suppressed Koreans who squinted up at the houses on the hill or jumped out of the way of the imported Japanese cars honking imperiously down their little streets.

After the surrender and once the protection of American occupation forces was assured, the people loosed all their pent-up pride and fury. In wild bursts of rage they rose in mobs and destroyed everything that reminded them of the Japanese. Only American M.P.'s and a vestigial feeling of awe kept them from tearing apart the Japanese themselves.

Night after night Koreans surged through the streets and up the hills to loot the many mansions our police were too few to guard. They overturned streetcars, and beat upon them with axes and clubs. They broke all the windows of the Japanese schools. They heaved boulders against factory gates, swarmed in to uproot and take away the big machines that under the Japanese had kept their country supplied with shoes and electric light globes and textiles and glass.

What happened to the machinery? The Koreans never throw anything away. Some of it was carted home, to rust in the back yard. Or maybe they could sell it. The whole three years I was in Seoul, a monster of a ring gear sat outside a shop I passed every day on my way to work. The shop sold pots and pans and knickknacks—and probably never will find a buyer for the ring gear. No Korean, one of our engineers told me, could ever possibly use it.

As for the schools they damaged, for a long time after the factories were sacked, there was no glass to replace the windows. When Military Government reestablished the school system that first winter, the Koreans themselves were obliged to occupy frosted classrooms—in earmuffs and mittens, if they had any. And most of the students had to walk miles to their classes, as only thirty-one streetcars were left to serve the near-million population of Seoul.

To most American working in Military Government, such unreasoning destruction was as exasperating as it was incomprehensible.

"Don't those damn gooks realize what they have done?" they would ask me, their voices rising to the falsetto of that desperate indignation which comes of being mad and not being able to go home. "The idiots expect us to help them progress *from* the Japanese era. The way things are now, we'll do well if we pick up the pieces and get the country back in the shape it was then!"

To me the situation would have been just as baffling, just as disgusting, were it not for a series of pictures from my childhood which will always be there in my mind—although I as well as the

Koreans might wish they could fade and be forgotten. In one, I see myself standing on a hill in North Korea overlooking the mines where my father worked. Great gashes in the mountainside above the little Korean village showed where the gold-bearing ore was being dug. The huge corrugated-iron stamp mill pounded in my ears. There, day and night, the ore was being pulverized and the precious yellow metal extracted.

The scene was familiar enough—in fact the only one I had ever known. But on this particular day there was an unaccustomed stir in the village; and out of this muted buzzing and milling, suddenly a long thin line of white-clad figures was winding its way up the hillside toward me.

As they got closer, a terror came over me and froze me—so that I did not cry, or run away. I stood and watched.

Most of the figures were women and children. Their white robes were dirty and torn, and bloody gaping wounds showed through. Weeping, or white-faced and silent, they made their way past me—on up the hill to the only refuge they knew, the company hospital of the American mine.

That was how I, a child of five, saw the passive Korean Revolution of 1919. It was explained to me, too, I remember; but I did not understand it then, any more than those women and their children understood it. Their wounds had been made by Japanese dumdum bullets. Unarmed, they had gone to the Gendarme stations to plead for the release of husbands and fathers taken into custody. Spring rice planting time was near, and the paddies lay dry and barren, with no men to hold the plow. . . .

The main event in this pitifully unequal encounter had taken place in Seoul. In February of 1919 the Old Korean King, who long before had been forced to abdicate, died under rather suspicious circumstances and it was rumored he had been poisoned by the Japanese. His funeral on March 1 was the occasion for what has become known as the Independence Movement, theoretically inspired by Woodrow Wilson's recent advocacy of "the self-determination of peoples."

On the morning of the Old King's funeral, thirty-three Korean men representing all religions, sects and classes met in a Seoul restaurant and read a carefully prepared Declaration of Independence based on the American document. They then called the Japanese police, informed them of what they had done, and said that they would wait at the restaurant to be carried off to prison. This suggestion was promptly complied with.

But the flare-up they caused was not to be so easily suppressed. Thousands of copies of the Declaration had been secretly distributed throughout the city, especially to a great crowd gathered in Pagoda Park. As the police drove through the streets the crowds broke into cries of "Mansei! Mansei!" (May Korea live ten thousand years!) Little Korean flags with their red-and-blue centers on white were brought out and waved wildly. Yet not a hand was raised in violence. The orders of the leaders had been strict:

> "Do not speak impolitely to the Japanese.
> Do not use your fists.
> Do not throw stones.
> For these are the acts of barbarians."

A new kind of revolution had begun.

On the wonderfully umbrageous grapevine which flourishes in Korea even today, the news spread over the country; and by nightfall in hundreds of villages such as our own, petitions had been presented and demonstrations begun.

The reaction of the Japanese was anything but passive. In Seoul, it is said, the police rode through the streets on their high-spirited horses catching the demonstrators on grappling hooks or trampling them to death. Tens of thousands were thrown into jail and flogged. Additional thousands were shot and killed.

The Japanese tried desperately to prove that the Christian missionaries had incited the people to rebellion. When they captured demonstrators they attempted to force them into "confessing" that they had been urged into insurrection by the "foreigners." We were horrified to hear that in a town called Suwon some thirty miles from Seoul, kerosene was poured over a Christian church and the church burned with its congregation in it.

When my parents returned to the states late in 1919 with such frightful tales still fresh in their minds, they repeated them—and told the things we had seen—in spite of veiled Japanese police threats that they would never be allowed to return if they talked. Good Americans were frankly incredulous. Japan was a civilized country! Its dainty and courteous people never would be capable of such barbarous cruelty!

Actually this particular aspect of Japanese "civilization" was not new to Korea. It had first been introduced much earlier than 1919—back in the sixteenth century, when Japan woke up and stretched and looked around her and saw the Korean peninsula was like "a dagger pointed at her heart." From then until modern times, Japan's every effort has been directed toward grasping the handle of that dagger.

We have long had in our home a token of the first attempt made in 1592 under the Japanese General Hideyoshi. It is a metal box dug from an old Korean grave. Such work, in which two metals are combined in intricate design, is a lost art in Korea but flourishes today in Japan — under the name of damascene.

Although Koreans finally succeeded in beating off Hideyoshi with their "turtle boat," the first ironclad vessel in history, the country never completely recovered from the effects of the Japanese invasion. The entire land was laid waste; and when Hideyoshi retreated he took with him Korea's master craftsmen in the fine arts of ceramics and metal design. They were forced to teach their secrets to the Japanese and then were killed, thus destroying forever these arts in Korea and presenting them to the world as "native" Japanese satsuma and damascene. Hideyoshi also carried off a fine collection of pickled Korean ears and noses. The "victory" mound where they are buried can still be seen in Kyoto.

For a number of years Japan plotted her revenge for the turtle boat disaster. The opportunity came in 1894 when an uprising in Korea caused both China and Japan to send troops into the country — China to protect her shadowy suzerainty and Japan to prevent China from extending her control. The result was the Sino-Japanese war, from which Japan emerged completely victorious and with a well-entrenched sphere of influence on the peninsula.

In her new role of big sister and protector, Japan prepared a list of reforms for her newly acquired charge. Some of them were excellent, such as those which abolished slavery, distinction between classes in vying for government office, and arrest of the family and relatives of a criminal.

However, the large number of Japanese advisors who arrived in Seoul prepared countless other ordinances to regulate and change age-old customs — just as large numbers of Americans were to do fifty years later. Some of these were deeply resented by the Koreans — for example the law forbidding the top knot worn in celebration of manhood by all Korean married men. To the Koreans this was as much a token of Japanese domination as in China the cutting off of the queue a few years earlier had been the token of Chinese subservience to the Manchus.

When my family first came Korea in 1911 immediately following Japan's formal annexation of the peninsula, Korean men in the back country where we lived were almost invariably refusing to obey this order. Even today one finds occasionally an old gentleman who still wears a twisted skein of hair on the top of his head, dimly visible through the mesh of a horsehair hat.

In other ways too we saw the Koreans humiliated — and reduced to second class citizens of the Japanese Empire, "hewers of wood and drawers of water." The Gendarmerie or military police, swaggering and clanking their sabres, carried the word of Japan even to our little mining village in North Korea. In the classrooms too, we could hear the Imperial teachers punctuating their eulogies on the glories of the Empire with the rattle of the short swords they wore in evidence of its temper and attainments.

In all textbooks and public documents the Korean language was supplanted by Japanese, and teaching of the 4,000-year history of Korea was forbidden. Every public utterance was closely scrutinized for evidence of nationalism, and swift arrest followed the least suspicion of disloyalty to Japan. A missionary told us that his pastor was promptly arrested for preaching a sermon on "Love your enemies."

> Korea had no enemy but Japan.
> So, this must refer to the Japanese.
> Ergo: it was disloyalty to the Empire.

Economically Japan's national policy was to turn Korea into a huge workshop from which the Zaibatsu, or great Japanese merchant families, could increase their own wealth and Japan's war potential. The Koreans became the not-too-bright youngsters who were ordered to oil the wheels or scrub the floor and do as they were told. Never were they permitted the glow of personal pride which comes of equal partnership. And eighty percent of their country's wealth eventually passed into the hands of the Japanese.

The most glaring sign of Military Government's unpreparedness was that we had at first planned to simplify our own task by directing the Koreans through Japanese colonial officials. It was soon obvious that such a course would be worse than useless, as the Koreans refused to work either with or for these bureaucrats. When we yielded to the

Korean demands on this point, we should have made a compromise. We should have insisted that we would send home the high officials of empire on condition that the Koreans would work with Japanese technicians and supervisory specialists until competent native replacements could be trained. But no; we did not give ground, we evacuated our position completely; we promised to get the 700,000 Japanese in Korea, engineer and bureaucrat alike, back to Japan as quickly as possible.

By the time I arrived, processing and repatriating these thousands of Japanese colonials had already begun. The undertaking was complicated by the additional thousands of Nipponese daily pouring into the southern zone from North Korea as the Russians sloughed them off. The refugees came across the border on foot, then rode down to Seoul on the South Manchurian Railway which bisects Korea like a spinal column.

Every day at Seoul Station I saw long lines of Japanese descending from box cars and plodding wearily to one of the Shinto shrines in the city for shelter. From all parts of Korea and Manchuria they came, on the long road back to Japan.

Near my billet, the Tanaka House, one of their relief centers was located. As the refugees straggled by I could not help being affected by the women and children bent almost double, heavy packs strapped to their backs. Their soiled and ragged clothing hung on bodies emaciated by months of near-starvation. In their eyes was unfathomable bewilderment at the disaster which had struck them—they who a short time ago had been the emissaries of an empire, and now were writing its epitaph.

Military Government entrusted the care and processing of all Japanese to the Sewaikai, a Japanese relief society working under the supervision of Americans in the Office of Foreign Affairs. The Sewaikai promptly set up twenty-seven refugee camps in the shrines and temples of the city, as well as a relief hospital. They did their work so efficiently that by the end of December 1945, 570,000 Japanese were back in Japan.

Those who remained were clinging desperately to their crumbling world. One evening I was invited by Lt. Wellington Wales, the American officer in charge of licensing Korean newspapers and familiarly known as "Duke," to visit a Japanese family he had befriended. Both of us were looking forward to the sukiyaki dinner, a welcome break from the canned meat or beans usually served in the officers mess.

The family spoke no English. I managed small conversation in halting Japanese, while the beef, cabbage, bean sprouts and bean curd—which would be ladled over our huge bowls of rice—simmered on the low table. Meanwhile we drank hot saki from tiny porcelain cups—and shifted uncomfortably from one awkward approximation of the Japanese eating position to another. At formal dinners they kneel, instead of sitting cross-legged as the Koreans do.

After dinner we adjourned to a large room with sliding paper doors, where we admired a gold-encrusted Buddhist shrine and beautiful hand-painted scroll or kakemono hanging in a niche in the wall. In Japan they change the kakemono each season, and this was a scene appropriate to the fall. Too late we remembered that in the Orient it is absolutely necessary to offer a guest anything he particularly appreciates. The kakemono was thrust in Lt. Wales' hand.

He put it from him almost in panic, and asked me to interpret a polite but firm refusal.

Next they turned their attention to the feminine taste. At first we thought it was merely for our entertainment that the stooped grey-haired grandmother opened a wooden box and carefully set up a round-faced doll in Buddhist robes. Then she was bowing low, asking me to accept it.

"Don't touch it!" Duke hissed in my ear.

"Why not?" I hissed back. "We don't want to insult them. Besides, they can't very well take a doll back to Japan." Each person was allowed only as much as he could carry in a large pack on his back.

"That's just the point," he whispered. "They don't want to go back to Japan. They're trying to obligate me, can't you see? They've even asked me to come here and live. They don't realize it wouldn't do them the least bit of good!"

Within two weeks the family departed. Their beautiful household furnishings were probably eventually sold in the Kanebo store, which was opened to dispose of all abandoned Japanese goods.

All personal possessions above what they could carry, the Japanese were required to pack and leave in Korean warehouses. The owners were given receipts, and evidently fully expected their belongings would someday be shipped to their new addresses in Japan. Instead these thousands of bundles were broken into and the contents sold to the occupation troops.

In spite of this the Koreans thought we were far too sympathetic toward the Japanese. They were furious that many of us had learned the Japanese language in Military Government school instead of Korean, which was much older and more honorable! Although almost all the younger generation could speak and write Japanese, when we tried to use it they only stared at us and pretended not to understand. Of course with only six months of the language behind us, we never could be quite sure that they did!

Koreans have always secretly looked down at the Japanese as mere parvenus, since their heritage dates back only as far as 660 BC—when their first Emperor Jimmu Tenno is supposed to have received the sacred sword, mirror and necklace from the sun goddess Amaterasu Omikami and founded the Japanese royal line. The Korean's patronizing attitude remains even today, though Japan has long since demonstrated her military and technological superiority.

In a sense the Koreans are right in claiming to be the cultural parents of Japan, since Japanese art, letters, ceramics and even the Buddhist religion came largely from Chinese sources modified in transit through Korea. But the truth is that while the Chinese were busy becoming the artisans and the merchants and the Japanese the industrialists of modern Asia, Koreans weighed down by a useless, corrupt but all-powerful ruling class, marked time for approximately the last five hundred of their four thousand years.

Unfortunately forty years of Japanese domination left the Koreans with a mass persecution complex. A Korean newspaperman once said to me accusingly: "You like the Japanese better than you do us. Japanese today are happier than Koreans."

"No, no," I protested. "I have been to Japan. They are not happier. They do not have nearly so much to eat. Here you see city street markets crammed with food. The prices are high, yes; but the food is available. In Japan prices are high and there is no food!"

He was not satisfied—probably because I had not strenuously contradicted the first half of his statement. I could not tell him that as time went by and we heard how docilely the Japanese were submitting to the occupation while Koreans were becoming more and more obstreperous, to most of my colleagues in MG the Koreans presented an actively unfavorable contrast.

The main difference between the two occupations lay no doubt in the difference between a conquered and a liberated people's psychology. And few, especially among the liberators themselves, fully understood how much more difficult is the liberator's role.

Woman Without a Country

At the beginning of the war, the Japanese interned in Seoul thirteen foreign nationals. Twelve were later repatriated on the Gripsholm.

The thirteenth was a friend of mine, Mr. MacFarlane. When he was told his wife could not accompany him to freedom he renounced his passage, even though their children had been sent back to Canada before the outbreak of hostilities.

I shall always remember Mr. MacFarlane with special affection. When I was about five, at least once a week he would stop by on his motorcycle to take me to the company store for a bag of candy. He had a son and daughter of his own—and he was busy at the mine. But this was before the day of the jeep, our family had no transportation, and Mr. MacFarlane knew how much an "outing" meant to a child.

I rarely saw Mrs. MacFarlane. Oh, once in a while she would accompany her husband, a large weatherbeaten Scotch-Canadian engineer, to our club. But we did not meet her often in the ordinary social way. Most of her time was spent in her home—or in the company of other Japanese ladies.

She was a beautiful woman, and not in the Asian fashion. She did not look Japanese, and may in fact have been of the Ainus, that Western-looking branch who inhabit the island of Hokkaido.

I have been asked whether the marriage excited comment or antagonism in the mining colony of Suan, a settlement as small and gossipy as any village in any other land. I do not remember that it did. The MacFarlanes, to us, were just another mining family.

We left Korea in 1919, but returned some years later to a different mine in the north. I was sixteen then, and just going to my first dances at the club. One of my partners was Mr. MacFarlane's son Johnny. I never saw Mabel, Johnny's sister. She was always away at school somewhere...

The Gipsholm sailed without him, and Mr. MacFarlane was released to house custody by the Japanese; but when I arrived in 1945 I learned that he was dead.

No one outside the country had heard from the MacFarlanes in over five years. Even after the liberation as the new Korean postal system was still unrecognized by international authority, one could get mail in and out of Korea only through the Army. I had been back in the country little more than a month when I received a letter from Mabel MacFarlane asking me to try to find her mother and learn the circumstances of her father's death. Her first news of her parents had come from an American Navy officer I knew, son of a former missionary in Korea, whose ship was at Inchon too briefly to permit his being of much help.

I turned for advice to Melvin Arick, who as a mining engineer in Korea before the war had also known the MacFarlanes. It was a chill and drizzly day in December that Melvin and I set out in a jeep for Sosha, a village near Seoul where the family home was located. I did not know whether I would find Mabel's mother there, but it seemed the only way to start.

If Melvin had not known the road, I would never have found the place. It was high in the sparsely settled hills back of the village.

As we drove up the steep grade a little white-haired lady dressed in a brown Japanese kimono rushed down the path to greet us. She knew Melvin, and greeted him joyfully. Then she turned to me, a well-bred question in her round, sparkling eyes.

It was a moment before I spoke. After all these years, I was still struck by her beauty. Her features a Caucasian would refer to as fine, or regular. She was tiny, not over five feet tall. Her hair was thick, pure white, in loose unparted coiffure—and wavy!

When I introduced myself she offered her hand and said warmly: "But yes! I not know you! Last time I see, you—" In a quick gesture she indicated "so high"—and it wasn't very.

I told her I had heard from her daughter, and gave her Mabel's message written in Japanese. She read it, crying quietly, as we ascended the path to her house.

It was a one-story frame house, white with green trim and green shingle roof, which her husband had designed and built—a house such as one might see in Canada or New England, or Canadians and new Englanders might build when they moved to Southern California.

In fragments of three languages—Japanese, Korean and English—we learned what Mrs. MacFarlane's life had been these past five years. Her countrymen had disowned her for her transgression in marrying a foreigner, and seemed determined to starve her husband to death.

"He have only one potato a day—so small," she said, and she held out her tiny clenched fist.

The rest of the story came slowly, in phrases chosen spontaneously from the Japanese, repeated for my benefit in a broken bit of Korean or English—all supported with quick, spirited gestures acting out what she had said, to make sure that I understood.

The Japanese police, she told me, continually dragged Mr. MacFarlane down to the station for questioning concerning the local Masonic chapter, records of which had been left in his care. They seemed convinced that anything as secret as the Masonic order must surely be an international spy system. That he was a good Mason is revealed by the police records we captured when we returned, which were later summarized for me by an officer of the American Military Police. No matter how they tortured Mr. MacFarlane, he never gave away a single secret . . .

Ironically enough it was on the day that the first American B-29's flew over Seoul that Mr. MacFarlane met his death. His wife rushed outside to see the planes; but he, thinking they would drop bombs, started for the cellar and pitched headlong down the stairs. Mrs. MacFarlane blamed his fatal fall on the starvation diet which had weakened him for so long.

We asked about her own condition.

It was bad, she said. Every time she tried to go to the village to shop—here she paused, made short overhand throwing motions—the Koreans threw rocks at her Japanese dress.

She could hardly stand up and say to them: "I am no more Japanese than you are. It was the Japanese who killed my husband. I am a British subject!" They would have shouted with laughter.

At night Koreans would break into her house to steal whatever they could. They had long since taken away her radio, one pleasure that had made her life a little more bearable. And when I went into the bathroom I saw that although it was fitted with American plumbing, the fixtures were useless because there was no running water. The Koreans had stolen her water pump, too.

The house was freezing, and I learned that for cooking fuel she was having to burn the young trees Mr. MacFarlane had planted on her hillside.

"House very cold," she said. "Very cold." It was not a complaint, but worry for our comfort. She brought out a little Japanese electric heater, knelt down to place it in the best position near our feet.

When she insisted that we stay to share the little she had for supper and some of Mr. MacFarlane's wine, I nearly wept. I was glad I had thought to bring a few cans of fruit and cream scrounged from the Army mess.

She went out to prepare the meal, and Melvin and I talked of ways to help her. Certain things must be done immediately. She must have Korean police protection, such as it was. Her funds at the Bank of Chosen must be "thawed" if possible. And the British Consulate must be informed of her situation, since we thought that she was legally a British subject.

As we drove away I was busy with my futile thoughts—trying to figure out why it is that when nations break out at each other, some of the most vital and courageous people in the world are left without any country at all. Once upon a time, according to my fifth grade American history text, a lot of people like this had got together and made a country of their own. But the world is not so wide as it was. There might be no place for Mrs. MacFarlane to move to; and certainly there was no place any more to hide.

The next time I saw her, her tiny figure was padding down the long marble corridors of the Capitol building to my office. She had come to tell me that the British Consulate would do nothing to help her because her marriage had been registered only with the Japanese.

Several times that winter I drove out to Sosha, sometimes with a bag of rice begged from the American major in charge of Korean food service, sometimes with a stock of canned goods purchased at the P.X. My "procurement" problem was complicated; for when I asked Mrs. MacFarlane what she would like, she said:

"I no eat meat. Buddhist. You understand?" And, to make sure that I did, she put her hands together and bowed her head briefly in an attitude of prayer.

I was still serving as their intermediary through the Army post office, so occasionally I could also take a letter or a package from her son or daughter. The mail always brought tears to Mrs. MacFarlane's eyes—especially one package containing a picture of her handsome son in his British naval lieutenant's uniform.

"Johnny good boy," she said. As she turned her head away, I realized that she never expected to see either of her children again.

From the beginning of my correspondence with Mabel, I had known she was anxious to get back to Korea. I thought I saw an opportunity to put in a word for her when I was asked by the colonel at the head of the Department of Public Information to recommend a friend who was a competent secretary.

"Just anybody," he said wearily. "We need at least two more."

I told him I knew just the person. And Mabel MacFarlane not only was a competent secretary, I said triumphantly, but also spoke both Korean and Japanese fluently.

He was visibly impressed. "And how in the world does it happen she can do that?" he asked.

I explained.

"Oh, no!" he gasped. "We can't have that! The Koreans in Military Government would never stand for it!"

I gritted my teeth and stifled an urge to ask him why the Koreans she worked with would have to be told about Mabel's ancestry. These "foreigners," I thought, eying the colonel with properly covert disgust, who get a few superficial points about the Orient, and then are stuck with them!

Mabel finally arrived—as secretary to the Canadian reprsentatives on the United Nations Temporary Commission on Korea, in 1948. Until she came I worried constantly about protecting her mother from Korean raids and insults, as the native police certainly did not have their hearts in the assignment.

It seemed incredible to me that all of Mr. MacFarlane's Korean friends should have deserted him. Now that danger of Japanese retaliation was past, surely even the faint of heart would come forward to help his widow, if they but knew of her trouble.

"Is there no one you knew before the war who is close?" I asked. A clumsily indirect way of asking 'Are you *sure* you have no Korean friends?'"

"Only the coolie stay," Mrs. MacFarlane said. "All during war he and family take care of us, then take care of me. He say he not afraid for the little he have to lose."

The coolie made me think of Huckleberry Finn. I remembered Huck's shocked suprise that Tom Sawyer, who was "respectable and well brung up and had a character to lose" should help him to be a "nigger stealer" and free their friend Jim the runaway slave, the only really good loyal and intelligent adult in the entire book. For himself, Huck concluded after considerable soul-searching, it was all right, since he was not handicapped by any such worth-while things.

"But how about the New Ilhan family?" I asked Mrs. MacFarlane, although I was afraid I knew the answer. It was the "handicap of worth-while things" that had made me think of the New Ilhans.

"I not see any more," she said softly, "since just after war come."

For years Mr. MacFarlane had been associated with New Ilhan in a very profitable drug business, and the two men were great friends. Later I heard from several sources that when war came, the Korean partner not only withdrew his friendship but used Japanese prejudice against MacFarlane as an opportunity to dissolve the partnership profitably.

It was literally true that the coolie became Mrs. MacFarlane's only Korean friend. I used to see him stoking the fire, or carrying her water up the hill in Standard Oil tins slung shoulder-bucket fashion. He was a big, engagingly clumsy Korean. His broad face was a universal study in young courage and kindliness, with slanted eyes. He looked very young, though he couldn't have been. I never learned his name.

Mrs. MacFarlane still badly needed another friend in the home, either Korean or American, who was "respectable and well brung up and had a character to lose" and could put the fear of the Lord in her enemies. The problem at last seemed solved when an American civilian attached to a nearby airbase consented to live in her home. Now, I thought, she will have someone to see that she eats properly and to keep her from harm.

To my horror, on my next visit I found that not only had this young gentleman contributed nothing to her comfort or protection, but—

"He like rice. He eat every morning for breakfast," Mrs. MacFarlane told me, nodding eagerly, "two big bowls."

He was supposed to be taking all his meals in the Army mess. But, obviously, "he like rice"—which, because of a severe native shortage, the Army was forbidden to serve!

It is true, as so many observers have charged, that Korea is a hatred- and prejudice-bound land, icy soil for the seeds of democracy we were trying to sow. But the hand of the sower was not always sure and steady. Too often his eyes were on the stars—or he could not see for his own stomach where he was putting his feet in this alien field.

Mrs. MacFarlane's, then, is the story of one woman without a country—with a moral for everyone in every country.

The moral is insulting in its simplicity.

The Traitors and the Patriots

Next to the Japanese themselves, the greatest thorn in the body politic of New Korea was the "pro-Japanese collaborator and national traitor." This typically long-winded epithet the Koreans pinned on any of their countrymen who had found favor with the Japanese, taken Japanese wives, or in any way appeared to prosper at the hands of the oppressor.

Military Government was at first inclined to ignore the entire matter as a bewildering maze of unsubstantiated accusation and counter-accusation. Before long, however, we were obliged to face the problem. As we feared, it had two faces.

My own participation began in a most informal way, but actually led to my first official assignment in Military Government. I was invited to preview the opening of the Kanebo store, where the silks and household goods and art treasures left by the Japanese would be sold to American troops. The captain in charge suddenly propelled me by the elbow and whispered:

"I want you to meet the Military Governor!"

That was the big boss, to me. Or at least according to the way Military Government was supposed to work. But already I had learned that even a first lieutenant in MG's Department of Public Information had two bosses. Maj. Gen. Archibald V. Arnold, who came to Korea in command of the Seventh Division, on September 12, 1945 had been selected by the Commanding General of our tactical forces to replace the Japanese Governor General. Theoretically then, General Arnold was alone responsible for Military Government, which took care of rehabilitation, health, law and order, public utilities—everything having to do with civil government, production and welfare. The Commanding General of the tactical forces, theoretically, would maintain an army of occupation, for assistance to Military Government in case of local trouble—and to guarantee Russian respect.

A good plan, in theory. But the Commanding General, Lt. Gen. John R. Hodge, who had started with full responsibility for both occupation and military government functions and had himself selected the Military Governor, was not at all inhibited by the theoretical organization. For one thing, he was always issuing press statements; and what he, the combat general who mopped up Okinawa, had to say to the Korean people usually gave them no chance whatever to save face and was often therefore disastrous to our "public relations." He had recently put his foot in it, I heard, by calling the Koreans "the same breed of cats as the Japanese." The second trouble was that he often decided that what the Military Governor decided was wrong—and would countermand it.

So I was very interested to meet the Military Governor. He must, I was sure, be either a gentleman of infinite patience or a very tired soldier who did not particularly care what happened.

I liked him immediately. He was tall, handsome, grey-haired—built like the former West Point football star he was. At the moment he was giving the Kanebo store his official seal of approval.

"So you're the WAC I've been hearing about," he said with a smile, "the one with newspaper experience who has lived in Korea before. Come up and see me tomorrow. I have something I want you to do."

When I reported this to my immediate boss, Colonel Glen Newman who was head of the Department of Public Information, he waved me out with the words: "Go right ahead. I don't monkey with two stars!"

General Arnold sat me down in his large paneled office, which had formerly belonged to the Japanese Governor General, and handed me a pamphlet.

"Have you seen this?" he asked.

I glanced at it. It was called "The Traitors and the Patriots."

The pamphlet was issued by a group calling themselves the Government of the People's Republic of Korea, and violently attacked General Arnold for a statement made to the press on October 10,

1945. The General had demanded that the People's Republic stop playing politics, disband and go to work—to feed, clothe and house their fellow citizens during the coming winter. In reply the Republic accused Arnold of surrounding himself with "pro-Japanese collaborators and national traitors"—and even produced some evidence.

"I don't see how they can be sure who collaborated and who didn't," General Arnold said with a frown. "Why, I've just talked to one of the worst of them, by all accounts, and he tells me he was actually sabotaging the Japanese war effort." He went on to relate the story of Mr. Pak and his airplane factory. He was clearly as bewildered as a General ever allows himself to be.

"I want you to write an answer to this pamphlet," he concluded wearily.

My heart sank. It was not only a very delicate task, but one of great responsibility.

"I'll try, sir," I said—naturally, to two stars.

In preparing the answer for the General's approval it was necessary that I draw on all I knew of the Korean people, and all I could possibly learn of their political resurgence since liberation.

During the years I lived in Korea under the Japanese, politics as such had not existed. There was no such thing as a political party, and what political leadership remained after the Revolution of 1919 had gone underground. I remember occasionally seeing a "political prisoner" dragged off to jail in chains by Japanese gendarmes. When I asked what he had done I was always told he was a communist—as often he was, even though that was also the Japanese name for any evidence of Korean nationalism.

The average Korean, following the disastrous Independence Movement, would refuse to discuss politics with anyone, knowing full well the ears of Japan sat on many an unsuspecting head, that no wall was thick enough—and that a man could suddenly drop permanently out of sight for harboring "dangerous thoughts."

Before I could even begin to write an intelligent reply to "The Traitors and the Patriots" I had first to understand the reasons behind the animosities Koreans had developed even against one another during the forty years of Japanese domination. But to understand the People's Republic I would start with recent history. I went back into the files to discover what had happened right after the surrender, before General Hodge and the 24th Corps arrived to meet any remaining Japanese resistance.

In the confusion of the surrender, apparently no one had given thought to what Korean reaction would be. It was soon evident that the Koreans interpreted the capitulation of Japan to mean their own freedom was immediate and complete. Accordingly, even as General Hodge's vessel swung at anchor in Inchon harbor September 8, 1945, three representatives of the "Korean People's Republic" arrived aboard and announced that they were ready to assume governmental responsibilities. As I understand it, General Hodge refused even to see them and they were very much put out about it.

The history of the Republic, the files told me, had begun on August 4, 1945. On that day Japanese Governor General Abe sent for Lyuh Woon Hyung, missionary-trained Korean socialist, informed him that the Japanese intended to surrender, and requested him to form a Korean organization to assist in maintaining law and order. The Japanese evidently selected Lyuh because they thought he would be acceptable to the Russians, who they believed would occupy all Korea.

Ever since 1919, when the peace conference at Versailles refused to recognize the Korean revolution, Russian-type communism had held a strong appeal for the Korean underground—largely because Russia was the one country in the world to offer a helping hand to the resistance movement. I was finding that almost every Korean leader, except for the extreme rightist Dr. Syngman Rhee, had at one time or another carried a Communist Party card or at the least been very friendly with those who did. This was true even inside Korea, in spite of strict surveillance by Japanese "thought police." In 1921-22 Lyuh Woon Hyung had visited Moscow with Dr. Kimm Kiusic, who under MG auspices was later to become chairman of the South Korean Interim Legislature.

With all this encouragement from the Soviets and little if any from the capitalist countries, it was clear to me that the first Korean attempts at self-government would naturally be tinged with red, both in letter and pattern. Lyuh Woon Hyung formed over 135 separate People's Committees throughout Korea with the avowed purpose of organizing a democratic form of government for the Korean people. These committees embraced all political faiths, but as a whole had a strongly communistic flavor. In the north the Russians readily accepted them for adaptation to their own uses. In the south, however, their sanguine cast as well as lack of elected representation rendered them entirely unacceptable to the American command.

By the time General Hodge's ship arrived from Okinawa, Lyuh's organization, originally called the National Founding Preparatory Committee, had assumed governmental functions hardly envisioned by the Japanese—and, I imagine, a bit startling to our Commanding General. General Hodge immediately denounced the People's Republic and all its People's Committees. We in the Department of Public Information were told to "watch out for them," and in everything that came down to us from 24th Crops Intelligence they were depicted as a syndicate who were trying to take over the Korean provinces, in which a political vacuum existed as we took out the Japanese.

Not at all subdued by the General's denunciation, the Republic moved into self-appointed offices throughout the provinces, gathering to itself farmers organizations and Student Public Peace bodies often composed, Hodge's Intelligence reports told us, of armed thugs and criminals.

After an extensive visit to rural areas in December 1945, Dr. Horace Underwood—of the typewriter Underwoods, and son of one of Korea's first missionary families—reported that the People's Republic was the strongest and most active organization he found, and no other group was allowed to exist beside it. Its persistence in calling itself the *de facto* government of Korea naturally brought it into open conflict with American Military Government as soon as we were established.

The majority of Koreans, when they somewhat recovered from their disappointment that complete independence was not to be immediate, settled down to watch warily what we were going to do. The first shock came when MG surrounded itself with an Advisory Council composed in majority of wealthy landlords and prosperous businessmen—well-dressed "respectable" Koreans who spoke a little English and knew how to make themselves agreeable. These men, said the People's Republic, were the very ones who during the war had worked most zealously for a Japanese victory. Now they were turning their coats and fawning on the gullible Americans.

"The Traitors and the Patriots," the loaded document to which I must now make reply, was the Republic's attempt to blow the lid off the Advisory Council. Among other things, the pamphlet said:

> "The birth of the People's Republic of Korea was an accomplished fact at the time of the American landing, by virtue of the Assembly which met on Sept. 6, 1945, in Seoul, and set March 31, 1946 as the date for the second convocation of the assembly . . .
>
> "It is absurd to ask the people of Korea to return to their jobs when the whole apparatus of Japanese imperialism still functions, the dogs are still permitted to bark freely, and even the Japanese army and police are not yet entirely disbanded . . .
>
> "We earnestly advise you (the Military Governor) to judge the situation in Korea by accurate investigation yielding honest information, and not on the basis of the mass of falsehoods spread by the nine traitorous Koreans who now serve upon the 'advisory council' only that they may advance their own interests."

The pamphlet went on to reprint from wartime newspapers enthusiastic recruiting speeches allegedly made by certain of these "nine traitorous Koreans" for the Japanese student volunteer corps. Among the statement attributed to them were the following:

> ". . . The Yankees and the John Bulls seem like religious people, but in reality they are the peoples of cupidity . . . The slave system is the best proof of their liberalism and individualism . . . We must shake off the yoke of the Anglo-Saxons which we have worn long enough.
>
> "The decisive battle has begun for the emancipation of our Eastern world. These vampires have sucked our blood until we are but skin and bone.
>
> "Storm and onslaught against these vampires! . . ."

> ". . . The Yankees are a people of cruelty and violence unparalleled in human history. As an instance, they maltreat, massacre and lynch the Negro in a manner too cruel for description. One American city is infamous for its slave market, to which Negroes were driven with clubs, and in which they were killed or burned at the stake for the slightest disobedience.
>
> "In statistics compiled to the Americans themselves, we find that 4,690 Negroes were slain during the last 58 years. Negroes are not permitted to travel in (American) tram cars, motor cars or trains, to lodge in hotels, or to be part of the audience at a public assembly, or to amuse themselves in the theater together with white citizens . . ."

The first is an excerpt from a speech by the chief of the general staff of the Korean Democratic Party, a rightist organization which we originally favored. The second is an attack on us by the Master of Jurisprudence of Seoul University, whom the pamphlet identified as advisor to the American

Military Government's "educational bureau." Another Korean prominent in recruitment of this type right after Pearl Harbor was the President of Chosen Christian College, an institution founded by the Underwood family and endowed in large part by the Underwood typewriter fortune.

After laboring for days over the problem the Military Governor had set me, I came up with a statement I considered fairly satisfactory. I tried to explain American policy and intentions in Korea as clearly and simply as possible, using the analogy of a child who is just learning to walk and must be assisted by its elders until it can stand on its own feet. I repeated our many promises to leave Korea as soon as she could support her populace, administer her own government and defend her newly-gained freedom.

I realized fully that this answered only the portion of the pamphlet which challenged our position, and that the American Military Government would have to demonstrate in actions what it said in words.

Not long afterward I was assigned to conduct a separate investigation on the wartime activities of the Advisory Council. A great mass of damaging evidence compiled by Korean undercover men in my office—investigators we hired to go out and question their fellow citizens, or to read through the newspapers and periodicals published during the war—showed that most of the Council members actually had said and done the things of which they stood accused.

Our inquiry was corroborated by the independent statements of many other Koreans, some of whom for fear of their lives would meet me only in my own home. One such was Dr. Pak Byu, commonly known as "Brown '05" because he always accompanied an introduction with the flash of his Phi Beta Kappa key and the murmur of his American university class numerals.

Brown '05 hurried in and out of my office one day, staying barely long enough to tell me he wanted to call at my home the following Sunday afternoon. He had something to tell me.

He came bearing a list of Koreans, written in a neat bamboo-stick marching of English letters.

"These," he said, "were disloyal to you during the war."

Many of the names I already knew—but there were others I did not, and in most cases he proved to be right.

"As a matter of fact," he said, "most of the Koreans you have in Military Government up to this time are questionable. And look at this! Kim Tai Won, receptionist in your own Department of Public Information, was a spy for the Japanese! All our people know this, and all the Koreans who visit your department must come to this traitor and beg admittance. You could not possibly have chosen more unfortunately!"

I later reported this, but we failed to find the necessary evidence and Kim Tai Won stayed on. After all, he was affable and could speak very good English . . .

"The real Koreans," Brown '05 told me, "the people who could appreciate and deserve this democracy you bring if it turns out right, they are all waiting to see what is going to happen."

Brown '05 was one. When he did choose to run, in 1950, he was elected to the South Korean legislature.

I thanked him for his help, being as profuse as I knew how in my acknowledgment of what he had done for Military Government—and possibly to himself—in bringing me the list.

"Would you have tea, or beer, and some bisquits?" I asked, when all three were already served.

"No thank you," he said. "And it is necessary that I leave now."

I went from the room to get his hat. When I came back I saw that the sugar, a huge lump in Army wrapper, had disappeared. I felt very sad that because of his country's terrible post-war shortages Brown '05 should have to do such a thing. And equally as sad for my clumsiness in not having thought to offer him the sugar.

I waited for a long time for Brown '05 to show us why he had brought me the list. But in the three years I was in Military Government, he was still "waiting to see what is going to happen." He never asked a favor of any kind.

Whether the Japanese by inhuman pressure had forced certain prominent Koreans to cooperate I never could discover; but it was plain that by their public stand they had irreparably lost the confidence of their countrymen. MG quietly filed my unfavorable report and as quietly dissolved the Advisory Council. However the entire question of proceedings against the "pro-Japanese collaborators and national traitors," for which Koreans were clamoring, MG felt it best to leave for action by "the future Korean government when it should be established."

When in 1948 the Korean government was established, their National Police burned the documents of a government committee investigating the subject and arrested the special police assigned to it. Thus "influence" still prevailed, leaving the problem as far from solution as ever, though Koreans are still shouting for the heads of the "pro-Japanese collaborators and national traitors."

Most Americans, on the other hand, are still wondering why the Koreans can't drop all accusations and start afresh, since in the long years of Japanese imperial residence in their country everyone must have collaborated to some extent in order to survive. Only after seeing the magnificence of Yun Chi Ho's residence set against a background of unhappiness, sickness and filth did I understand why for the average Korean such a sane and rational course is quite impossible.

Nationalism Versus Communism

When I first reported in at Military Government headquarters, I was told I could shop around for a suitable assignment. Because of my background in journalism I went to the Bureau of Public Information and asked Colonel Newman for a job. He promptly assigned me to the Political Research and Analysis Section, even though I vigorously protested my ignorance of Korean politics.

"Never mind," said the Colonel, "we need another body over there."

This piling up of bodies became known as "empire building." The more names a Chief had on his table of organization the more important he appeared. Perhaps some day his Bureau might even grow into a Department—as this one did.

Visualizing myself as a pinhead stuck in an organization chart, I obediently took my body off in the direction indicated. The duties of my section I discovered were to interview Korean political leaders, attend all types of political rallies and provide the American command with information concerning the rapidly changing political scene. Later I was mentally to thank the Colonel for this assignment, as Korean politics proved a fascinating and almost unreal experience. Most intriguing of all was the part played from the very beginning by the Communists.

The People's Republic, after a long and losing battle with the American command, finally gave up the struggle for governmental control and became a political party. This was only one of several Communist-tinged groups in South Korea, and all of them had strong ties north of the 38th parallel where the Russians were rapidly developing a Communist party of their own.

Although the reason for the division of Korea had originally been strategic—to fight and disarm the 200,000 Japanese troops in the country—by October 1945 the shooting war against a common enemy had degenerated into a political war between two former allies. The Russians opened fire by telling the Koreans that Russia had actually won the campaign against the Japanese—when as a matter of fact she had not come into the conflict until the last week and had engaged in only a few minor skirmishes. So strict was Japan's censorship concerning her defeats until the time of capitulation that the Koreans had no way of detecting the lie.

Of course the real reason behind the political war was that Russia, whose interest in Korea extended back to the nineteenth century, saw her potential sphere of influence threatened by our occupation. We, on the other hand, hoped to develop a friendly "democratic" Korea—lying as it does right across the straits from our vulnerable position in Japan.

Russia, to the Korean mind, had more reason to be concerned than we, for her Siberian border touches Korea's along an eleven mile frontier. By no stretch of the Korean's imagination could the protective borders of the United States be considered to extend so far. Thus the Russians had many attentive listeners among the natives when they proclaimed that our occupation indicated we had imperialistic designs on the little peninsula.

Actually the Korean from the moment of liberation was a completely nationalistic animal. Subservience once again to a foreign power, be it Russia or the United States, did not appeal to him in the least. His brightest hope was that the occupation forces on both sides of the parallel would go home, and the artificial boundary dividing his country be erased.

Although at the Cairo Conference the four powers had pledged that Korea was to become "free and independent in due course," up until December 1945 nothing had been done to implement the promise. Daily the two occupation armies became more deeply entrenched and the people of the two zones ideologically more sharply divided.

In an effort to break the stalemate and fulfill the Allies' wartime commitment, the Foreign Ministers Conference in Moscow in December 1945 took up the Korean question. The resulting agreement provided for an American Soviet Joint Commission to assist in the formation of a provisional government for all Korea. This commission was to submit its proposals to the four great powers who would then work out "an agreement concernng a four-power trusteeship of Korea for a period of five years."

We in the Department of Public Information first heard this Moscow Decision by radiogram a few hours before it broke in the Korean press. When we saw that it proposed a trusteeship for Korea, we knew we were in for trouble—and we had it!

Unfortunately Secretary Byrnes and the other foreign ministers met in Moscow could not know that "trusteeship" translated in Korean would come out "sintok," the very word the Japanese had used when they established the protectorate in 1906. From where the Koreans sat, it now looked certain that Russia and the United States were both playing the same old imperialistic game of gradual encroachment leading to final destruction of their newly-recovered liberty.

The morning after the "sintok" announcement the Koreans in our office gradually began drifting out the door. I thought nothing of it—until I looked up and realized we were completely alone. Our entire Korean staff had walked out. I picked up the telephone.

"They've *all* gone!" the operator told me. Only it wasn't the operator—it was the American supervisor. "There's not a Korean left in the building!"

Then came the sound of shouting in the streets: first a mutter, as when a dam is giving way—and then the roar that accompanies the crashing waters' release.

I ran to the office window. But it was a back window and looked out, as always, on the hushed gardens of the old Kwang Bok Palace, home of a long long line of dead Korean kings. I rushed to the front of the building.

The Capitol building—a hugely stolid and squat marble structure with an undersize dome, designed by a German architect and built by Japanese—was an island; and by now it fairly quaked in the flood of sound loosed against it from the streets. Pushing down the side alleys were the crests of a mob which spilled into "Pennsylvania Avenue" and eddied about the wall in front of the Capitol. At last I could read the lettering on the banners they carried.

DOWN WITH TRUSTEESHIP!
DOWN WITH AMERICAN IMPERIALISM!

It was a surging roaring show of feeling that reminded me of the distant din I had heard from the mine that morning in 1919, when the swarms of villagers in front of the Japanese police station had been shot. Korean political parties, youth groups and dozens of other organizations were comng toward us in an endless rush. An undulating mass of agitated banners and upflung arms, they moved along the walls of the Capitol and past the guarded gate shouting "Mansei! Mansei!" With each shout, in unison they raised their arms as high as they could reach, then all bent down as if to touch their toes.

The Communist Koreans were there too—at first as spontaneously anti-trusteeship as everyone else. But the Party line was to support the Moscow Decision, and before the day was over the gospel came down from North Korea and there were some changes made. Members close to the oracle hastily fashioned new banners out of their old ones, thus:

UP
~~DOWN~~ WITH TRUSTEESHIP!
JAPANESE
DOWN WITH ~~AMERICAN~~ IMPERIALISM!

But the orders were not sufficiently well-transmitted to reach all Party members in time. For the first few hours half the Communist banners bore the approved corrections, the other half did not. This ludicrous changeover to an unpopular attitude showed thinking Koreans just who was pulling the Communist strings, and caused the Party to lose a good deal of its prestige.

The demonstration began on a Saturday, a half workday in MG, and by noon we were quite ready to go home. The question was how to get there. Great masses of people blocked the streets from one end of Seoul to the other. I was standing in the motor dispatch office contemplating the situation when a major in a three-quarter ton truck offered to run the blockade.

We were prepared, at least mentally, for any turn Korean hostility might take; but to our amazement the crowd smiled at us, and parted to make way. We had to part the sea of faces three times before we reached the WAC billet, and each time they let us through without protest. Later worried friends sent me Stateside newspaper clippings with the headline: AMERICAN TROOPS STONED IN KOREA! No one I know of was stoned, nor did we in Korea hear of any such incident—except for the one little Korean boy who threw a pebble at a jeep!

After three days the demonstration finally flickered out—but not before certain interested parties took the general confusion as a perfect opportunity to dispose of Song Chin Woo, president of the conservative Korean Democratic Party. We were unable to solve the crime, but the facts we did find seemed to indicate the assassins had struck because Song's name was linked with those of the wealthy landlords and pro-Japanese collaborators.

Also under the cover of prevailing hubbub, Kim Koo, second president of the Korean Provisional Government in 1919, made an abortive attempt to move in as dictator of South Korea. His *Kim Koo d'etat* began with a formal statement that henceforth all government employees, both civil and police, should take orders from him. After all, hadn't the Moscow Decision called for a "provisional government"—the very words he used to describe his own? His henchmen took over a number of police boxes and made a futile attempt to storm the government-controlled radio station.

Meanwhile General Hodge was frantically trying to get an official State Department interpretation of the Moscow Conference. When it came, he asked the Department of Public Information to call all responsible Korean newspapermen in Seoul to the Capitol Throne Room, where his press conferences were held. The Throne Room, hung with gold-fringed red velvet, with a raised dais at one end, was originally intended for Emperor Hirohito should he ever visit Korea.

Naturally all of us in the Department attended this press conference, as on the General's words depended our entire future approach to the Korean people. Before a large and solemn assemblage the General officially confirmed his personal opinion that a trusteeship could be avoided if Korean political parties were overwhelmingly opposed.

The American State Department had decided that certain words (italicized below) in Article III of the Moscow Decision gave the Koreans a free choice in the matter—an interpretation with which Russia never agreed; and this particular semantic disagreement was to form the basis for many of our later disputes with the Soviets.

"III. It shall be the task of the (US-USSR) joint commission with the participation of the Provisional Korean Democratic Government and of Korean democratic organizations to *work out measures also for helping and assisting* (trusteeship) the political, economic and social progress of the Korean people, the development of democratic self-government and the establishment of the national independence of Korea. The proposals of the joint commission shall be submitted *following consultation with the Korean* Provisional Government for the *joint consideration* of the Governments of the United States, the Union of Soviet Socialist Republics, the United Kingdom and China *for the working out of an agreement concerning* a four power trusteeship of Korea up to a period of five years."

Armed with the official statement from James Byrnes, General Hodge also had words with the Great Revolutionist Kim Koo. They must have been strong words, for that evening Kim Koo took the air to broadcast a reassurance to the Korean people and to request that Military Government employees return to work and the country to peace and order.

Although this was the end of outright defiance on the part of Korean nationalists, shouting advocacy of trusteeship continued to be borne on the banners of the Communist party. Its firm cementation in official Soviet policy colored all future intercourse between the two zones.

On all other points, upon close examination I found all party platforms to be singularly alike— from the extreme right of Dr. Rhee to the extreme left of the Communists. They all advocated confiscation of Japanese farm lands and redistribution to the peasants. They all proposed nationalization of heavy industry, mines, forests, public utilities, banks, railroads, communications and transportation. To the Americans even the most conservative smacked of socialism, and the more radical were Bolshevism simon-pure. But in a country where seventy-five percent of the population had existed as virtual serfs for forty years, a program of nationalization and redistribution made sense.

The reduction of the seventy-five percent to a status of tenant farmers had come about in a number of ways. Under the Lee Dynasty many officials received land in lieu of salary, and some augmented their holdings by seizure. Sometimes landowners voluntarily deeded their lands over to court officials, since "palace" land was not subject to taxation.

When the Japanese came in 1906 they took over much of the "palace" land and gained control of additional acreage by confiscating it for military purposes or for non-payment of taxes. Koreans who collaborated willingly in these practices were often rewarded with a share of the holdings.

Much of the Japanese land was vested in the government-subsidized Oriental Development Company, an octopus which had a tentacle around nearly every phase of Korean economy. Besides controlling one sixth of the best rice tillage, it reached out to mines, orchards, dairy farms and even railroads.

While this forty-year process of legalized confiscation was going on, the land-hungry Korean peasant remained on the soil, working it for his Japanese or Korean master. And he continued to dream of a rice paddy of his own some day, with a bull to till it.

One morning as I was sitting in the Military Governor's outer office, a farmer, the grime of toil still clinging to his once-white garments, burst excitedly through the door. He all but made it – clear across the carpeted anteroom to the General's inner sanctum – before he was stopped by a Korean-speaking American officer who gently led him out, both chattering volubly.

"What did he want?" I asked when the officer returned.

"He had to see the Military Governor personally," was the reply. "He needs a new bull!"

If land redistribution to these earnest farmers made sense, nationalization of heavy industry was logical too, since practically all industry had been owned by the Japanese and now was left ownerless. And since all public utilities had been operated by the Japanese government there was no reason why a Korean government should not continue to operate them.

The difference between right and left was apparent to the Koreans chiefly on the land problem, and there it was largely a matter of degree. The rightist advocated confiscating only former Japanese-owned lands, redistributing them on a long-term payment basis. The Communist would confiscate large Korean holdings as well, and invest the control of all land in People's Committees who would parcel out the right of tillage free to The Most Deserving. The latter type of land program the Russians shortly put into effect in North Korea. We on the other hand in maintaining the sanctity of private property and wanting to be sure we did not violate any legitimate right, were tardy in our land program. Also, we put only a few small businesses on the market and insisted that the rest of this problem – like the question of the traitors and the collaborators – should be the responsibility of the future Korean government.

When news of the Communist land reform leaked across the border, many farmers trekked north to get their share of the bonanza. In the south rose a great clamor for similar "gifts" of free land. Disappointment in the north was swift, however. Taxes on the free land was 25% of the natural crop – and an additional 11% was levied by the People's Committees. All this took away nearly as much of the poor farmer's profits as the 50% rental formerly imposed by the Japanese.

In spite of this, South Koreans still felt we had failed them. When you consider that most of them were convinced their countrymen's wealth was either obtained or maintained through collaboration with the enemy, it is understandable that they felt our type of democracy, which to them meant a traitor had "rights," was a luxury they could ill afford.

Two early MG ordinances did lift a small part of the load from the back of the tenant farmer. One restricted rentals not to exceed one third of the natural crop, as opposed to the former 50%. Another forbade landlords to collect rent in cash or in kind from tenants. Instead the farmer was to take his grain to a government collection point where he received an inspection certificate. This he handed over to the landlord, who would receive payment from a government financial association. With this procedure we hoped to stop the common practice of shortchanging tenants; but there is no doubt that landlords and their agents managed to circumvent this reform, for MG's actual supervision extended only to the *kun* or county level.

All former Japanese lands, including those of the Oriental Development Company, MG vested in the New Korea Company. Here again, Military Government's American personnel was insufficient to supervise the strange and sprawling estate; so although the new company abided by the tenancy reforms, it was unable to rid itself of the Korean middleman whose squeezes increased the peasant's rental.

When the South Korean Interim Legislative Assembly was formed in December 1946, Military Government authorities urged it to give priority to land reform. The Assembly took up the question, but soon became hopelessly deadlocked because of the large number of land owners in that body.

By not coming to grips with the land problem sooner than it did, Military Government lost a great opportunity to benefit the ordinary Korean. It also lost prestige in comparison with the Russian zone, where a major land "reform" program was immediate. Furthermore, our delay availed nothing; for just before relinquishing control in 1948 MG had to work out a program for redistributing Japanese lands after all—to prevent the newly-elected Korean "nationalist" politicians from using land as a political weapon.

A Day In the Field

Everybody in the field always hates a headquarters, and Military Government headquarters was no exception. To the men in the provinces it was an ogre sitting up in the Capitol building devouring reports and spewing forth directives at such an impossible rate that it never left them any time for their real interest, the Korean people.

Whenever I began to feel stifled by the rarified atmosphere of the Capitol, I usually spent a day breathing the more-than earthy effluvia of the paddy fields and reassuring myself that we actually were dealing with humanity, not with little black marks on pieces of paper.

On one such occasion I rode in an open three-quarter ton truck to the village of Yangpyong with the American governor of Kyonggi-do, the province in which Seoul is located. Yangpyong was the capital of a *kun*, or county, which embraced a number of *myuns*, or townships, really collections of small villages.

Korean farmers are typically gregarious, building their houses huddled together in the center of surrounding rice paddies. These paddies are not laid out in neat, straight geometrical pattern, as in Japan. The borders are twisted and intercurved. When I asked the reason, an old Korean farmer said:

"It is so the Evil Spirit will get lost!"

This fear and propitiation of the Evil Spirit, by anthropologists called shamanism, is the principal religion in Korea; but as individuals they may profess Christianity or Buddhism — or Confucianism, which is the main influence in family relationships.

Bumping along over the rock-ribbed road I could see into courtyards and kitchens blackened by centuries of woodsmoke, where the farmers' wives were cooking the evening rice. From the doorways hung strings of red pepper and garlic used in making *kimchee*. Occasionally a rope strung with bits of charcoal tied across a gateway indicated the birth of a boy child.

You can't stand anywhere in Korea without seeing the dragon-tooth mountains, denuded of foliage by the centuries of woodcutting for the home fire. In the bowl formed by the horizon, the villages I passed were like paintings in the hollow of broken pottery vessels.

There had been some trouble with the People's Republic in this particular county, so the Governor had asked the *kunsoo*, or county chief, to call in all the *myunjohns*, the heads of townships, from their various villages for a little talk.

At Yangpyong we first met the American lieutenant who was assigned full time to the county, and with him we drove to the county seat, a former Japanese administration building taken over by the Koreans.

The *kunsoo* was a dapper little man in a blue pin-striped business suit. He led the Governor into an adjoining room where the *myunjohns* were seated around a table. They were all typical farmers dressed in their native costumes, big baggy pants and short jackets; but all were modern enough to wear their hair short rather than in the old-fashioned top knot.

Here was Korean democracy at work, for the *myunjohns* even under the Japanese were elected representatives, though the vote was cast by each family head rather than by every individual member. Military Government used this same method in choosing the elected half of the South Korean Interim Legislature.

The Governor made an impassioned speech explaining how the Americans had liberated Korea after a four-year-long war in the Pacific and now had come into the country to disarm the Japanese army and replace the Japanese civil government — and that American forces would remain only until Korea was strong enough to stand on its own feet. This was to counteract the insidious People's Republic propaganda that the Russians had really won the war against Japan and America was a johnny-come-lately intent on making Korea a new American colony.

When the speech was translated by the Governor's personal interpreter, the *myunjohns* accepted it impassively. It was difficult to tell if they were resentful, agreeable, or even interested. One knew only that they had come a long way from their native villages to this meeting, in bullcarts over bumpy roads, and so for them this must be an occasion of importance.

The meeting ended with the *kunsoo* leading us into his office, where he had spread a feast of tea, Korean apples, and a hard, tasteless American-style cake covered with gaudy frosting. One so often regretted all the eggs, flour and precious sugar the Koreans wasted trying to please the American palate.

On another occasion I came even closer to life in the field. Major Anson DeWolff, commanding the Military Government group at the border town of Kaesong just south of the 38th parallel, was the only American officer I knew who refused to use an interpreter. Like the rest of us Major DeWolff had spent six months studying Japanese in Civil Affairs Training school back in the States. But unlike the rest of us he kept on studying it even when he knew he would be coming to Korea. All his fellow officers at CAT school kidded him unmercifully all the way through—and even, at times, became annoyed with him. Not too many of them were as interested as they ought to have been in learning Japanese. But that DeWolff! Why, even at a party he wanted to talk Japanese. And when he went on a date, he took vocabulary cards!

By now quite proficient, DeWolff insisted on using the language in all his dealings with the Koreans, whether they liked it or not—thus avoiding the derisive term "government by interpreter."

While in Kaesong I accompanied the major on a tour of his district, where like an old-fashioned circuit judge he settled the accumulated disputes which had arisen since his previous visit.

The most important matter for arbitration this trip concerned a ferry—or rather two ferries—across a certain river. (A ferry in Korea is nothing more than a flat skiff with a man on a pole at either end.) It seemed that the more established ferry, or vested interest, had been given the sole right under the Japanese to pole people, cattle and pigs across this river. Then came the liberation—and with it entrepreneurs who, figuring all Japanese holds were off, started up a rival operation. The result was that the Korean boatmen spent all their time pulling passengers off each other's ferries, and nobody got to the other side.

The Major listened to both sides of the story delivered in rapid-fire Japanese. I found that Koreans were not at all adverse to using the hated tongue when they felt it would further their interests.

After considering the matter judiciously the Major decided to advise provincial headquarters in Seoul to issue a new license to the original ferry giving it sole rights to the crossing.

Next we must visit the village schoolhouse where the children had been lined up outside all morning awaiting our arrival.

It was a primary school. The little girls looked like dolls, just as the GI's said. Their "dutch" haircuts were those of our American 1920's, cut with the bowl around the head. They wore bright-colored Korean silks in brave contrast—such as a blue jacket, with red billowing skirt.

The little boys were toy soldiers. Their heads were shaved, and they were in military uniforms of grey—the same which the Japanese had forced upon their big brothers from the time they were in kindergarten. Every boy in the Empire was a soldier, as soon as he was able to leave his mother. The hand-me-down uniforms were old now, and pretty tattered and worn, but under the new Korean economy were all they had.

The children bowed.
The Major saluted.
The children sang.

We were then taken into the principal's office to hear his tale of woe concerning lack of Korean-language textbooks and other materials. After the Major had promised to see what could be done, we set out for home, stopping for dinner at a famous Japanese hotsprings resort where a company of American tactical troops was billeted.

The names of these men in the field rarely appeared in the newspapers or on official dispatches. Yet they were the ones who carried the message of democracy to the lowliest farmer in the farthest paddy—through rain, wind and snow, and over the worst possible roads. Without them, all headquarters' carefully written ordinances, proclamations and policies would have been only so many sheets of paper blowing in the wind.

Assassination of the People, By the People, For the People

As one wag put it, Korea is the "Land of the Night Soil, the Morning Calm, and the Afternoon Conference." Once the Japanese were off the lid, Koreans engaged in endless political discussions, releasing all the heat and steam of their long-suppressed volatile temperament.

By the time I arrived over 150 political parties had already been formed in South Korea, in striking "democratic" contrast to the one party in the north. However these parties hardly met our idea of the term, as most of them consisted only of a family and a few friends. One in particular, I remember, had just three members.

Bewildered by this ideological maze General Hodge, who from the beginning took an active hand in politics, made repeated appeals for unity and repeated attempts to persuade various groups to weigh their mutual interests and consolidate their forces.

One of my main tasks as a political analyst was to prepare for forwarding to Washington the official list of party names, platforms and lines of allegiance—in other words, who would join whom if what happened.

The heat and steam of Korean politics failed to offset the frigid conditions under which I wrote this report in late November and early December 1945. The Political Analysis Section was located at the side of the Capitol, in a small building formerly the Japanese office of movie and newspaper censorship. I began to gain some respect for censors as being extremely rugged individuals.

During the first winter a disinterested onlooker would have thought us gnomes in a Disney workshop, rather than Military Government officers. We sat huddled in hooded parkas and stiff wool mittens, vainly trying to hit only one key at a time as we typed, and frequently bending in grotesque concentration over our machines to separate the tangle of type bars which resulted from almost every dab of our clumsy paws.

Whenever we took a trip to the furnace room to consult with Korean stokers concerning the deplorable heat situation, we always got the same reply—complete with gestures and sooty grins.

"Capitol Building have *big* pipe," they would say, and describe a huge circle with their arms.

"Education Building have middle-sized pipe—" a smaller circle, using both hands.

"And you have *little* pipe—see?" A tiny circle composed of only the thumb and forefinger! "No can do."

And that, it seemed, was that.

And so back to politics... After some study the confused futuristic picture began to look like a pattern, and out of it emerged just seven parties worthy of consideration.

Since the Korean party leaders dominate their organizations, I tried that first winter to meet all whose activities might shape or modify the policies of Military Government in the months to come.

Following the unsuccessful Revolution of 1919 many of Korea's most prominent leaders fled to Shanghai, where they set up the Provisional Government. This government clung to a tenuous existence throughout the forty years of Japanese domination. Only the Free French and Nationalist China ever gave it even semi-recognition.

Since the Provisional Government did at least have a semblance of respectability, it was quite natural that when Americans came to Korea in 1945 they should look to it for leadership. Its first president Dr. Syngman Rhee was known to us, having for years kept the Korean question alive in Washington as a sort of unofficial ambassador. He, then, was our first hope—the first Korean politician-in-exile to return at U.S. Army invitation.

The fanfare with which he was greeted by General Hodge himself caused stirrings of envy and resentment among local politicians, many of whom had spent a good part of the past forty years brooding and "hatching" in Japanese jails.

The snow-thatched Rhee immediately set about organizing the National Society for the Rapid Realization of Independence. (All Korean party names are sesquipedalian.) He aimed at gathering all political parties into one fold—with himself as leader, of course. But since he was so violently anti-communistic, he never succeeded in winning over the left.

Rhee was followed to Korea in December 1945 by two other Provisional Government officials, Kim Koo and Dr. Kimm Kiusic. Kim Koo, called The Tiger by his contemporaries, had succeeded Rhee as head of the government-in-exile and was mainly notable as an assassin. As a young man of nineteen he killed a Japanese military policeman whom he believed responsible for the death of Queen Min, and wrote in large bloody letters on the wall: KIM KOO DID THIS. Imprisoned, he escaped and divided his time between study and organizing anti-Japanese movements. At the age of thirty-five he formed an assassination group to kill the first Japanese Governor, the harsh General Terauchi. The attempt failed, he was arrested again and imprisoned seven years.

After the Revolution of 1919 Kim Koo joined the expatriates at Shanghai. Here he engineered the bomb-throwing plot which resulted in the assassination of General Shirakawa and the loss of Admiral Shigametsu's leg. Twenty-six years later Shigametsu stumped aboard the *USS Missouri* to surrender to MacArthur.

To Kim Koo's *fortissimo* Dr. Kimm Kiusic was the grace notes. Of the three returning members of the government-in-exile, Kimm (spelled with double-M to distinguish him from all the other Kims, a name as common in Korea as Smith in this country) was probably the greatest scholar. He attended three different universities in the United States and went back to Korea to do Christian and educational work; but he found Japanese control so irksome that he departed for China, where he served the Provisional Government both as minister of foreign affairs and vice president. He was the young man who, after the Revolution of 1919 failed, journeyed to the Versailles Peace Conference to plead Korea's case before the world powers.

I met Kimm Kiusic at the headquarters of the Provisional Government in Seoul. I explained to him that it would be helpful to the American command to know his thoughts and attitude on current Korean political problems.

Speaking excellent English, he represented himself as the voice of Kim Koo. "Kim Koo speaks no English at all, you know," he said.

I did know. Even in Korean, Kim Koo was considered a "deze-dem-and-doze" man. It was Kim Koo, incidentally, who during the Anti-Trusteeship demonstration a couple of months later was to attempt an overthrow of American Military Government.

"The Koreans are now in such a turmoil," the soft-voiced Kimm Kiusic was saying in answer to my question, "it must be very difficult for your Command to make any sense at all of the political scene. But this is purely self-expression, which my people have been denied for so long. It does not mean they are confusion-prone. After a period of education in political science, and I cannot stress too strongly the need for education, they will settle down. Even now, they are beginning to understand that a consolidation of political parties is necessary."

Dr. Kimm was in his sixties, but his hair was coal black. He was not so well-fed looking as either Kim Koo or Syngman Rhee. In fact Kimm looked more like a professor of political science than a politician—and he talked more like a professor, a youngish professor with vitality rather than push. He was the only purely logical and dispassionate leader I met—the only one I instinctively felt had no axe to grind.

From this one conversation I saw why Kimm Kiusic won the confidence of Military Government to such an extent that he later became head of the South Korean Interim Government. He paid dearly for our confidence. The lines of concentration deepened to worry on his scholarly face; and before long, I heard, he developed an ulcer. From a "youngish professor" who walked briskly, he changed to an infirm patriarch who passed through the Capitol corridors on the arm of an aide. Before his long fight for the unification of North and South Korea was finally over and lost, he was getting about with ever-increasing difficulty, with an aide on either side.

The Korean Provisional Government had started out in 1919 with men of all political colors and creeds and for a time some of its members, including Kimm Kiusic, had dabbled in communism. However when they returned to Korea in 1945, their youthful radicalism had paled and they leaned mainly to the right.

The chief indigenous rightist group called itself the Korean Democratic Party—a paradox which we Americans in the Political Analysis Section had difficulty keeping straight in our minds.

This Democratic Party was composed of prosperous businessmen and wealthy landlords who had remained in the country during the war—the group from which MG selected most of its original Advisory Council, and from which the People's Republic selected most of its "pro-Japanese collaborators and national traitors!" Kim Syung Soo, the president, starred in "The Traitors and the Patriots" for his recruiting speeches; and Son Chin Woo, original leader of the party, had gone so far as to subscribe a sum of money for a memorial to Terauchi, the worst Japanese governor Korea ever had.

When I met fat heavy-lidded Son Chin Woo at Democratic Party headquarters I thought I was meeting a character actor—or in the flesh, the typical left-wing cartoon of a bloated plutocrat. I gave him my stock request, as politely as I could.

"It would be very helpful to American Military Government to have a brief statement from you," I said, "your views on the current political problems in Korea—"

He spoke very slowly, and the burden of his message was indeed just that. When I got accustomed to his particular breakage of the English language, I found that he was telling me a story. And making a great point of it.

During the years of the Japanese Empire in Korea, he had been a newspaper editor.

I nodded.

He had been thrown in jail by the Japanese! He said it proudly, and then went on to describe in great detail and almost with pleasure all the tortures he had endured.

All this, he concluded ponderously, was because the Japanese had not liked his editorials. They were too patriotic—too Korean!

In his own way, whether he knew it or no, he had answered my question. As we always did when a leader "protested" too much, I went back over the newspaper morgue files until I found out what Son Chin Woo had done for his country during the war.

It was true that he had been imprisoned, exactly as he claimed. But obviously the torture had done its work. From then on he had worked for the greater glory of Japan—and himself. The things I found out about him from the files undoubtedly every Korean knew; and they were unquestionably the reason he was assassinated a month or so after I talked with him, under cover of the Anti-Trusteeship melee.

The Korean politicians I have mentioned so far were all right of center. In Korea middle-of-the-road politics is practically unknown, but An Chai Hong and his Nationalist Party came as close to it as any. At the time of my investigation he and his followers gave the impression that they would join anybody who would take them—except possibly the communists—and eventually they did merge with Kim Koo's New Independence Party.

An Chai Hong, with his candid expression and toothbrush moustache, seemed cut of such innocuous material that MG selected him as the ideal Civil Administrator for the South Korean Interim Government, where he proved anything but harmless in his efforts to pass out favors and juggle personnel under the very nose of the Military Governor. An had been among those nominated for president of the People's Republic in its first and worst days, so actually we had little excuse for being surprised at the looseness of his political affections.

The communists and their fellow-travelers of course were always with us. Lyuh Woon Hyung eventually became disgusted with the infiltration of communists into his People's Republic and broke away, to form the leftist People's Party. How close his ties with Moscow remained after that is a matter of conjecture; but it is known that he took several trips to Pyengyang, the capital of the Russian zone, to confer with communist leaders.

Lyuh was a difficult man to meet, but I finally managed an invitation to the home of an American lieutenant colonel when I knew Lyuh was to be his dinner guest. He was one of the most distinguished-looking Koreans I have ever seen— short grey hair, military moustache, handsome face and hard athletic body. As a young man he had been active in promoting body-building exercises in the Korean YMCA.

Before I could even open my mouth he protested to me that he was not a communist, never had been a communist, and was trying to break away from their association.

"It is a very difficult thing to do," he said in perfect English. "I must proceed slowly. My life is in constant danger. Every night I move to a different house with my bodyguard. Even my wife does not know where I am."

Since Lyuh was the strongest representative of the non-communist left, MG made repeated attempts to draw him into wedlock with the moderate right represented by Dr. Kimm Kiusic. He continued to flirt with both sides but never gave himself to either. Koreans called him "the silver axe": he looked pretty but he didn't cut anything.

His mercurial temperament sabotaged the Representative Democratic Council, successor to the ill-begotten Advisory Council, and General Hodge's first great attempt to get all political parties to cooperate under government auspices. Although Lyuh promised to lend support, the day the new Council was inaugurated with much pomp and ceremony in the Capitol building he failed to appear. This literally and figuratively left a great big embarrassing empty seat right in the front row. The Council became only another ineffectual rightist organization.

The second attempt to draw Lyuh into the charmed circle was made by Lt. Leonard Bertsch, political analyst for the Department of Public Information. Feeling that the informal approach was best, Bertsch began by inviting Lyuh and Kimm Kiusic to a private meeting at his own home.

As Lt. Bertsch tells the story, Lyuh arrived early and settled down with a newspaper. He was still reading when Dr. Kimm arrived, and continued reading for another hour—an oriental way of expressing indifference to the whole situation. Finally, laying the paper aside, he apologized and indicated he was ready to begin the conversations.

For Lyuh's rudeness Dr. Kimm had the diplomat's answer.

"When you and I lived together in Shanghai," he said, "we often spent an entire evening reading together without feeling any need to talk."

With this beginning Kimm and Lyuh formed the nucleus of a Coalition Committee which embraced all but the ultra-conservative Korean Democratic Party on the right and the Moscow-supported branch of the Communist Party on the left. However, Lyuh's repeated "retirements" from public life for reasons of ill health (during which time he probably took another trip to Pyengyang) so hampered the work of the committee that it never went beyond the talking stage.

Finally Lyuh rounded out his vacillation by boycotting the South Korean Interim Assembly when it was formed in December 1946 as Military Government's halfway step to true autonomous government for the Korean people.

Even among the communists there was open schism—whether real or feigned it is difficult to say. One wing led by Pak Heung Yung seemed completely under the domination of Moscow. In the early days of the occupation Pak is credited by Richard Johnson, *New York Times* correspondent, with saying that he favored Korea's becoming a Republic of the USSR. The hullabaloo this statement aroused caused Pak to come out with a quick denial, but Johnson swears to this day that Pak's original statement was exactly as reported.

Pak eventually went underground when MG put out a warrant for his arrest on charges of inciting to riot and other offenses against the public peace. In 1948 he popped up in North Korea as Foreign Minister of the Russian-sponsored People's Republic.

The other communist wing was led by Hu Hun, who purportedly represented the now-Moscow left. For a time he "cooperated" on the Coalition Committee with the moderate right, but on all major issues proved intractable.

These then were the leaders upon whom MG had to call in attempting to form a self-governing body out of the chaos that was Korea following occupation. All had definite handicaps, the most obvious being their advanced age. Of the original "Big Four" of Korean politics, Syngman Rhee, Kim Koo, Kimm Kiusic and Lyuh Woon Hyung, the first two were over seventy and the others in their sixites. While this gave them a reverential aura in the eyes of their oriental constituents, for whom age is always synonymous with wisdom, it hardly augured a long and stable leadership.

Even more inimical to American aims than their calculated longevity was their bitter antagonism for one another. All our still-born coalition attempts were based on the false premise that Korean politicians could accept a majority decision. To a Korean the democratic theory of a "loyal opposition" was unthinkable. If you did not agree with your political contemporary you walked out on him—or better yet, you did away with him by assassination.

MG watched appalled as one by one the heads fell. The first to go was Son Chin Woo of the Democratic Party, the "bloated plutocrat" cartoon—

who on December 30, 1945 during the excitement following announcement of proposed trusteeship for Korea, was murdered as he slept.

A year later "the silver axe" Lyuh Woon Hyung, in spite of his system of secret sleep in a new place every night, was shot on the streets of Seoul by a young man from North Korea. The afternoon of the assassination I met Richard Johnson at the bar of the Chosen Hotel just before he went upstairs to write the dispatch.

"I wish the real story of Lyuh could be told," Dick said. "There was a guy who tried to get along with the Commies!"

Another gentleman who tried to get along with the Commies was Kim Koo, The Tiger. As a result he fell victim to his own terrorist tactics.

In April 1948 just prior to the UN-sponsored general election for South Korea, Kim Koo and his voice Kimm Kiusic journeyed to Pyengyang for a meeting with the North Korean People's Committee over a proposed election for all Korea and the simultaneous withdrawal of both American and Soviet troops. Kimm Kiusic violently disagreed with the UN proposal to hold an election without the North, and just the month before had resigned his chairmanship of the South Korean Interim Legislature in protest—even though the reason for the UN Commission's decision was that its representatives had been denied access to Russian-controlled territory. Kimm evidently sincerely felt that such an election would divide the country permanently.

Dr. Kimm returned from the Soviet Zone with glowing reports of the Conference's approval of his withdrawal program—which General Hodge flatly rejected. The General's statement:

"There is every reason to believe that if such a withdrawal (of American troops) were carried out as demanded, the North Korean Communist Army and its horde of power-hungry camp followers and stooges already selected and trained for the job would take over control of the rest of the nation."

A now very weak and very weary Kimm Kiusic, once the fair-haired boy of Military Government, proceeded to denounce the American administration of South Korea as corrupt. He reported that he found factories in the Soviet Zone in fuller production and the Russians less obtrusive than the occupation officials of the South.

"Americans," he said, "meddle too much... Koreans in forty years of Japanese occupation learned to work with dishonest Japanese officials and now they use the experience in using Americans to help work their corruption. Several Americans have gone home rich."

Kim Koo was less vociferous but more deadly. The story goes that he made a private agreement with the communists to spread rebellion among discontented members of the South Korean constabulary (now the army of South Korea) and the police. Of this program Kimm Kiusic was terrified, and he went into permanent retirement "for reasons of health."

Kim Koo, backed by the communists and the Russians, is credited with responsibility for the bloody uprisings of the constabulary at Yosu and Sunchon in November 1948. Much to Kim's surprise, enough of the constabulary and police remained loyal to Rhee's government to quell the riots.

Seeing that the anti-communist Rhee was the greatest obstacle to the success of his schemes, Kim Koo stationed a member of the constabulary, a certain Lieutenant Ahn, above Dr. Rhee's home with a battery and bombs and orders to await an opportune moment to blow up the master and his house.

One day in June 1949, Lieutenant Ahn called at The Tiger's home to discuss the matter.

The plot was faulty, the Lieutenant declared. From here on in, they could count him out.

Kim Koo ordered him to fire the battery.

Ahn refused.

Kim Koo repeated the order, with characteristic threats—whereupon the Lieutenant drew a .45 caliber pistol (American Army issue) and shot the seventy-three-year-old terrorist four times, killing him instantly. Ahn later confessed that he had slain The Tiger to keep him from "using part of the Korean Army for his own purposes."

The dead Kim Koo still had enough prestige to command at his funeral the greatest crowd of Korean mourners since the death of the Old Korean King. But his demise left the seventy-four-year-old Syngman Rhee complete master of South Korea's political field, with only the ever-present threat of the communists to challenge him.

Syngman Rhee – Dictator or Democrat?

Winter was just getting well under way in 1945 when we decided that, at least for our own benefit, we must sort the Somebodies from the Upstarts among the dozens of politicians who were representing themselves to us as Korean leaders.

To do this, we must conduct a survey in the field. "A survey in the field." Sounds so simple, doesn't it? Here's what it meant, that winter.

As political experts for the Department of Public Information, a teammate and I were given a list of the politicians—the same men I discussed in the previous chapter—and a sheet of carefully prepared questions, and told to go all over a certain section of the map of South Korea and find out what the Koreans thought of these politicians. We took along a Korean interpreter.

The three of us traveled by jeep over the glassy pock-marked roads in sub-zero weather, from one Korean opinion to the next. It is nothing like ringing doorbells in the States, where a solid block of houses may start you well on your way to a cross section of the people's thinking. In the Korean province we were to cover, the villages are tiny and the farms remote—and sometimes where it said on the map there was a road, we would find a mere track where we alternately wallowed in drifts of snow and side-slipped over hard patches of ice-bound earth. We found our first Korean leading his bull and cart home from Market Day. He had just sold the straw shoes which he made in his spare time these cold months, and a little of the rice he still had left from the year's bumper crop.

The interpreter hailed the Korean and offered him a cigaret.

The bull stood placidly munching his cud and emitting small puffs of warm white breath from his nostrils. The Korean citizen and our interpreter, stamping their feet and hugging themselves in the cold, talked politely of the black market in rice—in accordance with the Oriental custom of never coming with indecent haste to the point of any meeting. Then, at a nod from the interpreter, we came forward. We were waddling figures in hooded parkas, two pairs of fatigue pants each, and high-topped field boots. I fished in a side pocket for our list of names and questions, grasped a pencil firmly in the huge wooly fingers of my mittens. The interpreter took the list of names, and began reading.

Our first question: "Have you ever heard of this man?"

At each name, the farmer shook his head.

Finally, his face brightened. "Cho Man Shik! Yes, know him!"

"Do you know anything about him?" my partner asked.

There is no such thing as a quick answer in Korea. The farmer scratched his head, studied carefully the turned-up toe of his rubber shoes—and at last appeared to consider with equal care the question we had put.

"Him Christian," he told us. "Preacher."

"Do the people like him?"

"Yes, they like. He good man."

But Cho Man Shik was in Russian custody, north of the 38th parallel. A Presbyterian minister known as the Ghandi of Korea because of his advocacy of passive resistance under the Japanese, Cho would be someone we could depend on to help the New Korea—if we could reach him. He was being held incommunicado.

So, wearily, we proceeded with the list of names. And we were almost to the end when the farmer smiled.

"Syngman Rhee!" he exclaimed. "Everybody know Dr. Rhee!"

And that is where we came out, almost every time. Many knew Cho Man Shik. And, even among those who could neither read nor write, "everybody know Dr. Rhee!"

Our five-in-one rations (five men for one day, or one man for five days) were down to the cans and the little cellophane sacks of the fifth day, and we had almost covered the rugged little section of map the Colonel assigned us. I was sitting beside the road, opening a cold can of beef and vegetables.

"Sure, everybody know Dr. Rhee," my teammate growled into a canteen cup of synthetic lemonade. "But what do they say when we ask what they know about him?"

The translator had excused himself and disappeared over the side of the roadbed, so I replied accurately: "Great scholar. Good family in Korea. Travel many places."

I made my own effort to get to know Dr. Rhee. And instead, I got to know his wife.

I was to have just the one interview; and as I made my way up the low gradual hill to the brick mansion with the blue tile roof, I was gathering my resources for one big super-human effort to understand. The time would be so short; and it was so important that I see, if I could, the man behind this name which all Korea knew.

My escort and I were received by Mrs. Rhee, who led us into the Western style room in which the visit would take place. The room was stiff and unlived in—Victorian decor, as interpreted by the Japanese. Aging velour drapes breathed out stifling dust particles to dull the oblique rays of afternoon sunshine. An upholstered davenport squatted sullenly at an awkward angle. A dead fireplace yawned bleakly. A garish Western-style glass vase sat on a lace doily in the middle of a round long-legged center table. And a light dust was over everything, for the Korean idea of dusting is to dab with feathers at the places that show.

The rest of the house, formerly Japanese and furnished to Dr. Rhee by American Military Government, was undoubtedly as charmingly simple as the others I saw in the Gold Coast area; and I am sure Dr. Rhee himself was no more at home in the ghastly "Western" room than I. We faced each other on hard wooden rockers, Dr. Rhee looking as if he would rather have sat cross-legged on the floor.

He was in Korean dress—a grey robe of heavy worsted, with white trim. Underneath he wore white trousers, tied at the ankles over low-cut American shoes. Rhee was of average height even among Western men, and almost stocky in contrast to those of his countrymen who have lived for so many years on the rice and dried fish diet of Korea. When he crossed the room to the ridiculous little rocker, I noticed that in spite of his years in the western world, he still moved in the shuffling gait of those who wear heel-less Oriental shoes.

Today, though still firm and erect, he was not the Dr. Rhee I was accustomed to seeing on the platforms of Korean political rallies. He was weary; and his face was expressionless, somehow, in its gravity.

In contrast Mrs. Rhee, her face peculiarly determined in its regularity of feature, was young looking. Her hair was grey, but the face could have been in its forties. She was wearing western clothes, probably from our country—in the style of the war years when seams and hemlines took into consideration the fabric shortages rather than the limitations of individual physique.

Sometimes, when beside her husband on the platform at a public gathering, Mrs. Rhee would wear the native Korean costume. But the people were not pleased by this gesture.

"And when they find fault with the way she ties the *chogeri*, the short jacket," a missionary-trained Korean friend said to me behind his hand at a Sam Il Day celebration, "it is not this Mrs. Rhee that they are criticizing. It is the other Mrs. Rhee that they are remembering. After all, Dr. Rhee represents himself as a Christian. He should not, then, have two wives."

The "other" Mrs. Rhee was a Korean woman he had married before he became quite such a great scholar and traveled quite so many places. Still legally Mrs. Rhee, she now lived in one of the provinces north of the 38th parallel.

"This" Mrs. Rhee, my hostess, was an Austrian Dr. Rhee had met and married while an unofficial delegate to the League of Nations in Geneva.

"We have worked many years for Korea," she was saying. I had asked her how she liked Korea. "For my part this work was done on faith—faith in Dr. Rhee. So I am particularly happy that I like being here—that I find the country charming, and my husband's people worthy of the lifetime he has given them."

Dr. Rhee's face was amiable, blank.

"Do you feel your people are making satisfactory progress in consolidating their political viewpoints?"

I asked him. "Will they be ready soon to show us the leadership they want?"

But the answer came from the other wooden rocker.

"Dr. Rhee feels," she said firmly, "that there are far too many political parties registered. It is frankly ridiculous that anyone who wishes should be allowed to form a party."

"I know," I said. By now there were over two hundred. And one I had just registered was a tiny group calling itself something like "The Objectors to The New Society for The Earliest Possible Formation of a Coalition Party."

"But they will disappear," I told Mrs. — and Dr.— Rhee gently. "It was the same in our country, you know, after 1776. There will be a converging of interests, once each group is given a chance to express itself."

"But Dr. Rhee feels something has to be done *now* about the communists," she said. "Your government is permitting them complete freedom, when instead they should be exterminated."

"The Russians were our allies," I said. "We are trying very hard to come to an agreement with them on a government for all Korea. If we should injure the people who represent their way of life, or even fail to allow them freedom of speech, we might destroy any possibility of bringing about the unity which is so important to your country.

"You need not tell me the great value of political unity," Dr. Rhee said testily. "There is no one in Korea who understands it better than I do. As you will observe from my speeches, I have frequently said that I want all Koreans without exception to follow me."

Dictator, or democrat? That was, and still is, one of the most frequent questions asked about Syngman Rhee. Dr. Rhee's history could have produced either one, for it is the history of a revolutionary.

For the first ten years of his political life Rhee was a minor character fighting in company with the Progressives for reform of the Lee Dynasty of old Korea. His activities led to his arrest immediately after the assassination of Queen Min; and he spent the following seven years, until 1904, in prison.

Now as he pushed the wooden rocker into gentle motion with the flat of his sole, he was gently touching together the tips of his fingers, then rubbing them. For the first seven months of his imprisonment he had been tortured daily, and his fingers so badly mashed that after forty years he still was soothing them.

"It will take a long time," I said, "to form a Korean republic in the democratic way; but do you not feel it should be done that way?" I looked eagerly at Dr. Rhee.

"We feel," said his wife, "that more should be done immediately to strengthen Dr. Rhee's position in the country, if he is to be asked to assume the burden of its leadership. For instance, this coalition of the right with the left that you expect him to tolerate. The non-communist left, your Military Government calls it." Mrs. Rhee's English was faultless, its preciseness the only hint of her European origin. "Dr. Rhee feels there is no such thing here as a non-communist left. And, after all, he does know Korea."

This last was a statement currently in common dispute among Koreans. Many of his countrymen, especially the political leaders who had spent the past forty years working inside Korea for independence, claimed his long absence had put Rhee completely out of touch with Korea and her problems.

"What are the principal changes, Dr. Rhee, since you were here in 1913?" I asked.

"All these political parties," he said softly. "Nobody talked politics under the Japanese. I am very happy to see my country liberated . . . And have you, too, found many changes?"

"Yes, even since 1939, when I came to spend a summer with my family at the Unsan gold mines."

"Tell me," he said, "what is being done now about these mines. Are they starting up again?"

"I really don't know. They're most of them north of the 38th parallel, and we've had no word."

"But why is nothing being done? Why doesn't your government try to find out something?"

"Probably because gold is not the thing your people need most urgently at this time," I said.

"But *I* would very much like to have a gold mine!" For the first time, he spoke eagerly.

During long years as a professional politician and unofficial ambassador and minority crusader Dr. Rhee had been dependent on the contributions of the dwindling number of people who still believed enough to give their money. Sometimes, it is said, his personal friends had to help him. And now, he was tiring . . .

Mrs. Rhee was still talking about his knowledge of Korea and its people, saying: "Your people should listen more to Dr. Rhee."

At first Military Government had listened, and gladly. But the fanfare of Dr. Rhee's triumphal return had barely died away when he and General Hodge began to discover that they did not see eye to eye at all.

Rhee's main quarrel with Military Government was, as Mrs. Rhee said, that we were tolerant of leftist groups in the country. To Rhee, all the leftists were communists in thin disguise, and what we so smugly fancied was "middle ground" was a quagmire in which we would shortly find ourselves sunk if we did not listen to him.

Rhee also at this time was strongly advocating withdrawal of American troops, and the granting of complete and immediate independence for his country. He made it quite clear that he felt the Koreans could work out their problems much more quickly without our interference.

So Dr. Rhee was definitely not, as so many observers were hinting, a Military Government man. He was his own white haired boy. Although in the beginning we might have liked to, we were not grooming him for the presidency—nor did we even want him in the job.

But even as I sat with him in the depressing nineteenth-century Western room, I knew Rhee would be Korea's first chief executive. At the moment to Koreans he was still a private citizen—just one of nearly two hundred aspirants for their leadership. But he would win it—because he was the one man in South Korea known to every farmer in every paddy field.

"Dr. Rhee, would you mind discussing your political platform?"

"It is very simple," he said. "You know most of the issues already, I assume, since your officials have—ah—discussed them with me so often. Immediate independence is the main one . . . For the rest, I would distribute former Japanese land to the people, I would nationalize banking institutions and heavy industry and public utilities."

"That is very similar to what the Russians are doing in the North, isn't it," I said, "except that they are redistributing all the land." I meant it as a suggestion of unity, but it was an unfortunate one.

"There is nothing similar about our plan and the communist plan," he said acidly. "They are the opposition, whether your people like to face the fact or no." And I remembered what Rhee had said to the press, immediately after his return to Korea—and before his return to diplomacy: "When I come to power, I shall crush the opposition!"

Not out-vote, out-think, or even out-maneuver —crush!

Dictator, or democrat? The best answer had come from one of my fellow officers in Military Government, and I considered it now:

"Rhee is not a fascist, nor is he a democrat. He could more truly be characterized as the last of the Bourbons. You remember what they said about the Bourbons: they never learned anything, and they never forgot anything."

Here was a man who got his Ph.D. at Princeton, while Wilson was still president there. But he had never truly learned the meaning of Wilson's words about self-determination of peoples—words Rhee himself used in his long fight for recognition of Korea's sovereign rights.

The thing Rhee never forgot, apparently, was his seven year stretch in prison. He never forgot the police methods he suffered and saw there— beating with bamboo rods, water torture, summary shooting without trial. For these are the methods he has used, since he came to power, to "crush the opposition."

When I asked him whether he did not favor immediate reform in Korean police methods, he said: "The country is in turmoil. The communistic influence is strong, and if Korea is not to go entirely communist, strong measures are necessary against it. In the United States you can still afford to treat communists 'democratically'—clear on up through the Supreme Court—because the force of their infiltration has not yet faced you with the issue of survival. In Korea, survival is the issue."

For a moment the room was in silence except for the creak of Dr. Rhee's wooden rocker and a faint drying sound as he rubbed his palms, then lightly caressed his fingers together. His face was closed down again; and he lidded his eyes as if in dismissal.

Mrs. Rhee rose from her rocker.

We stood too, and I looked disconsolately about the room. The tawdry velvet drapes were swelled and sucked back in a rising late afternoon breeze. They rose and fell as with operatic breath, and I saw the musty cloaks of a stock company chorus in *The Mikado*. The fireplace still yawned its black and dusty boredom. Empty, Mrs. Rhee's wooden rocker fidgeted against the parquet floor. Dr. Rhee seemed to be asleep; and although he only seemed to be, we stole out behind our hostess—at first without realizing we were on tiptoe.

Rhee was a powerful name long before she took it, I was thinking. Here was no "woman behind the throne." But certainly she and her husband were of a single mind on the abilities and qualifications of Dr. Rhee.

When the climb grew steep and he wearied, she would get out and push. That was the way it was with them, I decided. And she talked when she knew he would want her to do the talking. In their public appearances together on the platform, she never talked. She sat—in Korean costume. But with us he had evidently felt that it would be better for her to have most of the say. That way he would be committed to nothing—and his praises would of course fall more sympathetically on our ears.

Mrs. Rhee had led us back through the mahogany paneled passageway, back to the front door of the yellow brick mansion with the blue tiled roof. We thanked her, and she thanked us in turn for the visit.

Then she looked closely at me and said: "You understand, of course, that Dr. Rhee wants nothing for himself?"

I nodded.

But I could not see clearly the Dr. Rhee she so urgently wanted me to see. I could not see the Father of Korea, the Lodestar, the dispassionate humanitarian, the Western-schooled statesman in the iron-grey robe.

I saw a weary traveler who had come over many paths that only seemed to lead to freedom. I saw an old man, soothing tortured fingers. A man whose eyes had lighted only once in an afternoon—at the thought of a gold mine.

I Meet the Russians

Everybody wanted to meet the Russians. Even in the first few months of occupation this was not easy, and later it became well-nigh impossible.

In the early days there were stories of parties up along the border, where the Russians officers would drink our own into a state of semi-paralysis and then amuse themselves by crashing through the paper *shoji* which served as walls in their Japanese houses. By January 1946 the high command of both armies had put a stop to all such "informal" meetings between personnel of the two forces.

As time went by and our troubles with them increased and multiplied I became more and more interested, and personally curious, to know what our Russian allies were like as people. At every opportunity I sought out Koreans who had known them. After talking with quite a number, I still did not know what the Russians were like; but I did form some picture of conditions in Russian-controlled territory as far as the Korean who owned a little property was concerned. The stories these Koreans brought down from the north proved far better anti-communist propaganda than anything MG's Department of Public Information could devise.

Miss Cho, whose father had been a wealthy landholder in North Korea, told me how her father's house and lands had been requisitioned at gunpoint by the Russians, and the entire family forced to flee. She told how the Russian soldiers lived off the land, robbing the Koreans of their cattle and their rice. She also saw trainloads of Korean cattle being shipped farther north, evidently for Russian troops in Manchuria.

One of my informants was Mr. Huh, son of the fine old Korean gentleman who had been my father's chief assayer at the mines in North Korea before the war. A number of times he crossed the border, and each time reported to me what he saw. Early in 1948 he told me all able-bodied men between 17 and 25 in North Korea were being drafted for the North Korean army and those from 25 to 30 were being taken to Russia to work. He himself was taken to the police station and questioned for two weeks on conditions in South Korea. Even his old mother and his wife and baby were held for a week by the police. The Russian and Korean police together, he said, relieved him of about two million yen.

I questioned him on food conditions in North Korea. He said that the Russians had collected all the rice and were rationing it only to the families whose men they had taken. What little there was for sale in the black market cost ¥1,000 for small mal (about eight quarts). During this same period the black-market price of rice in South Korea was about half that, and two hop (two thirds of a pint) a day was rationed at the government price of ¥140 a small mal to all non-producers.

It seemed that the first Russian soldiers to effect occupation of North Korea were a lawless and disorderly lot. Hundreds of instances of rape and looting were reported by both Koreans and Japanese. Some of the Russians even admitted to the Koreans that they were recently-discharged convicts who had been conscripted for the outbreak of hostilities between the USSR and Japan. When Korean representatives protested, they were told that these men would soon be replaced by more orderly troops, but that for the moment nothing could be done.

Originally the Russians placed Cho Man Shik, the Christian merchant-preacher known as "the Ghandi of Korea," at the head of their Executive People's Committee in Pyengyang. Cho was very popular, and it is felt that he accepted the position to be of service to his countrymen. By January 1946 he had crossed swords with his Russian masters over Trusteeship and thenceforth was kept in "protective custody" in his hotel. His position was filled by the puppet Kim Il Sung.

Local People's Committees were organized in every community and armed by the Russians to preserve peace. According to refugees, they subjected the people to a wave of terrorism far different from the democracy that had been promised. Citizens were killed, jailed, beaten or robbed for speaking openly against the Committee, for being well-to-do, or for in any way causing Committee members to think that they represented an anti-communist element.

In listening to these tales of rapine and vandalism, I had always to keep in mind that their bearers were the disaffected element from the North, and that there were many thousand Koreans who seemed perfectly content with the way things were being done up there. And we had no reason to be smug or even confident about our own half of the occupation. The fact that the traffic between the two zones was largely one-way could be taken only as proof of capitalism's appeal as opposed to communism when that was the only choice.

As one Korean said to me: "It's not that the Americans look so good; it's that the Russians look so bad."

Actually the average Korean's desires, as shown by many opinion polls, fell somewhere in between what the two zones had to offer; for what he really wanted was a socialist state.

Not until the first US-USSR Joint Commission met in Seoul did the Russians show beyond any doubt that their object was to make Korea a communist satellite.

Before this meeting only electricity and mail had officially crossed the border—the latter twice a month by special arrangement between Soviet and American postal authorities. This state of bisection was rapidly proving disastrous to Korea's economy; for the south is the rice bowl and workshop, while the north is supposed to be the supplier of raw materials such as coal, iron and lumber which made the wheels in the factories turn and kept the urban populace housed and occupied.

In March 1946 a long train filled with Soviet officials, from three-star generals to interpreters and stenographers, puffed into Seoul station—ostensibly to confer with American delegates concerning the removal of the artificial barrier dividing the country, and the establishment of a provisional government for all Korea as provided by the Moscow Decision.

The Russians immediately took an adamant stand on a delicate issue: no Korean political parties or individuals should participate in the government if they had in any way demonstrated against Trusteeship. Now we knew why the Communist Party of South Korea had been required to reword their banners in the exciting days of early January! Compliance with the Soviet demand would mean the Communist Party would be in sole control of the new Korean Provisional Government from its inception.

American opposition to the demand finally led to a Russian compromise: they agreed to consult with any Korean parties who, regardless of former opposition, would now sign a declaration promising to abide by the Moscow Decision. This compromise blew up when General Hodge announced in answer to anxious inquiries: "Signing the declaration for consultation with the Joint Commission does not indicate that the political party or social organization favors Trusteeship." To the Russians, this allowance for a legal opposition was amazing and completely unacceptable.

When no headway could be made in forming a government the Commission turned its attention to the economic pressure of the 38° parallel that was like an iron ring, squeezing Korea in the middle and cutting off free circulation of goods and services from one zone to another. Maj. General Arnold, who had patiently but firmly been dealing with the Russians on the matter of trade, dramatically suggested at an eleventh-hour meeting that the division at the 38° parallel be entirely abolished. Although Koreans desperately needed to exchange the industrial goods of the north for the agricultural products of the south, on this proposal too the Soviets proved intransigent.

So after a month of futile wrangling the Soviets packed their bags and huffed out of Seoul station— without a single thing being accomplished on either side. And thus ended our first attempt to do business with the Russians.

I talked with Vladimir Pekarsky, a white-Russian-American Army sergeant who often served as General Hodge's personal interpreter, and who had been with the joint US-USSR survey party when the 38° parallel was officially marked off.

"What's it all about?" I demanded. "I can see the Russians are being completely impossible on this Trusteeship thing. But isn't there *any* way we could get along with them better on other things?"

"I do not know," he said. "Personally, it is possible to get along with a Russian person if you do not make him uneasy with talk of your philosophy. But officially—" he paused. "On that survey party, we got along very well—and not because we did all the giving in, either. On that party there was—how would you say—a congenial meeting of self-respecting personalities, supported by definite and unchanging instructions on both sides.

"On other matters where I have served as interpreter, I have often witnessed vascillation on our part. Sometimes it would happen that the officer charged with negotiating would first say one thing, then he would receive a later directive from higher authority and be forced to retract. This occasionally involved the breaking of a promise given. And when we broke a promise in this way, the Russians could hardly believe it! Why, they were like children, when a birthday party is called off. That is, at first they were child-like. Later they became like the bear, when this would happen. You see, they in their government are not equipped to understand that democracy often means a change or a shilly-shally in the order of things. They can only regard disappointing official change as a promise broken, an evidence of bad faith."

The only American women I knew who had met the Russians on the other side of the border were ten Red Cross workers. I heard their story when they landed in the WAC billet after spending two whole days behind the iron curtain.

Their plane from Tokyo to Seoul missed Kimpo airport in the fog and sailed on up into the Russian zone. When Russians began to uncover their fighter planes, the bewildered pilot thought he had better land to explain.

A cordon of Russian soldiers immediately surrounded the troop carrier, and passengers were ordered to descend. I would like to have seen their faces when ten American girls crawled gingerly down the ladder, instead of the bristling platoon they were apparently expecting.

"How did they treat you?" I asked eagerly.

"Very politely but very firmly," was the reply. "They insisted that we have dinner with them that evening. A Russian officer firmly took each one of us in charge and escorted us to the officers mess. The dinner wasn't bad, but the vodka was terrific. If we refused to drink, or tried to take it in small sips, our escort—again firmly—placed his hand under our elbow and forced the whole glassful down at one gulp."

"Fattening you for the kill?" I suggested.

"That's what we thought," replied my interviewee, "and each of us was prepared to defend her honor to the death!

"After dinner our escorts took us to a barracks where some beds had been made up. This is it, we thought. Then they politely bowed, thanked us for a pleasant evening, and left. After two days we were extradited by 24th Corps, and that was that."

"But still," I said, "you can say you have lived with the Russians!"

On a day in January when the hills were sere and brown and covered with patches of snow, a woman news correspondent and I set out to meet the Russians. We had no idea how we were going to bring this "impossible" meeting about; we had simply decided to trust to fate and our friends. As it happened, both were kind.

One of our friends, Major DeWolff, had already invited us for a week-end visit on the edge of the Russian zone, at Kaesong. Our next problem was how to get there.

The solution was furnished by another friend in charge of the South Korean railways, the southern segment of the former South Manchurian Railway extending from Kaesong to Pusan on the tip of the peninsula. He promised me a "private steam-heated car" to make the journey to the northern terminus.

The car turned out to be private enough, in that a couple of G.I.'s scraped off the Koreans who tried to swarm aboard; but it had no form of heat whatsoever. We wrapped ourselves in our blankets, sipped our thermos of hot coffee, and shivered all the way to the border.

That night the private car was left unguarded on a railway siding. Some Korean refugees from north of 38° slipped in, built a fire on the floor to keep themselves warm, and sent it up in smoke. If the claims against our occupation are ever totalled up, I suppose I shall be in debt to the government of Korea for one railway coach.

Major DeWolff had met us at the station and put us up in an Army field hospital nearby, but was powerless to bring us closer to the Russians.

Two miles beyond the town lay the first Russian outpost, a signal corps outfit whose main duty was to keep the telephone lines open between Pyengyang and Seoul. From a discreet distance one could view the field tent which housed the advanced guard of an opposing ideology. But the space intervening might have been a glacial crevasse.

Officially I had requested this trip to investigate political conditions along the border. The next day I went out to get my information, and contacted the intelligence officer of the American regiment which held Kaesong.

I learned that over a thousand Koreans a day were crossing the border into the southern zone. The chief danger to the North Korean emigrés lay in the no-man's-land between the zones, controlled by Korean bandits who took their money, goods, and sometimes even their lives. The Russians, for their part, did not molest them—in fact were apparently glad to be rid of these unregenerated capitalists whose lands, houses and cattle they could then confiscate with far less trouble.

The intelligence officer who gave me this information happened to be a White Russian whose parents had come from Lithuania. Since he spoke the language, one of his duties was to contact the Red Russians on any local business between the two zones.

He also happened to be an amiable young man, and we happened to be the first American women to arrive in Kaesong.

One of the paradoxes caused by the arbitrary division of Korea along the 38th parallel, he told us, was that the Onjin peninsula, which was in the U.S. zone, could be reached only by going through Russian territory. He urged us to stay over and join the one weekly convoy the Russians allowed. By no stretch of the imagination could I extend my official duties so far, and I regretfully refused.

"I'm sorry too," he said. "Haeju, the largest Russian-held town the convoy passes, is really something to see. It looks like a set for a class-B movie on dictatorship—all hung with pictures of Stalin and Kim Il Sung!"

"The so-called Kim Il Sung," I corrected wryly. By this time we knew that the figure the Russians set up as head of the People's Committee of North Korea was not only a puppet but an imposter as well. The real Kim Il Sung had been a Korean general fighting with the Chinese army against the Japanese; and vital statistics showed us that if he had survived the war of Nippon and the peace of the Russian zone, he would by now be a man fifty-five years of age. The puppet was a fat sleepy-eyed youth not more than thirty.

It was probably coincidental that the telephone line between Seoul and Pyengyang went out the night we arrived. But it was hardly coincidental that our new-found friend met and picked us up on his way to ask the Russian officer to do a little trouble-shooting on his side of the line.

As we drew near the Russian headquarters after giving our sentry the proper password, the wan shafts of our headlights began to pick out American-made material. We drew up behind a GI two-and-a-half ton truck, in front of which was parked an equally familiar jeep, both distinguishable from our own only by the red star on the bumper.

As we entered the tent, which also appeared to be of US Army origin, the Russians snapped to attention and saluted with unanimous precision. I was impressed that they saluted under cover and without particular attention to rank, contrary to the custom in our Army.

In a hasty glance around while our friend was attending to the social amenities, I saw that the tent stove, field telephone and folding table were all duplicates of those we had back in Seoul. For the first time I realized the magnitude of lend-lease. The only thing Russian about the outpost was the Russians themselves.

The officer in charge was a first lieutenant. He offered us folding US-Army camp stools while he and our intelligence officer went to work on the intricacies of the telephone breakdown.

At an order from their lieutenant, two of the men "looked alive." They went to a box in the corner, took out tools and climbing spikes and safety belts, adjusted small battery lamps over their caps and went out into the darkness. The rest of the enlisted men were now seated on the ground, facing us in a stolid circle. I was amazed at their lack of curiosity. In my mind was a contrast between this arrival of ours and the reception two Russian women would get if they were to visit, even properly escorted, an American barracks tent in an isolated post. Was it fear, discipline or inertia that made the Russians so different? I had the feeling it was inertia.

Only one among them, the sergeant, seemed to have any life—or whatever the vital quality which in any army or any society makes a man an individual. Whether out of initiative, intelligence or a certain graciousness, the sergeant decided we might be feeling out of place in the strange atmosphere or shut out by the wall of Russian-language conference between the two lieutenants. He knew very little English and my one word of Russian was the equivalent of "bottoms up," hardly appropriate for the occasion. But the sergeant, a handsome lad with a blond crewcut and an engaging grin, bravely persisted.

When I did not understand his fragmentary questioning he smiled, waved his hands like semaphore flags signalling error, and took out his wallet. Carefully he extracted a worn picture and handed it to me.

"Me—" he said, tapping his left breast, "marry."

She was a buxom dark-haired lass, that much I could tell; but the photography was the amateur variety that is so candid as to be virtually anonymous. "She is very pretty," I said, handing back the picture as carefully as he had tendered it.

"No see," he went on earnestly, "no see—" and he held up six fingers.

"Six years?" I suggested.

He nodded, pleased that I had understood his "English."

"Me—" He looked helpless for just a moment. Then he fished in his wallet, more hastily this time, and brought out a picture of a little valley full of tiny trees and tiny houses. "Ukraine," he said. "No go home—" six fingers held up. He plucked at the sleeve of his uniform. "No—"

"No leave?" I prompted.

He did not understand. Later our intelligence officer told me the sergeant had indeed been in the Army six years with no leave—as had many others in the area, all transferred to Kaesong direct from the Eastern front. This contradicted the rumor that most of the Russians north of 38° were the Mongoloid type, drafted from the Siberian wilds.

I looked carefully again from face to face, still trying to decide just what type they were. My first impression was of their extreme youth. The privates seemed no more than sixteen or seventeen. My second observation was of their slovenliness; and it came second only because their uniforms were so bad I had been making an effort not to stare openmouthed. I now gave up and looked them over.

It was, as I have said, winter. The men's uniforms were not of wool, and they had no overcoats—a fact which they compensated by underpadding the garments into shapeless knobby cocoons which had lint in the creases and shone with grease and grime on the protrusions. I was sure they could not have been taken off or washed all winter. One could blame this on lack of facilities if our own soldiers living exactly the same way a few hundred yards back had not managed to look fairly clean—and if these men had not actually looked worse than underprivileged natives. I later learned that even the Koreans were shocked at Russian standards of cleanliness. Miss Cho told me in horror how she had once seen a very grimy Russian soldier wash his hands and face in a bowl and then drink the water.

The officer and the sergeant alone looked as if they had paid recent attention to their personal appearance. But even as I made this comparison, I was beginning to think I understood the men's lethargy.

The lieutenant's uniform was of wool—an immaculate, smartly tailored ginger-brown with red epaulets. The sergeant too wore wool—a tunic with no padding, since his uniform was warm enough—and he looked fairly clean and had some shape to him and some pride in his bearing. In fact, compared to his buddies the sergeant looked like a student prince.

I talked later with our intelligence officer about this, and he told me it was the same with all the Russian units he had seen.

"But how can those soldiers live like that and go on swallowing all this Russian talk about beautiful, ideal, classless brotherhood?" I asked indignantly.

"Maybe they just dream different," he said with a grin. "In the States we say anyone can get to be President. In Russia, when a boy baby comes, perhaps the neighbors all crowd around and burble: Maybe he'll get to be a *sergeant* some day!"

"Boy baby indeed!" I sniffed. "You're not as progressive as the Red Russians!"

The sergeant, seeing my glance travel among the men, spoke to them. One or two grinned bashfully.

"I ask," he said, hesitating over the new English word he had just heard me use, "years." He pointed at me.

"My age?"

"Yes." He held up ten fingers, then ten more, then two. Then he smiled with impish inquiring sweetness, very pleased with himself.

I laughed outright, and shook my head; but I too was pleased by this age-old male gesture of under-guessing the lady's years.

It developed into a game. Urged on by their sergeant, the comrade with the most vitality and good will, all the men joined in and underguessed my age, then my friend's. Then we guessed theirs—tactfully holding up more fingers than we thought were right. They looked like highschool boys; but we learned to our surprise that all the men were over eighteen and some were in their twenties.

By this time our escort had finished his conversation with the lieutenant, and he turned to us.

"Are there any questions you girls would like me to translate? Stay away from politics, though," he warned.

I cudgeled my brain for a safe subject that would be of any interest and finally came up with a question about the Russian WAC.

"Are there many in North Korea? And what do they do?"

"There are quite a few in our forces here." The lieutenant's reply was clipped; and since he did not answer it, I saw that I had made a mistake in putting even a general question about their duties.

I then asked what the lieutenant's group did in the evening for entertainment. In reply he dragged out a tattered scrapbook and slowly turned the pages. Pictures of Hollywood stars, cut from American movie magazines. He stopped before a stylized photograph of Deanna Durbin and asked the question I had already heard several times in Manila, Japan and Korea.

"Is she dead?"

I assured him she was very much alive, but said I could give him no recent news of her.

Though we had not heard Miss Durbin in two or three years, we had not worried. Changes were the order of our lives—especially the kind of change decreed by Hollywood. But I wondered who had started this rumor; and further, why from Manila to Moscow Deanna Durbin should be our most popular candidate for world citizenship.

Her picture reminded me that Russians are noted for their magnificent choral work. If one were to believe what comes out of Hollywood (which apparently I did) when any group of Russians get together, they just naturally burst into soul-stirring pipe-organ chords of song.

In a last effort to keep this strictly non-political party going, I asked the officer if he and his men would sing us some Russian ballads.

But the men didn't know the words to any of the traditional ballads he led off with—and didn't seem to care. It ended in a duet by the lieutenant and the sergeant. The officer, the older man with a suggestion of the Hollywood Russian about him, made a courtly apology in which there was also something of sadness.

"But perhaps they were born in the wrong time to learn the old ballads," he said.

Or perhaps they had never felt like singing.

"I am so sorry I had no vodka to offer," the lieutenant said as we rose to leave, "but it is issued only once each month—and it is always gone the next day." There was a joshing smile on his face as he looked at his men.

No change of expression visited their faces as they heard the lieutenant's good-natured jibe. They had risen as we rose—and were standing as they had sat, a stolid circle of man-flesh.

I looked about the tent—and through its wrinkling flap, where a lightless night extended. It would be the same here every night—only colder outside, perhaps, or warmer.

My glance fell once more on the worn scrapbook, still open at the portrait of Durbin.

I thought of Tolstoy—and of war, and peace.

United States Military Government in Korea and Economic Cooperation Administration 1945 – 1950

Civil Affairs Training School – Stanford University.

First WAC at CAT School Lieutenant Ada Leeke graduates in April 1945.

April 1945 graduates: Lieutenant Leeke second from left in front row.

Civil Affairs Staging Area, Presidio of Monterey: Post newspaper staff, Assistant Editor Leeke front row, far left.

The author as Liaison Officer to General Archer L. Lerch, Military Governor of Korea.

1946: Going to press with CHUKAN (WEEKLY) DIGEST.

Editor with her Korean counterpart at CHUKAN DIGEST. (Man with wo-man shot.)

Editor with her Korean counterpart at CHUKAN DIGEST, and with his staff.
(On reverse of this picture is an inscription which if translated may be relevant. Original manuscript in archive of Center for Korean Studies, University of Hawaii at Manoa.)

(On the reverse of this portrait of the author, for translation, is what appears to be some kind of citation — dated December 1946.)

Aerial view of Seoul with Capitol – headquarters for United States Military Government in Korea – at center. Photograph by US Army Signal Corps immediately following World War II.
—*National Archives*

General Douglas MacArthur leaves SHAPE headquarters, Dai Ichi Building in Tokyo with noon crowds of GIs and curious Japanese looking on.
—National Archives

This photo's credit line, like all previous pictures of the United Nations personnel, is DEPT OF PUBLIC INFORMATION US AMGIK. On the back is written:

> LST arrived Inchon from Tientsin 11 May (1946?) [year not given] with 1091 repatriates from Mukden. Father George Carroll (standing, left rear) Catholic representative on LARA, accompanied LST to Tientsin and back to Inchon with refugees. Carl Judy (sitting left foreground) is Protestant representative for L A R A.
> Some of groups were flown from Mukden to Tientsin. Others walked. Will stay 12 days at Receiving Camp at Inchon before going to permanent residences in provinces.

15 August 1946: Repatriation arrivals listed as left to right.
KIM LAH KOH DR. KOO CHANG

17 October 1946: Happy UNRRA baby trying on new clothes.

Communist Party members gather at South Gate, Seoul during a demonstration. Shots were fired from the building in the background later in the day. 1 March 1947. —National Archives

Seoul, Korea 25 June 1947: Colonel General Terenty F. Shtikov, Chief Commissioner of the Russian delegation, chairman; and Major General Albert E. Brown, Chief Commissioner of the American delegation during the first meeting of Korea's democratic parties and social organization with the US-USSR Joint Commission held in the Legislative Hall of the Korean Legislative Assembly.

—123rd Signal Photo Detachment

28 August 1947: View of the partially completed Bal An irrigation storage dam near Suwon. The spillway is at the far end of the dam. The area in the foreground is the reservoir site. Estimated completion date March 1949.

28 August 1947: Mr. Stanley I. Phillippi, advisor to Irrigation and Land Reclamation Section, Department of Agriculture inspects the Wang Sang Dam near Suwon. He is shown consulting with the engineers at the spillway site.

22 September 1947: Under-Secretary of War William H. Draper arrives at Kimpo Army Air Base from Tokyo.

Duk Soo Palace as home of US-USSR Joint Commission on Korea. The center pole had flown the red flag of Russia, which left with the Soviet delegation following recession of the commission 31 October 1947.

—National Archives

Three Korean merchants shovel snow from in front of their store on Bong Chang Street in Seoul, after the heaviest snowfall in 30 years. They are utilizing the famous Korean three-man shovel. 24 Jan. '48.
—National Archives

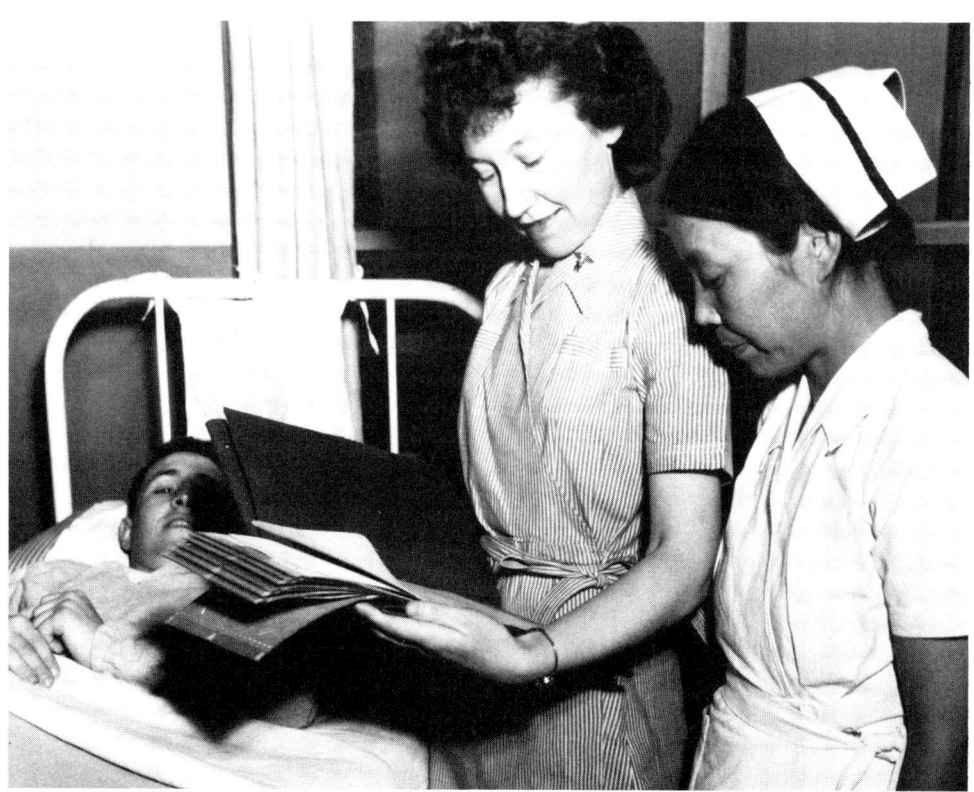

1st Lt. Sara Tapp, Army Nurse Corps and a Korean student nurse, Cecilia Kim, check the progress chart of patient Tec. 5 James Burnett, at the U.S. 377th Station Hospital in Seoul. 3 Feb. 1948.
—National Archives

Department of Public Information USMGIK at work on news for the world.

Koreans lining the roadways from Kimpo Airbase to Seoul awaiting the arrival of the United Nations Commission.

At Kimpo Airport Major General William Dean greets M. Gobaoa Menon, delegate to United Nations Commission on Korea and Under-Secretary of External Affairs for Hindustan.

Petrus J. Schmidt, Principal Secretary of The United Nations and Netherlands member of the United Nations Commission on Korea.

With the United Nations Commission on Korea.

Olivier Manet, France and Costelses Costhiles, France.

Left to right Mr. Graham J. Lucas, Assistant Secretary of the United Nations Commission from the United States; Mr. Langdon, U.S. Consul in Seoul; S. H. Jackson, Australian Delegate to U.N. Commission on Korea; Mr. Marc Schriber, United Nations Legal Aide.

Members of the UN Commission were welcomed by Koreans bearing flowers. Left to right: R. Yasin Mughir, Syrian Secretary; Dr. Zeki Djabi, Syrian delegate; M. Gobaoa Menon, Hindustan Under-Secretary of External Affairs; Dr. Yu Wan Liu, Chinese Consul General in Korea and Chinese delegate on the Commission; and Dr. Victor Chi-Tsai Hoo, Assistant Secretary General of the United Nations.

Mr. Yu Wan Liu, Chinese Consul General and delegate to the United Nations from China, reads an announcement from the United Nations that Korea will have a UN-supervised election this spring (1948). He speaks to a mass of some 80,000 Koreans crowded into Seoul Stadium to commemorate Korea's 1919 Declaration of Independence from Japan. 1 March 1948.   — National Archives

Miss Muriel McGuire, representative of USAMGIK Department of Public Information shows Mr. Pak Sang Byu, Korean education leader, through the newly opened library in the United States Information Center. Mr. Pak, known as "Brown '05," is a graduate of Brown University and was the first Korean Phi Beta Kappa. He is now executive president of the Korean Red Cross. Seoul, April 1948.
— National Archives

Seoul, 30 July 1948. Mr. Jack Newman of Santa Barbara, director of the OCI information center and Mr. Kim Wha Seon, a Korean counterpart at the center, show a poster prepared by the visual section of OCI to Mr. Leo Hart of Bakersfield, Mr. Jack Anderson of San Jose and Mr. John A. Morton from Billings, Montana. Mr. Hart is advisor to elementary and secondary schools, National Department of Education, USAMGIK. Mr. Anderson is trade and industrial education consultant with teachers training center, and Mr. Morton is assistant director and consultant to the TTC.

— National Archives

Seoul, 30 July 1948 Left to right: Mr. John Latrash, administrative assistant with Office of Civil Information in Los Angeles conducts Mr. Robert E. Gibson, Mr. Lee Chun Ho, and Mr. Wallace Moore on tour of the OCI Information Center Library. Mr. Gibson is advisor to the director of the National Department of Education, USAMGIK and Mr. Lee is assistant director. Mr. Moore is one of 20 distinguished American educators who arrived here last month to work with Koreans in a teachers training center for teachers and administrators.

– National Archives

Korean elections 1948.

Korean elections 1948: Polling booth closeup showing picture/hashmark balloting system.

Economic Cooperation Administration 1949-1950: Koreans bring supplies ashore under supervision of American Army personnel.
—*National Archives*

ECA cargo offload: Pillsbury flour. —National Archives

KOREAN CONFLICT. Pak Chong Moon, Civil Affairs representative, organizes the townspeople to form a community self government, at a village in Korea. 19 November 1950.

—National Archives

The preceding pictures were from the official record. Those which follow are a part of the author's private collection.

– Korean Gentleman

Farmer –

Korean Dancers
   Chang Chu Wha
   Cho Taik Wan

Dancers
   Chang Chu Wha
   Cho Taik Wan

Farmers Dance Festival

Farmers Dance Musician

Girls on See-saw

Scene from a Korean Opera
Lee Do Ryung

Sam Il Day
South Mountain

Korean Cradle

School Children

Children

Rice Fields

Farmer Plowing

Planting Rice

Drying Grain

Drying Ginseng at Kaesong

Threshing Grain

Shoeing a Bull

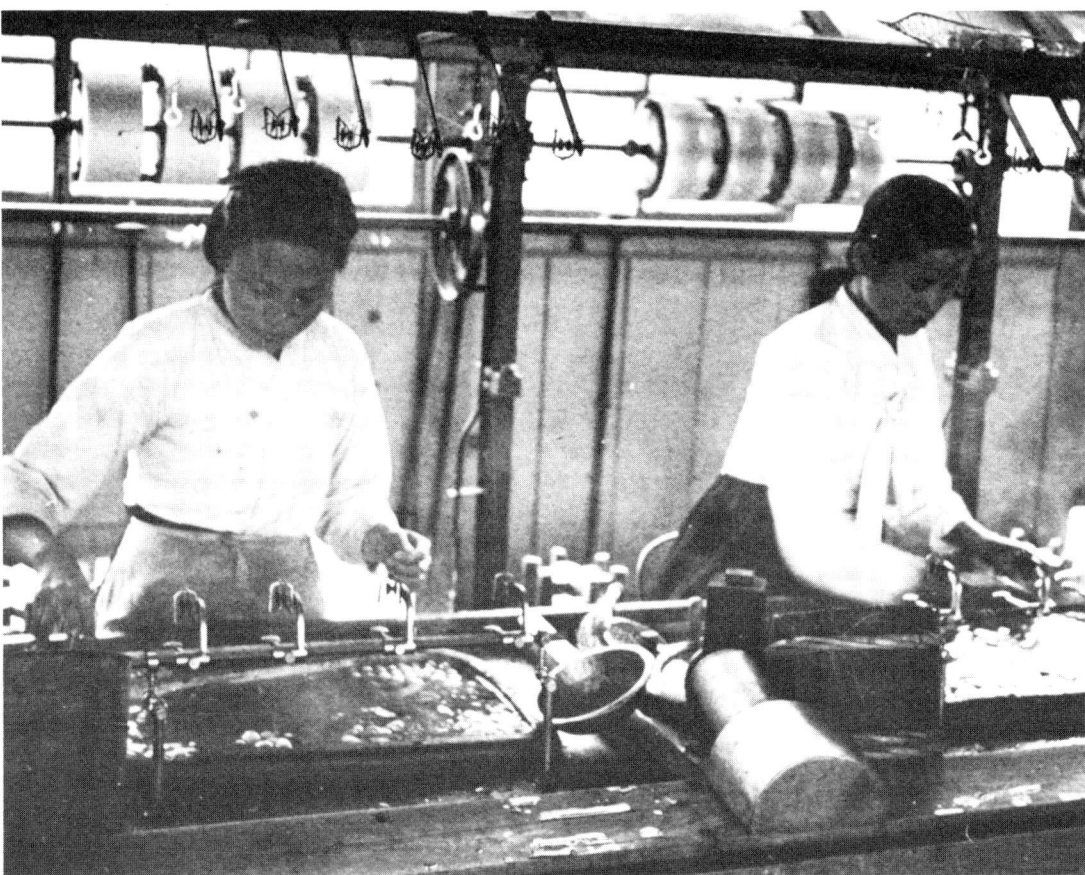

Unwinding Silk Cocoons — Suwon Experimental Station

Korean Roofs

Building a Korean House

Cutting Wood

Shinto Shrine

Tombs of the Eastern Kings

Tombs of the Eastern Kings

White Buddha

Seoul's South Gate

Gold Buddha

Anti-Trusteeship Demonstration January 1946

Student Demonstration October 1946

Student Demonstration October 1946

Trolley Scene

Market Scene

Capitol

Duk Soo Palace

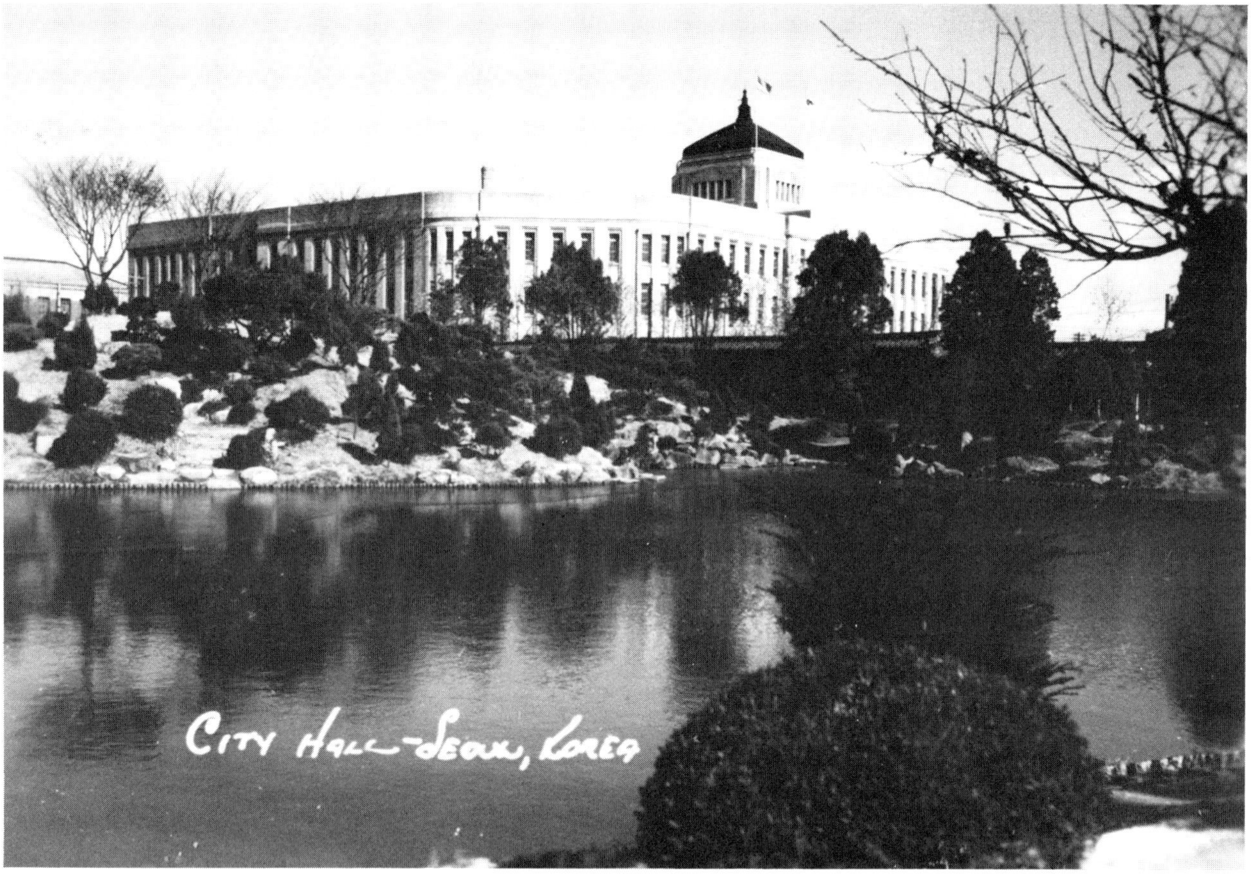
CITY HALL-SEOUL, KOREA

BANK OF CHOSEN
SEOUL, KOREA

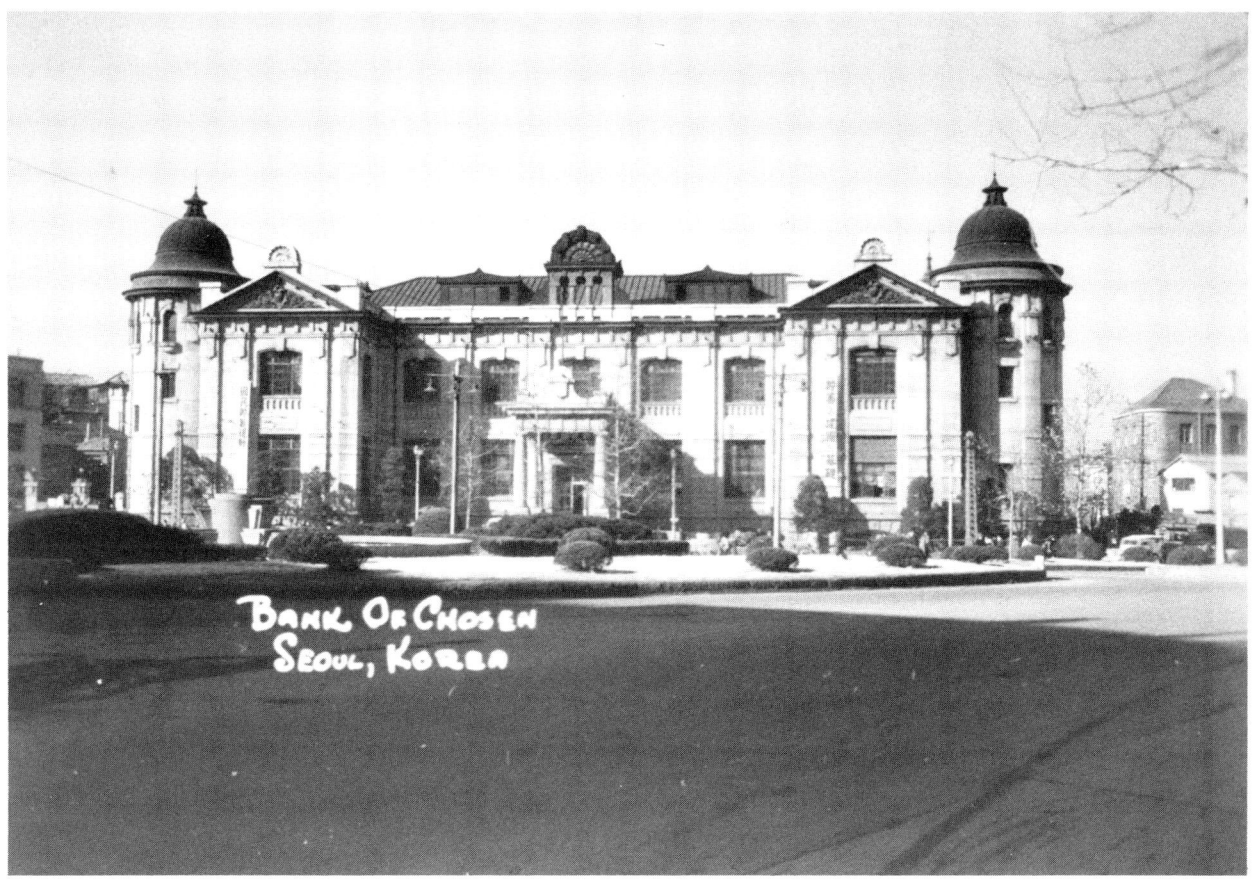

Main Street to Capitol

Han River Bridge

French Cathedral

Secret Garden Chang Duk Palace

Che Dan Shrine at rear of Chosen Hotel in Seoul

Honey Carts

Washing Clothes

Village Scene

Mountain Retreat

Mountain Village

Pastoral Scene Kaesong

Man Trouble – Korean Style

I knew I would run into man trouble when I was placed in authority over Korean males, and I did. Just how do I define man trouble? Well, I am afraid I am voicing the complaint exactly as so many other women before me have voiced it, in every language and in every period of history. I refer to the condition of being ignored!

At the time of this latest assignment I was still working on political analysis. When General Hodge sent down to our department to get information on a Korean politician, my office was supposed to find the facts for a report – and I was supposed to write it. But the Korean undercover men in the office were refusing to report to me. Instead, when they finished investigating they were going with their long closely-stroked notes and their interpreters to the sergeant who kept my files.

The agent would talk to the interpreter, who would talk to the sergeant, who would talk to me. I understood of course why they were doing it. According to their way of looking at me, I simply had not been born with any of the right equipment! They would lose face, reporting to an oversized girl child.

The sergeant was an intelligent man and could have handled the situation; but I am a patient woman only to a point, and I could not. It was just too complicated. It meant that when I wanted to ask for further details on a report, I had to talk to the sergeant who had to talk to the interpreter who had to question the investigator. And the more people you ring in on passing the word, the more like hearsay it becomes. So I was determined not to go through the channels the Korean men had established for me. I was just as self-conscious as they, just as much burdened with the awkwardness of strange custom. But why should we not all learn to be people together?

The first Korean male I bearded was the chief investigator. He was quite a personage, both in the office and in Seoul, and had much more face to lose than any of the others.

Not many people have had the opportunity to observe that the same essential types exist in all nations, stations and climes. There are Koreans who look like Herbert Hoover, there are Koreans who look like Eleanor Roosevelt, there are Koreans who look like your Aunt Susie and Uncle Theobald. This of course will seem exaggerated to anyone who has not seen a sufficient number of Koreans. But the familiar types are there; and as you get used to and forget the marks of racial origin and climate, you see them more and more clearly.

Mr. Lee, "my" chief investigator, was the Leslie Howard type. He was a tall slim bony English philosopher in baggy tweeds – the disinterested observer, the relaxed variety of thinker. He used to sit at his desk after he came in from an investigation, and smoke and think, and think and smoke. Then he would lean over his writing paper and make little notes, and smile whimsically, sometimes a little sadly, and make more notes – which he would give to the interpreter to give to the sergeant!

If I went up to him and his interpreter and asked questions direct, Mr. Lee was polite and made answers, but there was never any information in them. The information would arrive later, through the sergeant. I still don't know what would have happened if I had sent for Mr. Lee to come to me. I didn't go about "liberating" him in quite that way.

I chose a time when there were no other men in the office, just Mr. Lee and his interpreter. They were an oddly congenial team. The interpreter was the type the films so often used to cast as a French count – a dapper little man with good western clothes sharply pressed, and patent leather hair. I never quite knew what he thought. It was as if he didn't think, until Mr. Lee spoke. His name was Mr. Hyun.

I went up to Mr. Lee and Mr. Hyun. For just a moment Mr. Lee looked cornered, but then he replied civilly to my good-morning.

"I wished to thank you for the latest People's Committee report," I said—to them both, even though it was Mr. Lee who had gone out to get the information. "General Hodge was very pleased."

"The General told you this?" Mr. Lee's look was one of polite interest, which on a Korean face often denotes complete surprise.

"No, the word came through channels. Like everything else," I added—a rather sad attempt at lightness. "Colonel Newman told me. But you must admit that it is rather rare to have the channel bring a word of praise."

My smile was tentative, theirs imperceptible. Before I left them, I reached in the pocket of my field jacket and took out two packages of cigarets which I offered as graciously as I knew how to offer small gifts to discomfited Korean males. I meant it graciously, that much at least was right. And I didn't have any too many cigarets myself!

Mr. Lee, Leslie Howard, accepted his package just as graciously—and pocketed it, whereupon he took out his pipe, a pencil-stemmed Korean pipe with tiny round blister of a bowl. Mr. Hyun accepted his package like an insurance agent accepting a cigar from someone he thinks may still buy the insurance. He opened the pack, and offered me one. I declined, and left them.

The next time I saw Mr. Lee at his desk thinking and smoking and smoking and thinking, I noticed that at least he was smoking the cigarets.

This was the beginning of a better relationship in the office, although we were still awkward with one another. I continued a sort of "ice patrol," in which I would periodically arm myself with cigarets and a subject to discuss, and seek out Mr. Lee and Mr. Hyun—at first only when we were alone in the office. The subject I discussed with them was often the Army. I was trying to get across to them what it was like, to us. I wanted them to understand that my position in the office was as much a matter of being *put* in a spot as they thought theirs was. But I wanted them to understand all this without my having to say it, of course. A woman, after all, has a "face" of her own to consider.

Things gradually got better and easier all the time. Mr. Lee and Mr. Hyun were now bowing and saying good morning and good night, and even smiling when they said it. And when Mr. Lee finished his reports he was bringing them to my desk, again with a bow and smile, for translation.

I could tell, however, that Mr. Lee was still not entirely at rest in his mind about the situation.

His bows were mere inclinations, and his smile a bleak anglicized version which still bespoke some reservations. But about this time it happened that General Hodge sent down for information on a certain political leader who had been kicking up a particular row against Military Government.

Mr. Lee went out to get his facts, and then he came in and sat down at his desk and smoked and thought. Great clouds issued from his pipe, and diminished only as the haze seemed to lift from his mind. Then he wrote. And this time he was not smiling.

When the General received the thick report, he sent it back by messenger to our colonel. "This is not what I want!" the General's note shouted at us. "It's too complicated! What I want to know is, IS he, or ISN'T he?"

Was this leader, or was he not, a communist?

I had read all the evidence painstakingly and found it one of those very interesting and intricate cases in which a leading citizen raises a righteous ruckus, and some of his cheering section are righteous loyal Koreans (or Americans, or whoever) and some of the people in it are subversives who think his name will make an honest thing out of their reputation. Does the leading citizen want these subversives in his cheering section? Did he figure the more the merrier, and does he belong with them? Or does he not even know they are there?

They are not questions I would care to answer, unless I was sure I knew the truth and could prove it.

I went to Mr. Lee. "Do you feel," I said, "that you have got all the information it is possible to get on this case?" I was looking at Mr. Lee, of course, not at Mr. Hyun. When you speak with a deaf person, you do not after all stare at or shout into his hearing aid.

Mr. Hyun's voice came, then Mr. Lee's, then Mr. Hyun's. "I am afraid so. The situation there is very complicated, and I do not feel that we can be any more definite without calling down upon our heads a possible charge of character assassination. Naturally your government does not wish this. Nor can Korea spare any able leader who may even possibly be honest. Later there may be more information. Not now."

And later, I understand, Mr. Lee heard what difficulty I had in getting the report accepted. When a General sends down for a yes or no answer, I have always believed that he needs one, but certainly would prefer the truth. There are, among officers junior to a General, two schools of thought on this point. After a lot of talking, and a little stolid sitting, mine finally prevailed. And that is how it happened that to Mr. Lee I became a person, and he and I—and Mr. Hyun, of course—got to be people together.

The other men in the office had not been so difficult to win to this casual view. For one thing, their "faces" may have been smaller.

As time passed and more and more American women arrived in Korea, it seemed that all the native men began to look upon us as some sort of neuter, half mother and half male.

This was forcibly brought home to me when in the summer of 1946 I was given charge of the *Chukan* (Weekly) *Digest*, a Military Government newspaper with a circulation of 600,000 throughout South Korea. The *Digest* employed six or seven Korean men as reporters, translators and editors; and in my position as editor-in-chief it often seemed to me I spent more time looking after "my boys" than I did writing and editing the news.

There was Mr. Kwack, for instance. The house of Kwack was for some reason or other continually on the move. As each new shift was in the offing he would approach me with a pleading look in his eye. The request never varied.

"Today I move. Please I need truck."

For an Army truck in those days one practically had to promise one's soul. But rather than face Mr. Kwack's absence for days at a time as he laboriously pushed his lares and penates from old home to new home in a hand cart, I would call up the motor pool and on some pretext secure a couple of hours' big transportation.

One fine day Mr. Kwack, after what had seemed like a normal enough family move, sent the truck rumbling back from an outrageously long journey— and with the driver, a polite note of resignation:

So sorry please I now go country.
No can work. Thank you very much.

Then there was Mr. Chai, my assistant editor. Mr. Chai was a former Christian pastor, a slight nervous little man who never looked me in the eye. He had produced a prodigious number of even littler Christians, all of whom had to be fed regularly even as the heathen. With the small salary he made on the *Chukan Digest* Mr. Chai was never able to accomplish this, prices being what they were. So when he would maneuver me into transporting free rice from his nephew's farm to the Chai house in the city, I never had the heart to protest.

Mr. Chai would never ask, of course. But I got so I could recognize the symptoms. When he came to my desk looking littler and more nervous than usual, and his eyes, searching some invisible spot on the wall, shifted and blinked, then I would know that he wished to go with me that day to the printers, whose shop was on the edge of Seoul nearest the farm of his nephew. Chai would putter around the printshop for a decent interval, then disappear.

When we were ready to go back I would find our jeep loaded with the "free rice," which I would then graciously offer to take to Mr. Chai's home "on our way back to the office." I felt very oriental indeed in making the offer in just those words, for his home was about as far out of our way as it would be possible to go without abandoning it entirely.

Finally there was Mr. Kim Tong Soo. Mr. Kim's face reminded me of the wrinkled brown skin of a walnut, and Mr. Kim's mind worked more like an American's than any Oriental I ever knew. Perhaps this was because he had spent eight years traveling for the Salvation Army, and had seen more of my own country than I.

Mr. Kim tried very hard never to ask for anything. But Mr. Kim's son, as staunch an enemy to MG as Mr. Kim was a friend, was continually getting thrown in jail for joining in anti-American student demonstrations. At such times Mr. Kim's natural reticence would break down, and he and I would journey together to the police station.

Later I was placed in charge of all publications emanating from the Department of Public Information. This involved the supervision of fifty-five Korean men, and the maternal aspect of my job reached its peak.

Unless the publications were wrapped, addressed and circulated throughout the country by rail, truck, bicycle or bullcart they were just so much waste paper, and very expensive waste paper at that. The man in charge of the Dissemination Section was well named—Mr. Kim Young Buk. At the age of sixty, he had produced a new son.

One day I was sitting at my desk, Mr. Kim thrust his yellowed teeth in my face and enveloped me in his high *kimchee* breath, whispering:

"My wife, you know he have new baby?"

He waited for my polite verbal applause, then squeaked: "My wife, he have no milk!"

I waited, knowing he would tell me what he expected me to do about it.

"American store, you have big can milk," he suggested.

Ah, powdered milk. But I had no commissary card. "Maybe no can get," I replied judiciously. "I look see."

"Thank you," breathed Mr. Kim, "thank you very much." And he bowed himself out with all his teeth showing, perfectly confident that everything would be taken care of without any further effort on his part.

They expected us to be everything from father confessor to wet nurse, I thought impatiently. But I knew very well why. Whether we liked it or not, we had inherited Japanese paternalism—which from the Korean point of view made us responsible for every man in our employ and all his family, from birth to burial. What the Japanese had done in forty years, we were not going to be able to undo in four. But more than that, I knew that as a woman I in particular had to do these little "family" things to keep the loyalty of my men, without which it would have been impossible to edit publications in a language I could neither read nor write.

I picked up the phone to call an American dependent I knew who had just had a baby.

"I can get you the milk all right," she said. "But it's supposed to be given according to a formula. How old is the baby?"

"I don't know, but I'll find out."

The obliging lady's doctor made out a complicated formula which I duly presented to Mr. Kim together with an outsized can of Klim. Although from Mr. Kim's disinterested expression I knew perfectly well he would never use the formula, at least I had done what I could to help one more Kim from his cradle to his destiny. And what was more important at the moment, Mr. Kim's mind was at rest.

I was gratified to learn that in spite of my anomalous position in relation to these Korean men, I had not completely lost my feminine standing. When I left Korea, "my boys" gathered around me as I passed out the last cigarets. Mr. Kim Tong Soo was their spokesman.

"They want to tell something to you," he said.

"Fine," I replied, "go ahead."

"They like you very much." He giggled with oriental embarrassment. "They want when you go home, you get married."

Propaganda is a Two-Edged Sword

"Propaganda knows neither right nor wrong; it only knows what it wants."

—Goebbels

Traditionally American, one of General Hodge's first acts upon entering South Korea was to grant the Koreans freedom of speech and freedom of the press. The agency charged with guarding these freedoms was the Department of Public Information. To the Koreans this was an anomaly, for under the Japanese an agency by almost the same name had been chiefly concerned with suppression.

The Japanese had brought all modern printing equipment into Korea and closed down one native newspaper after another, until when we arrived not a single paper was being published in the Korean language. Military Government proceeded to turn over to supposedly-qualified Koreans the operation of the newspaper plants until their final disposition should be decided upon, presumably at the Japanese peace conference.

Most of the Koreans who represented themselves to us as journalists had in reality worked only as copy boys, advertising solicitors or circulation managers in the Japanese newspaper plants; and in granting freedom of the press to these "newspapermen," we opened up a hornet's nest.

Dozens of Korean scandal sheets immediately sprang into being, most of them in outright support of some political party. Try as it would, the Department of Public Information could not keep these upstarts from malicious slander nor instill in them a sense of newspaper ethics. The bitterness and hate they had harbored so long against the Japanese they now turned on each other and on the Americans. Day by day the attacks grew more scurrilous, with the Communists always leading the rest, until finally Military Government was forced to close down the worst offenders.

The *Chukan Digest* itself indirectly fell victim to Korean lack of responsible journalism. One day I was called into the Colonel's office.

"Sit down," he said. "You may need to. The publisher at the plant where you print your city edition has been thrown in jail and we've shut the place down."

"But why?" I protested. "He seemed like such a nice guy—so especially helpful and cooperative."

"Maybe he was," said the Colonel, "but we're trying to teach these Koreans something none of them seems to understand—that the editor and publisher is responsible for everything that appears in his paper. Now this fellow has certain Communists on his staff who have been writing anything they please. He says he can't get rid of them; so he and they together are thinking about it in the clink."

"Where do I go from there?"

"We'll send you down to Kyongsong Ilbo and see how you get along."

To my surprise and relief Kyongsong Ilbo and I got along beautifully. Instead of resenting a woman clambering over their huge rotary presses they actually seemed to consider it something of a distinction. I didn't fully realize this until the publisher insisted upon taking my picture in front of one of his crouched behemoths.

The next time I returned to the plant the picture had been framed and hung in the pressroom.

"To inspire our workmen!" the publisher told me proudly.

The business manager of the plant was a young Korean eager to learn English and adopt all American ways. During the picture-taking episode he sidled up to me and whispered:

"In America, is it rude for man to have his picture taken with wo-man?"

"No," I said. "In America we like it very much."

"Will you take your picture with me?" he asked shyly.

My man-with-woman shot I prize highly as an example of how ancient barriers were breaking down in the new Korea.

Even with their presses shut down, the Communists still carried on their vituperative campaign—by handbill, by word of mouth, and by broadcast from Radio Pyengyang.

With Soviet troops living off the land in North Korea, Party organs had the nerve to criticize the Americans for bringing food into the country, saying that our real aim was to make Korea a trade colony of the United States. Similarly they spread the tale that we were collecting rice in South Korea not to feed the non-suppliers in the city but to smuggle out to America or Japan. This rumor was so persistent that two years after it was started it could still be found lurking about the countryside, mouthed by illiterate farmers.

The abuse rose to a harsh crescendo in the summer of 1946 when Party members at Inchon circulated the story that Military Government had transported barges loaded with lepers out into the Yellow Sea where they served as targets for our naval gunnery exercises. Later in the same year the North Korean Party-controlled radio in Pyengyang broadcast the amazing and wholly fictitious report that American troops operating the tanks had machine-gunned and crushed to death some two hundred Koreans in Kwangju.

What was the purpose of this vicious propaganda campaign? It was to denounce, deride and distort everything the American Military Government did in South Korea—to bring about disorder and an ultimate uprising in the southern zone. Then the Communists would set up a new Korean government on the Soviet pattern. This, as uncovered in late June of 1946, was the Master Plan. The authority for the plan was definitely pinned down when copies signed by Major Nicholai Kusnor, Chief of the Soviet Army Headquarters in North Korea, were discovered at Communist headquarters in Seoul:

> "At an opportune time the Soviet forces will offer to withdraw from North Korea, provided the Americans will also withdraw from Korea. Soon after the Allies have withdrawn various incidents and disorders in widely scattered areas of the country will occur. On the excuse of restoring order, the trained Communist armies and police will begin action in all parts of the country simultaneously . . . While 'order' is thus being restored, the government will be taken over by the Communists, and during the same period objectionable persons such as national traitors and pro-Japanese will be eliminated."

This plan, exactly as delineated above, very nearly succeeded. The clever seduction of the Rightist leaders Kim Koo and Kimm Kiusic and the bloody outbreaks caused by Communist infiltration into the constabularly and police at Yosu and Sunchon in November 1948 were the preliminary steps. They were to have been followed by a Communist *coup d'état* in South Korea. However, when the main body of the constabulary and police remained loyal to the Rhee government, the plot was foiled. The only remaining course was civil war, the step which was taken in June of 1950.

What was the Department of Public Information doing all this time to counteract the spread of the insidious Communist propaganda and stalemate its deadly aims? At first, very little.

For one thing, under Military Government how free was our own free press?

Any newspaperman knows that the vital part of this thing we know as a free press is giving to the reader some credit for a decent degree of intelligence and discrimination.

I remember once finding a Korean legend of particular charm, which I thought illustrated to perfection the point I had been instructed to make in my editorial for the week—that freedom is everybody's job. It was the story of a peasant—a clever fellow with a truly legendary sense of elemental justice, who outwits the bearer of a false but to all appearances legal claim against his little farm.

The villain in the legend was a Buddhist monk.

"We can't use this," the colonel said impatiently. "It's sacrilegious!"

"But it's a legend, Colonel," I protested mildly. "It's the one kind of literature we can use that all the people know and will understand. And surely they see as well as we do that there are all kinds of human examples, good and bad, in every calling." That's exactly what the legend is all about, I screamed mentally. That's why it illustrates our point!

"I can't help it," he retorted, "it's not to be used, and that's flat. I don't want the Organization of Buddhist Priests presenting a delegation to my office!"

If the pro-democracy aspect of our propaganda was ineffectual, our anti-communist output was something less than that. At the beginning of the occupation and for a year thereafter D.P.I. was ordered to follow a hands-off policy with regard to counter-propaganda. We were to point out the constructive things which American Military Government was accomplishing in South Korea—food and heavy-machinery imports, flood control, stamping out the cholera epidemic, and so on. Contrast with the communists' way of life was implied, of course—but was never to be mentioned. In fact, the word *communist* was not to appear in print *ever*—even when we reported terroristic activities or uprisings well known to be communistic in origin. Such circumlocutions as "agitators" and "subversive elements" must be used instead.

We were instructed to listen to the issues raised by the Koreans and to interpret these to our Chief— who would acquaint the Military Governor and the Commanding General with the details. From these one- two- or three-star conferences would come our orders.

We were told what to tell the Koreans, in explanation of the good our side was doing for their country. And it was very important, the orders reminded us solemnly, to say these things in a way the Koreans could understand and accept. Only we mustn't say This. And if we said That, we would have to be very careful not to be too definite about it, because later developments might change the situation and . . . !

The first Chief of the Department of Public Information listened to just so many Korean problems, and accepted just so many orders on what to tell the people—and then one day he was seen running down the hall of the Capitol building toward an open elevator shaft, shouting at the top of his lungs. He was restrained from flinging himself down the shaft—and sent home in a straitjacket. This man was an MG-trained officer I had known at the Monterey staging area, a former newspaper executive.

His successor, our Chief, was a combat man—a West Point coast artillery colonel. I can see some superficial reason for such an assignment. Perhaps the Army felt a man untrained in public relations might, in this job for which there was actually not yet a receptive public nor any satisfactory relations, suffer less and do more. But the fact remained that the new Chief did not know the Korean people and was not acquainted with Military Government or its design for propaganda, and he shouted his way through the most delicate problems—the more delicate the problem, the louder the shouts.

Over a period of two years our Chief gave his best, and he learned a lot—and so did we. But it was none of it in time to inspire Korea to love either us or the democratic form of government.

There was unfortunately nothing inspirational about the voice of Military Government in Korea. There was nothing in our propaganda which said, as one people to another, that one loves a country for her faults as much as for her successes. There was nothing which said: Bear with us a while. We don't know yet what we're doing, but we do want to help you . . . There was only routine announcement and instruction—which, sired as it was by Red Tape out of Caution, could not help being either deformed or sterile.

To the very last, no writer in the Department of Public Information was permitted anything so dangerous as simile, metaphor or direct appeal. I remember going to the Chief with my story about the Korean Interim Legislature—the first government of the Koreans, by the Koreans, for the Koreans.

Today at high noon, I had written, *a new democracy was born. For the first time in Korea's 4,000-year-long history, a representative body met to legislate . . .*

"In the first place," the Chief shouted, "it *isn't* a democracy! It's just another *step!*"

The Koreans were, metaphorically speaking, weary and footsore. We had told them again and again and *again* that this or that or the other was "just another step." We never permitted them, in our propaganda, to stop and rest a while and think—and to look back, perhaps, at where they had been before we came . . . I tried to convey something of this to the Chief.

He handed back my story and waved me away.

"We aren't writing Christmas cards!" he snapped.

Perhaps we should have been.

Not until early in 1947 was our policy modified and the communists and their activities pointed out and called by name. And not until January 1948, nearly the end of Military Government, did we get the green light on counter-propaganda. The change was immediately noticeable in radio, where a program called "News Behind the News" was begun on January 3, prepared by Americans and definitely of a propaganda nature. Another such program was "News to North Korea," begun on February 14 and prepared by G-2. The effect was also marked in press releases, leaflets and airdrops where blame for the failure of the second Joint Commission and of the UN to bring about the unification of Korea was definitely laid at Russia's door.

To the Koreans we must always have seemed feeble, frightened and futile. There were many reasons for our lack, some of which were insurmountable.

The Russians when they moved into their zone found a whole army of Korean communists, zealots well trained in Marxist doctrine and only too eager to spread the good word without encouragement from their masters. Russia was at last rewarded for the years of assistance she had lent to the underground movement in Korea after 1919 while the rest of the world turned a deaf ear to the little country's entreaties. Now the Soviet underground work was paying off, in that native movements which rose to the surface immediately following the Japanese surrender were almost entirely communistic in pattern.

We on the other hand found no Korean leaders with a true philosophy of Western democracy. Among the Rightists we found only the wealthy landlords bent on maintaining their status quo, and the aging returned politicos such as Kim Koo and Syngman Rhee. Unless we allied ourselves with these, which after the first few disastrous attempts we knew we could not do, we had to conduct our own propaganda campaign—hampered by faulty translations, lack of knowledge of Korean psychology and custom, and the stigma of "foreign" ideas.

While the Russians' main propaganda gun was the most effective medium in the world, word of mouth, we had to depend mainly on press releases, MG publications, and the government-controlled radio. Only 20 to 30 percent of our press releases were carried in the native Korean papers. As for our own two Military Government newspapes, the *Chukan Digest* and the *Farmers' Weekly*, we had paper enough to print only 600,000 of each, a mere trickle, for the 23,000,000 people in South Korea. Many times even this number did not reach its proper readership, as on the lower levels we had to depend upon Korean *kun* and *myun* officials who took little interest in a service for which they were not paid—or not punished for failing to perform. I remember visiting the capital city of Chunchon, province of Kwang Won Do, and finding in the provincial office thousands of old and dusty *Chukan Digests* stacked against the wall. Even in our own province of Kyonggi-Do, where dissemination was at its best, I would journey through village after village without seeing a single MG poster.

The South Korean Broadcasting system too was hampered, by lack of parts-replacement for its Japanese equipment and by the fact that only a comparative handful of Koreans possessed receiving sets.

In the long run we found our most effective media to be airdrops over the isolated villages and a "Friendship Train" carrying trained Korean speakers to the larger cities. But unfortunately these too bore the obvious print of the guiding American hand.

Our greatest virtue was perhaps our greatest handicap; we conscientiously tried to tell the truth.

Plain and ordinary truth, we found, does not stand up very well against vivid and sensational lies. Stealing a page from Goebbels' book, no lie was too big for the communists if it could turn the gullible Koreans against the United States.

The communists with their nutshell phrases found it only too easy to whip up Korean hatred for an America which came "bearing the almighty dollar in one hand and the atomic bomb in the other." We for our part used no quick "ad-man" appeals; and we failed to wed plain and ordinary truth to either emotion or inspiration.

Particularly confusing to the Koreans was the fact that everybody was using the word *democracy*. The Russians used it to describe the totalitarian state they were developing in the north, and we used it to describe every act of Military Government from compulsory education to the establishment of the South Korean Interim Legislature.

The South Koreans did not know whether to admire us for our generosity and the political freedom we allowed them, or to consider these a sign of weakness. They did not know whether to despise and fear the police control and dictatorship in the north, or to respect these as proving the strength of Soviet "democracy."

Certainly we had nothing so definite, nothing that offered such lurid appeal, as the loud Russian outcries against "reactionary, capitalistic, and imperialistic America!" or "suppression of the liberation movement of colonial peoples at the point of a gun!" We could only try patiently, with our truth, to teach the turbulent Koreans to live peaceably together under the law imposed by their elected representatives—a conception as alien to their historical background as Confucianism is to ours.

As Mr. K. I. Yun had said, you cannot give democracy in a package. But communism the Russians could wrap up and deliver neatly tied with red strings—which they did.

Vladimir Pekarsky, General Hodge's interpreter and by now my authority on the Russians, had something to say about this, too—something that made such beautiful, human good sense. And which of course I was powerless to put to any use!

"Our propaganda!" It was a horrified hush of an exclamation; and from the impatient wave of his expressive right hand, the slight twitch of his nose, I knew I was in for it.

"You know I do not mean—" He hesitated. "I know you write much of it," he said lamely.

I laughed. "Please, I want to hear what you have to say. There could be nothing less personal than the fact that I write it, sad to say. And certainly there is nothing confidential about the way it smells!"

He smiled, the assurance of his quiet, objective self restored. "What I want to say that will be more constructive is this: The Russian propaganda is excellent—although I would not dare to be so enthusiastic to anyone but a trusted friend. Certainly it is lies—all lies; but it is so *interesting*! And very cleverly the Russians tell their lies about subjects which affect the feelings, even the very life, of each individual Korean. We who make so much of telling the truth—we are staying away from the most vital and interesting subjects, because our officials are afraid to be controversial. So do we really tell the truth at all?

"And suppose," he went on excitedly, "suppose we were to decide that tomorrow we will begin to tell the truth, whether it is controversial or not; how would we do it? We would do it in the language of official decree, with whereases, and with the meaning still left open for escape or so tied in legal squareknots as to be killing in its dullness. There would be no drama, no— Well, maybe I am being too dismal. Your radio station is doing a good job."

I nodded eagerly—and then remembered that the Koreans had no radios. We had brought over huge shipments, but they were a mere spit in an ocean; and by now most of the receiving sets we had distributed were out of repair.

"And there are some good movies your department has made," Pekarsky said eagerly. "That one showing the Koreans how to vote, and educating them against being influenced by the man next door or the pressure politician, that was superb. We should spend all our money in media of direct, dramatic presentation. As it is, we are spoiling even the media we have. Your *Chukan Digest* which you give to so many hundred thousand Koreans—what was in that last week? A whole long boring speech by the Commanding General! Sure, it is not his fault that it was boring; someone else, the higher authority, is restricting what he shall say and how say it. But did you have to print it all? Why, it took up the whole paper! There was *nothing* else!"

Appalling as it will be to anyone who knows journalism, this was true.

"I had to print the whole speech," I said feebly. "Orders. There was no room for anything else."

"Well," he said sadly, "our propaganda is doing us more harm than good, and I mean that seriously. If we would only tell truths that are as big as the lies the Russians are telling! Then we would gain respect even from the Russians, and the Koreans would get to know us. As it is, the Russians are laughing at us—and the Koreans do not know what to believe."

No one has ever said it better.

Our propaganda knew right from wrong, but it did not know how to say it; so it did not seem to know what it wanted. And when it does not seem to know what it wants, propaganda is indeed a two-edged sword—which may well end by biting into the bearer.

You Can't Print That — Unless You Get the Paper

The difficulties in which I became embroiled trying to print an American Military Government newspaper in the Korean language on broken-down Japanese presses now seem utterly fantastic. Looking back, I marvel at the fact that we never missed an issue.

Take, for instance, the matter of translation. The MG press releases, world news, and editorials came to me in English. These I rewrote or edited and turned over to Mr. Chai, who would pass them around to the "boys," who would get out their little dictionaries and go to work.

We were all of us continually involved in squabbles over the proper Korean equivalent for an English word. The boys' bilingual abilities I soon found to be pitifully weak, but they were the best we could purchase at government salaries. Many a time I cursed Military Government school for not teaching me Korean instead of Japanese — and myself for not taking it more seriously years ago; but I never dreamed that a knowledge of Korean would prove invaluable to my fourth occupation of Korea.

Things went along fairly well on the *Chukan Digest* until one dreadful day in December 1946, after Maj. General Archer L. Lerch had replaced General Arnold as Military Governor.

General Lerch's great learn-by-doing experiment in teaching the Koreans practical democracy was underway. In September each American was asked to choose a Korean "counterpart" to sit at his side and thoroughly learn the operation of his job. For me this was Mr. Chai, while Mr. Kim Tong Soo became head of the Publications Section.

In December all Americans moved out of the Capitol building into another building on the grounds, while the Koreans took over our titles and supposedly our work as well. "Koreanization" this was called. We became known as "advisors" to whom our Korean counterparts should come for help on any difficult problems. The system worked better in some departments than in others. In the Department of Public Information it was difficult to make it work at all.

On December 12 the first representative law-making body in all Korea's 4,000 years of history convened. Half the members of the South Korean Interim Legislative Assembly were elected by votes cast by household heads throughout the country, and the other half were appointed by General Hodge from among prominent Korean political leaders.

That the rightest elements managed to control the election was evident from the fact that only two leftist delegates arrived in Seoul. They had traveled all the way from the island of Cheju Do, which was highly communist-organized; but when they found they were outnumbered they disappeared, evidently too frightened to show up at the Assembly.

The leftist representatives appointed by General Hodge were very few, because the Communists and the "silver axe" Lyuh Woon Hyung had boycotted the idea. Thus the Legislature became almost entirely a rightest body — but even within these limits many disputes arose.

The *Chukan Digest's* part in the picture was strictly non-partisan. As Military Government's official organ it merely presented favorable publicity for the Assembly, without political comment.

Then I had a brainstorm. Koreans throughout the country, I reasoned, should become familiar with the names and faces of their law-makers. I would run a series featuring their pictures and a thumbnail biography. With a great deal of effort I persuaded the Army Signal unit to set up a portrait studio next to the Assembly chambers, and I ran the Assemblymen through, while my reporters stood by with pencil and paper to take down interviews.

The entire job took several days, and when it was over I sat back with a sigh of satisfaction. As soon as I wrote a lead to the story and sent it over to Mr. Chai, the series would be ready to go.

When the next issue of the Digest was distributed to the Korean press conference presided over by my Department chief Colonel Newman, I thought I might possibly get a word of commendation. Instead I received an angry note from the Colonel, still closeted with the Korean reporters.

"What do you mean by writing a sarcastic lead to the Assemblymen story?" it demanded.

I was filled with the dismay of the innocent. My lead had surely been innocuous enough. How in the world had it turned sarcastic in Korean?

I dashed across the intervening ground to the Capitol and ran up the three flights of stairs, a very undignified advisor indeed.

"Mr. Chai," I panted, pointing to the story, "translate that lead back to me immediately!"

Mr. Chai, licking his lips and trembling like an aspen, glanced desperately about the room, his eyes searching three blank walls at my back. Evidently he too had gotten wind of the uproar downstairs in the press conference.

The translation he handed me seemed harmless, but it wasn't what I had written. I scented a rat.

"Give me my original copy," I demanded.

"Take this to the Colonel," I said to the messenger who had obediently trotted after me. "Tell him this is what I wrote and that I'll find out what happened."

Seeing the Mr. Chai didn't have the truth in him, I snatched a copy of the *Chukan Digest* and raced down to the office of the Military Governor, where the best translators were located. Cornering one, I requested an accurate literal translation of the lead I knew was not mine.

"This is very bad," he said. "You say here that you are introducing the legislators who have made a lot of promises to the people and you wonder if they intend to keep them."

"I never said anything of the sort," I replied, "but thanks a lot."

Faced with the evidence Mr. Chai broke down. He admitted in his hurry to get the copy to press he had stuffed my lead in his drawer without even bothering to translate it. Instead he had slapped on one written by a new Korean reporter who evidently had his own ideas about the success of the Legislative Assembly.

By this time the *Chukan Digest* was already out on the streets. The Colonel came frothing out of the press conference and ordered us out in trucks to pick up all the papers we could find before they fell into Communist hands. The Communists, he pointed out, would like nothing better than to sabotage us with our own material, hoist us on our own petard.

The reporter immediately underwent a stiff investigation to find out why he had turned columnist for the opposition. Since we could establish no connection between him and the Communist Party, we decided he must have felt the story dull and decided to add a little spice of his own. Needless to say, we found it impossible to dispense with his creative services.

Translation was one thing, getting the material to press was another.

After the copy was translated it was rushed across town by Mr. Kim and myself to a Korean printer, who set the type by hand. No linotype has ever been invented to handle the thousands of Chinese characters considered essential to an average Korean newspaper. Thus dozens of hands reach into hundreds of type trays before even a small two-page paper like the *Chukan Digest* can be made up.

The same plant which set the type also put out the provincial edition on flat bed presses. A high-speed rotary press on the other side of town printed the city editon, which was supposed to beat the Seoul papers to the streets the following morning. To save time as well as money, the completed forms were taken across the city in a jeep from one plant to another. Ordinarily I picked up Mr. Kim in the evening and we transported the type together. One dark night, however, political trouble caused all Americans to be confined to quarters after six o'clock. This left poor Mr. Kim, who was doing the proofreading, stranded at the first plant with no possible way for me to get in touch with him.

"Well," I thought as I fell into bed, "I guess the Seoul papers will beat *us* to the streets tomorrow morning."

But when I arrived at the office Mr. Kim was proudly laying a freshly-printed copy of the *Chukan Digest* on my desk.

"However did you do it?" I asked.

"When you no come I take type across city in Chinese horse cart," he replied, as if it were the most natural thing in the world.

Even on the days the *Chukan Digest* was correctly translated and safely transported to press, there still remained the problem of procuring the paper on which to print it. In a land of shortages, each issue of the *Digest* ate up five tons of a commodity suffering post-war shortage all over the world.

Military Government took over all paper stocks left by the Japanese, as well as operation of the one roll-paper mill in South Korea. The stocks were soon exhausted and the mill limped along feebly with untrained personnel, worn-out blankets, and a rapidly-disappearing wood pulp supply. The paper it produced was the poorest conceivable quality, tearing every few minutes during a press run.

Finally came the day when the pulp gave out altogether and the mill shut down. And that was the day we in the Department of Public Information really began to scramble, for without paper we withered and died.

Can you imagine a government denouncing blackmarket activities on the one hand, and dipping into that very market with the other—to buy the paper on which to print the denunciations? That is what we almost did.

The Department of Commerce had set a ceiling price on paper but could provide no paper at the ceiling. Yet every day on the main street of Seoul I saw Koreans hauling from one place to another huge rolls of newsprint tied onto bullcarts. Where had it come from and where was it going? We had no idea.

I was resolved to find out.

On various tips I raided Korean warehouses, hoping to turn up Japanese stocks which had escaped Military Government. Always I found the paper either had a perfectly legitimate reason for being there or was unsuitable for our publications.

One day the Kyongsong Ilbo boys whispered in my ear that they could get me in touch with a Big Blackmarketeer with tons of roll newsprint to sell. I called up the Department of Commerce, told them what I was going to do. Resignedly, with mild good-natured profanity, they blessed me on my way.

All that afternoon in the cold and dreary office of the Kyongsong Ilbo building I waited, warming my fingertips over a Japanese "stove"—a few bits of charcoal resting in a pottery bowl filled with sand. But the Big Blackmarketeer never showed up. He was evidently as much afraid of doing business with the government as the government was of doing business with him.

The day we were down to our last roll of paper the American advisor on foreign trade called me jubilantly. He had managed to purchase some newsprint in Macao, the great Portuguese smuggling den off the coast of South China. It had just arrived in Inchon, and he would turn it over to me—for a suitable consideration, of course. The paper, Norwegian stock, must have already passed through a dozen black markets, for the price was fabulous. But it had come into Korea legitimately, which was the main thing; and we were beyond haggling.

Hurriedly negotiating an eleven-million yen supplement to our Departmental budget, I rushed down to Commerce to present the check before anyone else could get his hands on the precious shipment. Then I ordered a fleet of Army trucks with Korean drivers to go to Inchon and pick it up.

Sometime later that day I received a call from Military Government at the port.

"They're some Koreans in trucks down here," said the voice at the other end of the line. "Are they yours?"

"They're supposed to be picking up some paper at the Customs warehouse on the docks. What on earth are they doing in your office?"

"Korean customs won't release the paper because you haven't got a permit," said the voice. "I'm afraid I can't do anything to help. We're Koreanized, you know."

Koreanized. That terrible word which relieved us of authority yet left us with all the responsibility.

I met the empty trucks rolling back to Seoul.

Next day I contacted the American advisor to the Korean Customs.

"The Department of Commerce should have arranged all that for you," he said. "But since they didn't, we'll have to make you a customs broker."

Nursemaid, editor, blackmarketeer—and now customs broker! What next?

The answer came swiftly. I became a farm advisor!

Even as a customs broker I was unable to find enough paper to feed both the *Chukan Digest* and the *Farmers' Weekly*; so the day came when the poor little *Chukan Digest* went to bed for the last time, and I was given the *Farmers' Weekly*.

Although there was a pulp shortage the world over, if our government had thought propaganda was really important to Korea, we would have got the paper.

The *Chukan Digest* was just a little two-page sheet, tabloid size, that came out once a week. In the States, thousands of big fat papers hit the streets dialy. So there was paper, for those who thought it was vital—without incidentally, the necessity for going the rounds of an international smuggling center like Macao, where my last shipment was found.

It is true that the paper we did get was often wasted because we were so timid about setting realities down in black and white. But the fact that the paper supply, too, was inadequate proves beyond any denial that we failed entirely to recognize the part good propaganda could have played in our occupation of Korea.

Life Is a Bowl of Rice

It was in 1947 that the *Chukan Digest* finally folded and I began to concentrate my customs broker's license and my maternalism on advising the Farmer's Weekly. In the spring I traveled out with the American agricultural expert in charge of production. Officially our mission was to inspect the coming rice crop. But it was a personal errand too—for one of our fellow officers in Seoul.

"I think it must be right around here," I said. My companion slowed the jeep, and we searched with our eyes over the rice paddies laid out like a jig-saw puzzle on the slope to the wooded mountain.

"What a maze! Why on earth do they lay out their fields in such crooked lines? I must admit it looks pretty; but I should think it would be damned inconvenient remembering whose is which!"

"Oh, they know," I said. "The pattern has probably been the same for generations. And there's a very important reason for the maze: it's so the Devil will get lost."

The Expert guffawed, then abruptly sobered. "What am I laughing at? These rice farmers have Kelly-green thumbs—and ours are a sickly yellow! Their average yield is 55.4 bushels an acre—more than ours at home." He sighed.

"Why is that?" I asked.

"For one thing, the Koreans use land we would consider unarable; and for another, they do all the work by hand. In California, in the San Joaquin Valley, most of us do the sowing from airplanes. And because the climate allows us to get by with it, we don't transplant at all. The Koreans would say we are scattering the seeds wastefully and that to be at its best rice must *always* be transplanted—by hand! And they'd be right. You know, it's hellishly embarrassing trying to help these farmers. There's a lot I could teach them; but I know so little about rice, compared to them, that they don't think I know anything at all!"

I nodded somberly. "You remind me of my last effort to do something for the Korean farmer. Remember when that shipment of chemical fertilizer got in from the States?"

The Expert nodded. The fertilizer, so needed to supply nitrogen and phosphorus to Korea's weary farm lands, had been part of our "incentive goods" program. In other words, if the farmer would turn in his rice quota to help feed the city folks, Military Government would give him a bonus in goods. Or sometimes he was given a certificate which entitled him to buy from us at a token price such things as rubber shoes, cloth, matches or other items he could not otherwise find at all on the depleted Korean market.

"Well, when the farmers didn't seem interested in the fertilizer," I said, "I promised your department to make a little propaganda. I decided a story comparing this 'wonderful new chemical fertilizer' to the 'old-fashioned night soil' might be a help to you, so I sent a reporter out to interview a farmer on the outskirts of Seoul, where I knew the chemical was being tested. The farmer was very polite about our fertilizer. He said he had just used it on his rice seedlings. 'But,' he said nostalgically, 'night soil really has much more *kyun*.' *Kyun* means power. Needless to say, we never used the story!"

We were still bouncing along the raised roadbed between the pieces of ricepaddy jigsaw, still not sure where to find the paddy of the farmer we sought.

"Maybe we should have asked in the village," the Expert said wearily.

"It wouldn't have done any good. These villagers are like the colored people in a deep-south settlement. If a stranger comes asking after one of them, no one has ever heard of him! We'll just have to keep looking. Carl said it was through this ravine that they made the last part of the survey. It can't be too much farther; the fields end about three miles up."

Three miles. In the States, short journey. But as our jeep continued to nose up and down the rocky road and switch its tailboard this way and that, 'losing the Devil,' we had plenty of time to talk.

"The Koreans are back in the Bible days," said the Expert—and punctuated with an *oof* as the jeep plumped its left rear tire in a deep rut. "They harvest with sickles, thresh their grain with hand flails, dig irrigation ditches with a three-man shovel and then painfully lift the water from one level to the other with crude wooden scoops. All right, so they get the job done. And even if we wanted to and they'd let us, we couldn't modernize their farms for years. We haven't got the equipment, or the personnel to train them. But one thing I do wish, and that is that we could get it through their heads about the relationship between reforestation and farming."

Jerkily I nodded. The road by now was so rough that my comment was limited to a few involuntary grunts.

For centuries the farmer had ruthlessly cut down the trees on his neighboring mountainside for firewood and manicured to the roots all the grass, weeds, hedges and bush for compost. When the Japanese came into the country they put a stop to irresponsible lumbering and ordered an extensive reforestation program, protecting the new growth with rigid police protection for more than twenty years. To our consternation, immediately after Japanese police controls were removed the Koreans began felling their trees all over again.

And it was true they could see no relationship between the axes of men and the terrible floods of June 1946, which washed away villages and hamlets that had stood for thousands of years. To the Korean farmer these were the acts of the gods. This year he might have a bumper crop, but next year the floods might come and bury his land under a rush of mud and stones. These things had always happened so, and they always would. Survival, not science, was the answer!

I laid my hand on the Expert's arm, and pointed. "This must be this place," I said as the jeep slowed again and the noise of its labors lessened to a growl. "Why didn't Carl just tell us it was the next-to-last field below the mountain, instead of giving us all that list of landmarks up a one-way track!"

"He's been in government service too long," said the Expert with an evil little smile.

Oblivious to our approach, a farmer stood in the next-to-last paddy. A weary figure he was, with a white sweatband wound around his head and white cotton pants rolled up at the knee. He stopped to caress windward a single straw rice shoot.

The Expert looked at me and grinned. But it was a nice grin. "See what I mean?" he said. "He's probably just a tenant farmer—and he *still* slicks down every little wisp just so."

A modern Millet could have painted this man as he stood there, and to millions of Koreans the picture would be a symbol of the centre of life. For his name and his face and his figure are legion. He is not an individual; that is not the kind of statement which could ever touch him, ever mean enough to him to please him. Perhaps if we could have told him that to us, to the Americans who would help him, he represented three-quarters of the country . . . If we could have expressed our feeling that he was Korea, not just a Korean . . .

He straightened, looked at us. And then, probably thinking that we too were lost in his maze and wanted direction, he sloshed to the bank and climbed to where the jeep was stopped.

"Your name is Chung?" I asked, nodding in response to his bow.

He said it was, and looked inquiringly at the two of us.

"I bring you good wishes for health, and a message from one of our officers in Seoul, whose wallet you found in your field and so kindly returned by your cousin. Our friend was not in when your cousin called at his office, and—"

The farmer held up his hand, and I saw by his confused smile that he had not understood anything except the good wishes for health!

"You come my house," he said gently. "My wife missionary girl. She speak English."

He wiped his feet carefully on the grass tufts at the side of the roadbed before accepting our invitation to get in the jeep."

"Thank you," he said. "Not have bull. My house far."

His house was indeed far—five miles at least from the last-but-one paddy in the fields surrounding his village. But I knew he would rather commute on his calloused feet an even greater distance than be separated from his friends the way our prairie farmers are in the States.

At the distant edge of the district paddies, secure in the elbow-crook of a guardian mountain range, was Chung's village.

His house was like most of the rest—U-shaped, of clay and stone, with a thatched roof which was getting a little mouldy but would be renewed again as soon as the annual harvest was in and more rice straw available. Chung led us into the house, then went out to the courtyard where the usual company of chickens, a pig or two, and several children were engaged in the universal activities common to each and all together. Summoning a boy child, he asked him to find the *poo-een*.

Mrs. Chung came back from the river where she had been doing the family wash, and I began again with my message.

An Army Engineer Corps major and a detachment of men had the month before, following the spring thaw, made a survey of road and bridge conditions in the mountain country back of Mr. Chung's village. The major had lost his wallet — with all the usual identification that in the Army it is so hideously hard to explain the loss of, or to replace. Not only that, but his whole month's pay, in cash. We all knew it isn't smart to carry around a lot of money. But we all did it. There was in Korea so little for us to spend it on that it had almost lost is importance — unless, of course, we lost it and had none to send home.

Mrs. Chung nodded brightly as I told her how the major had appreciated the return of his property and regretted not having been in to receive the distant Chung cousin with whom it had been sent back.

"In our country," I said, "it is the custom to share with the finder the contents of the purse. The major begs that you accept in token of his thanks this money, with which he hopes you may get whatever you most want that so small a sum could buy."

I was addressing my talk in the Eastern mode, for actually it was a huge sum. The major's generosity was in due proportion to his amazement. Had his wallet been found by one of the million people of Seoul, it would almost certainly have been stripped and thrown away. In this country as in our own, the values of the people seemed to have become confused in direct relation to the crowding of their everyday living. Only in the rural areas now did one find the stiff-starched honesty my father had found in his early meetings with the Koreans.

Mrs. Chung was shaking her head gently and saying in her little-girl English, which the missionaries had taught her twenty years before:

"But we cannot take the money. It belong your friend. We feel happy he have it back."

"He is happy too. That is what I wanted you to understand. He wished to share his pleasure in the only way he knew." But, on my advice, he had been prepared for a refusal. I changed the subject, planning in the accepted manner to return to it later. "How is everything with your farm? Our officials would be glad of word from you about conditions."

She turned to Mr. Chung, then interpreted for him so: "We do well enough here. There are questions we have, that make wondering in the village — questions about American governor. Is it permitted to ask you?"

"Of course," I said. "If I know, I will answer. Or I can find out for you."

"It has been said to us by some of the city Koreans passing through our village that the Americans are sending our rice away, to their own homes across the ocean. Is that so? Of course, if your people have need—"

Inwardly I groaned. The communists had done their work well. Here over these same paddies was probably hanging like poison gas the story about the lepers, too; but of course the Chungs would be too polite, too judicious, to mention that.

I tried to tell the Chungs the whole story, in terms they could readily visualize. In our own terms, it was like this:

In the few briefings our MG officers had on board ship en route to Korea, they were told, "At least you won't have a food problem there, as they have in Japan. The Korean taste is simple, and there was a bumper rice crop this year. Now that the Japanese aren't shipping any out, there ought to be plenty for everyone."

Yet by May of 1946 the United States was shipping food in to Korea, the one occupied country in the world that was not supposed to have a post-war food shortage. What had happened to Korea's bumper crop and to the large surplus she was reputed to have? Mr. Chung's question was only natural.

The rightists would have answered that it was being hoarded on the small farms, such as his own. The leftists would have told him it was locked in the bins of the wealthy landowners. And Military Government would have to say quite honestly, as I did, that we had no accurate record of where it had gone. By now it was fairly well established that the crop never had been as large as reported, and that it had been dissipated in a number of ways.

Under the Japanese the collection and distribution of rice had been rigidly controlled.

"Know well." Mr. Chung nodded grimly. "Japanese tell how much rice must grow, how much must sell, and make take price they say."

Again in our terms, this meant there was no open market for rice in Korea. The Japanese carefully rationed to the non-producers a predetermined amount, and the rest they took for themselves, sending most of their haul back to Japan.

When we came into Korea in September 1945 the problem of how to handle the first "liberated" harvest was imminent. Because most of the original Advisory Council were wealthy landholders they pressed for a free market in rice. And because we sincerely believed this in keeping with democratic principles of private enterprise, we promptly complied. The results were catastrophic.

"I remember," Mr. Chung said, in vocal appreciation of my simplified report. "People long time have not very much, long time told what must do with rice. All-a-sudden have plenty, no one make buy or sell or lay away. All farmers here eat—" In elaboration he indicated a big fat stomach with the circle of his arms. "All make rice wine, rice candy—"

"So you see," I said, "that is where a lot of it went. And some of it was sold to people who saved it for the hungry months of spring and summer, when the price would be high."

"Saved" was an inanely charitable word. They were blackmarket hoarders, just like those in any other country in troubled times.

It was mid-day, and Mr. Chung insisted we should lunch with him. The three of us sat on the earthen floor, and Mrs. Chung waited on us. She did not sit down to the meal, and it was most unobtrusively that she continued her function of interpreter.

On the mat before me was a bowl of boiled rice, with dried fish; and at the side of a smaller bowl of *kimchee. Kimchee* is Korea's only winter vitamin food, although I imagine most Koreans eat if from instinct rather than with any conscious knowledge that it is the only thing that saves some of them from beri-beri and scurvy. It is a pickle made of Chinese cabbage, red peppers, Korean pears and sometimes meat or fish. This melange is placed in a large earthen jar, covered with brine and buried in the back yard, where most foreigners feel it should remain. After about a month, the Koreans dig it up and eat it.

I never had learned to like *kimchee*. The smell is not precisely one of putrefaction, but it is a very strong combination of garlic and soured cabbage—an odor so clamorous, in fact, that I found it difficult to concentrate on conversation.

Mr. Chung, apparently satisfied with my rueful explanation about the rice, asked me another. "When I turn in rice quota to your people," he said, "I tell them it too high—that my family need more to live. But your officer say people in city hungry; and if I give, then they give me paper and I can buy cloth and matches I need. Okay, I give rice, they give paper. I go to place where the paper is to be traded—and they say hab-a-no!"

Mr. Chung, out of regard for my face, was putting it mildly. This, then, was our "incentive goods" program. The idea was excellent. But since the goods were purchased in former Japanese factories now operating at only 20 to 30 percent of capacity, there was never enough to go around. And the farmer who didn't get his incentive bonus was sure to spread the word that it was only another foreign hoax, to separate the Korean people from their precious grain.

I explained the situation to Mr. Chung. And then I said: "It would give our friend the major much pleasure to see that you get these goods you need, since you will not accept his gift. If you will give me a list, I shall take it to him."

And so that was how the major's debt was finally paid. As he said, and Mr. Chung himself would have agreed, here was an American doing what ought to have been done long ago, for a Korean who had done for him what most other human beings should do and don't.

The last thing Mr. Chung said as he and his wife bowed us into our jeep was: "You do something soon about rice? Our cousin last year come down from North Korea, tell us plenty hab-a-yes."

The Russians were officially our allies; and it was much too hot an afternoon to go into any plausible detail with Mr. Chung and still be certain of my diplomacy where the difference in the two zones was concerned. I made Mr. Chung a wilted bow and said I too hoped we could do something soon about rice.

It is true that the Russians were at first much more successful in dealing with the rice question. By retaining the Japanese collection and rationing system they avoided the obvious pitfall into which the American command had stumbled. Furthermore they used rationing as a political weapon, refusing a card to anyone who failed to fall in line with the desires of the People's Committee of North Korea.

The communists in South Korea did their bit for the Party by making political capital of our unhappy food situation. They craftily pointed out how the hoarders were profiteering off the people. They accused the Americans of shipping rice out of the country; and the Koreans knowing as little as Mr. Chung about the facts of their rice crop, were quite ready to believe it.

Our condition was further complicated by the thousands of non-producers daily pouring down from the North, and by the fact that Korean land had been depleted by lack of chemical fertilizer during the war years, when Japan diverted all available chemicals to her own immediate needs.

From the disastrous lesson in rice that first winter, Military Government learned that however "democratic" the free enterprise system might be, the Koreans were not yet ready for it. Strong controls were obviously necessary. So in April 1946 MG placed the collection and distribution of all foods and beverages in the hands of the newly-formed National Food Administration. The "quota" Mr. Chung speaks of was assigned to each farmer, supposedly not so large as to work a hardship on him. This was purchased at a government price much under the black market, and sold to the non-producers in the city at a still lower price—the first year at ¥85 per small mal as against the black market price of between ¥450 and ¥550. The government absorbed the deficit in an attempt to stabilize the economy and curb the black market.

From first to last, our collection and rationing program was completely unpopular with everybody concerned. The farmers complained, few of them so mildly as Mr. Chung, that the quotas were unfair and the government price much too low. Only under duress was 83% of the quota gathered in the second harvest. The city dwellers complained that the daily ration was never enough. This, in fact, was precisely the thing Mr. Kim, the editor with the skin like a walnut and the mind like an Occidental gentleman, wished to discuss with me the minute I returned from my trip to the rice paddies.

"How is the crop?" he asked earnestly. "Will we soon be able to raise the ration?"

"I don't see how," I said. "Anyway, we have raised it. The people said they needed three hop a day. Since last year we've been allowing one and a half hop rice and one hop of some other grain, which brings it to two and a half hop. At that rate, they may not feel replete—but certainly no one is underfed."

"Oh, but they are," Mr. Kim said, his eyes wide. "This 'other grain' you speak of—they probably throw it away. Most of them do not know what to do with wheat. And corn they consider fit only for cattle."

"But we've been importing rice for them, too," I said impatiently. "Surely—"

"Louisiana rice," Mr. Kim reminded me quietly. "They do not like that either. They say the kernels are too long, and the flavor inferior to our Korean rice. And as for your packages of three-minute rice—time is one thing our people have plenty of; and such short-time rice, they say, is apt to be sticky." At something on my face, Mr. Kim quickened his speech: "Do not misunderstand me, please. I tell you this not because I think they are right, but because I think it right that you should understand them." He placed on my desk a copy of a Korean newspaper.

The story he had marked should logically have been a simple report: Military Government was placing Army surplus cans of candy and turkey on the native ration store shelves. Instead it was an attack, of banner headline fury. "Candy and turkey!" it screamed. "When Koreans are starving for rice!"

At that time I seldom saw a can of turkey myself. I was finding it a little difficult to sympathize. But Mr. Kim's gentle voice took the burden of thought from me.

"You with your years in this country understand that food to the Korean means rice—three times a day."

I did understand. If he knows it at all, the Korean cares less than nothing for the fact that centuries of his diet have made his people a small, reluctant race. There is, to him, no acceptable substitute for rice. His bowl of rice is bread, potatoes, ice cream. It is life itself.

Even though the South Koreans were not happy, under MG's collection and rationing measures the general food situation in the South eventually improved while in the North it grew steadily worse. Refugees from the Russian zone reported that rationed rice there sold for ¥300 per small mal, while the black market rice was about ¥1,000. It was no wonder they wanted to cross the parallel.

Always dependent to some extent on the South for food, North Korea ws beginning to feel the full effect of the Soviet Army's living off the land. On this point too, we missed an opportunity. If we had only explained to the Koreans how differently our Army lived—how careful we tried to be!

Not only did we ship in all our own food, but the troops were strictly forbidden to buy food in the Korean market or take meals in a Korean eating house. And the one time the American Army mess served rice, even though it was 'inferior' Louisiana longkernel, an UNRRA official made formal complaint to the Military Government: No American should eat any rice at all in Korea as long as a single Korean had to go without!

One more thing we ought to have done that we did not do, when we knew we were going into Korea, was make it our business to learn everything there is to know about the Korean and his rice.

Before the Japanese came, Korea was literally the hermit kingdom she had so long been named — and this was largely because of rice. As long as the Koreans had plenty of rice, the outside world held nothing they wanted. And in that era, before the time of instantaneous communication and power balances and spheres of influence, Korea had so little besides rice that no one coveted what was hers.

We, with our chemical fertilizer, our suggestions of irrigation projects and reforestation and crop rotation, were paying a visit to a hermit. This was very much the feeling we had as we made our rounds of the paddy fields. And we were just as uncertain of our effect as the city fellow who pays a visit to a wise old man in a country cave. We never knew, for instance, whether most of the Koreans actually used the fertilizer we gave them. I can just see them burying it in a hole, if they could get night soil instead and thought we wouldn't find it out.

Just before June 1950 Korea was again self-sufficient where food was concerned — which in their language is to say that once more there was a-plenty of rice in every bowl. Part of this recovery was certainly due to the efforts of agricultural experts such as the one I accompanied through the fields; but no one can estimate how much of the credit is ours, and how much is due the instinct and ingenuity of the Korean farmer — who grows better rice than we do and grows more of it, and always has. Of our earnest fumbling efforts to restabilize their economy, which of course meant the rice market, I can only say we did the Koreans no worse wrong than we have often done ourselves at home, with our subsidies and controls.

As a whole, then, we did not fail Korea on the rice question.

It is rather as if we had never been there at all.

How Black Was the Black Market?

The black market in Korea was a creation of Military Government, for actually it extended only to those items upon which we set a price ceiling.

Take for instance the case of rice, the first item to be hit by price control in the early days of the occupation and thereafter the number one black market commodity. We had thought that a prior announcement of coming controls would drive rice out in the open. Instead it caused it to disappear from the stores and the stalls altogether; and with hoarded rice the first black market was opened for business.

There was nothing surreptitious about this. Every day I saw blackmarket rice lying quite openly in large round straw baskets in the streets markets of Seoul. There was no way for the government to prosecute the vendor, for it was impossible to determine whether the rice had come to him illegally from a profiteer or legally from some poor farmer's hoard.

In the second year of Military Government's rice-mixing, when a more effective collection system was established and each farmer given a quota to turn in to the government, theoretically the quota left only enough to feed the farmer's family and provide for next year's planting. In some cases, such as that of the Chung family, there were claims that the quota imposed a hardship—that not enough rice was left for the needs of the farmer. In others, a substantial surplus remained to the grower—and there was nothing to prevent his selling it on the black market, where prices were at least four times what the government paid.

In Korea, as in our own country in times of stress, the privileged class talked about how unpatriotic it was to patronize the black market—and, for the most part, continued to patronize it. The poor people did not talk about it—did not think about it. They simply patronized it, whenever they could possibly afford to do so. To them, it was sometimes a matter of survival.

As Mr. Kim had told me, the Seoul ration which was supplied to non-producers at the legal price satisfied no one. We claimed it was plenty. And in 1948, by a wide survey of 25,000 people from all walks of life, we found the daily intake to be 2,480 calories—hardly a starvation diet in any country. But we count in calories; the Korean counts in rice.

Just who was right, MG or the Korean consumer, I cannot say. I do not know who conducted the survey or how reliable it was. I do remember that I was surprised by the result—and that even our boss in the Department of Public Information indicated that 2,480 calories sounded like a pretty "dreamy" intake to him.

The black market grew steadily. Soon Army rations found their way there as Koreans stole them—or as they were bought or "borrowed" by Army personnel who sold them or traded for Korean goods. This black market in American goods was principally a surreptitious traffic in cigarets. Cigarets became money. Americans found that for a ninety-cent carton they could get Korean goods worth ¥2,000, or about thirteen dollars at the legal Army exchange of fifteen yen to one dollar. The theory behind this unrealistic fifteen-to-one—which went to fifty-to-one in 1948—was to keep down inflation by discouraging American purchases on the Korean market. In practice, it caused every article of possible interest to the occupation troops to have two prices, one in yen and the other in cigarets.

The Commanding General's answer to all this was, naturally enough, an Army ultimatum. Many of them, in fact. There were a whole set of ultimatums—one for every possible evil, past, present or future. One of our brother officers christened them "beanos," for they always started out so: There shall *be no* trading on the Korean market by personnel of the U. S. Army . . . Or: There shall *be no* exchange of gifts between Koreans and Americans . . . And of course the "beano" took care of the Commanding General's obligation—since, thereafter, theoretically, there *was no*.

There were obvious and good reasons for the "beano" on exchange of gifts with Koreans. But in the Orient there are just as good reasons why its literal observance would have made us look small and feel small. As we know, the Korean places a great deal more emphasis on a gift than we do— and quite a different emphasis. To him it is a necessary and gracious part of any business or social relationship. So we—everybody but the Commanding General, perhaps—went right ahead passing out little gifts of candy and cigarets to the Koreans working in our offices. Maybe the Commanding General did it too. After all, his "beano" was really intended to catch the big fish operating in the black market with PX items for personal gain—though in spite of it many of the biggest fish got away, returning to the States rich in Oriental *objets d'art*.

The pathetic part about the small "presentos" we gave the Koreans we worked with was that they so often turned up in the black market. As time went by we saw trays of cigarets and candy bars appear in increasing number along Seoul's main thoroughfares. These "branch PX's" as we called them, could easily be picked up and spirited away in case of a police raid—which seldom occurred, however, for Koreans have a very strong feeling about every man's right to "earn" his livelihood.

"The people's livelihood." In my work with original Korean articles submitted for the *Chukan Digest*, I found this to be the Korean's main concern. And the elements of their conception of the people's livelihood were as roughly basic as the granite outcroppings on a Korean mountain peak. "The people's livelihood." Not hot-and-cold running water, nor privacy; certainly not television and a car, but *can you exist? Can you feed yourself and your children this winter?*

In Korea as in all war-devastated countries, morality broke down in the face of necessity. The Koreans stole. It was months after I got back to the States this last time, that I finally broke the frantic habit of going back every few minutes to see whether my car was still standing where I had parked it. And no one dared leave any object of value lying about—even right in our own MG office. To this day, if I pause too long in the middle of a thought I am trying to put in writing, I still cap my fountain pen and pocket it; for in the Public Information Office it could have been stolen as I turned my head!

So the Koreans stole. They stole food, and clothing. Or they stole valuables which could be exchanged for food and clothing. One Korean employee of MG put it to me this way:

"It is a fine thing to make a right decision between goodness and badness. But in a time of national disaster—Let us say your neighbor is cooking a fine, stolen meal; and you smell the goodness of the food, and you see your own family getting hungrier and hungrier . . . You will talk righteously against your neighbor for just so long, and then you will go out and steal for yourself—and for your family. Morality is a thing you have to be able to afford, sometimes."

And I noticed that he had said steal *for yourself—and for your family*. I commented, since I knew him well, and he said:

"But of course that is the order of importance. If you die, what can you then do for your family?"

Eventually Military Government's price controls—and the black market—extended beyond food to cloth, shoes, soap, matches and light bulbs. But here the controls were effective only on goods produced by MG-operated factories taken over from the Japanese. Since for lack of raw materials and trained technicians these factories operated on only about 20% of capacity when they were operating at all, there were never enough controlled commodities to go around—and that of course is how these items got into the black market.

The answer to a black market is increased production, and MG tried to increase it by importing American civilian experts in various fields. These well-meaning experts were always bogged to the eyeballs in problems—lack of materials, broken-down neglected machinery, too little understanding of the language or psychology of the Koreans. In the main they were highly paid "advisors" working at top level without sufficient trained personnel under them who were willing to get their hands dirty.

The Executive Officer to the Military Governor had the right idea, I thought. "We have too many high level people working on this thing," he told me. "We need to get some *foremen*. Sure, they may have their front teeth out, and calloused hands, and they may not know how to get through a cocktail party—but they'll get this production started!"

And he volunteered, officially, to return to the States and recruit workers and technicians of the caliber and experience we needed. I do not know how his idea was received—but I do know that nothing was done about it!

In the North the Russians were doing a little better. They had shut their ears to the loud Korean outcries against Japanese technicians, and placed these technicians under the supervision of the People's Committees where they were used extensively to keep up production and to train Korean replacements.

Inflated currency was another complication which the Russians handled better than we. When the Japanese left they purposely dumped their currency reserves, paying every Korean in their employ a bonus amounting to about five months' wages. This raised the money in circulation throughout all Korea to about eight million yen.

The Russians soon replaced the currency in their zone with a Red note, causing most of the original Chosen Bank notes to find their way South. In addition the MG printing presses began rolling night and day printing money to pay for the occupation. When the total amount in circulation reached thirty-one billion yen in 1948, the only bright note in our official statement was that "the increase is now decreasing."

To the average Korean the whole situation was completely confusing. Our amah who came down from North Korea put it in these words:

"Before time, I make ¥25 a month and it plenty. Today I make ¥2,800 and it not enough. I not understand our money!"

In such a situation it was difficult for a Korean, particularly one working on a government salary which was deliberately held down, to "afford" morality. Take the case of Mr. Kim Tong Soo, who tried as hard as any Korean I ever knew.

Mr. Kim made about ¥2,500 a month, on which he supported his wife and three children. Mr. Kim always dressed in foreign clothes, as did most of the officials in Military Government. As time went on I saw that Mr. Kim's one pair of shoes was gradually wearing out. Finally the day came when he was replacing his soles with cardboard—and he a Bureau Chief in the South Korean Interim Government!

Mr. Kim confided in me that a pair of shoes on the black market, the only place they were available, would cost him half a month's wages. Fortunately an American in the Department whose brother owned a shoe store back in the States had taken a particular interest in Mr. Kim; so Mr. Kim got his pair of new shoes without sacrificing his integrity, but there were many who did not.

Since we are back again at the subject of integrity, I shall speak of the true color of the Korean black market. How black was it?

In the main, it was as I have written—the Korean layman's traffic in little things, cigarets and candy and trinkets, to buy the big thing he wanted—rice. It ranged from the struggle for survival to the age-old struggle to keep up a habitual standard of living. There were Koreans who operated big-time on the black market, I am sure of that. And the Korean when he is dishonest is fabulously, flamboyantly so. He makes a real production of it! I do not think in this country I have heard anything to equal the story of the Korean contractor who was hired to build a burglar-proof warehouse for the American Army Commissary. He then accepted a second contract—from himself—to tunnel under the warehouse and in-lay on its flooring a concealed trap door through which he could remove the Army's supplies as fast as they came in.

But in the main, the Korean's black market in Korea was pale grey in comparison with our own. I have already mentioned our small-time operators. But our Big Time Operators astonished me.

I had been back in Korea barely a week when I got the first indication. I was sitting at breakfast in the officers mess—mentally minding my own business, which was a very small and struggling one at that point. The conversation was general and I listened only at intervals until the talk turned to Oriental *objets d'art*, a hobby of mine. But the man who spoke loudest had quite a different appreciation:

"Why, it's as if the streets were paved with gold!" he cried. "Priceless things, just lying around—all over the place!" He took a huge bite of something, and the sound of his munchings suddenly began to grate on me. He swallowed, gestured with his re-loaded fork, and then it came: "Anybody's a *fool*," he said, "who doesn't go home at least $50,000 richer!"

Here was a man I had known at the Presidio of Monterey, and thought was a pretty nice guy!

And, since no one at the table answered him, I assumed he was not alone. But then I did not answer him either—and I hoped even at the time that I did not show my feelings. Perhaps my error was no less than his, in that I had long since decided that in trying to "keep" my brother I would probably succeed only in becoming unkempt myself. Perhaps my attitude is precisely the reason why he and his kind can exist so loudly among us.

I do not know whether he ever got his fifty thousand, but I know another officer who did. This BTO was Governor of one of the provinces; and as such, he made occasion to ship back to the States the entire contents of a Buddhist temple.

He was found out. But even that, perhaps, is not a crime any more. He was relieved of his command with only a reprimand, the contents of the temple remaining in his possession. I personally heard him say with a chortle that he thought he had come off pretty well in the deal.

Another case I knew of seemed as equivocal to me; but it was more difficult to be critical of the Americans involved. In the back of a former-Japanese Geisha house, some compatriots of ours unearthed a cache of Oriental art treasures of the type whose value is literally inestimable. Originally confiscated from Koreans, these things had recently been buried by Japanese Colonials who evidently hoped to return to Korea after the dust had settled, to reclaim the hoard.

I never heard how the Americans happened to find these treasures, but find them they did, and send them back to the States. In this case, however, the motive seemed rather pride in ownership than any desire to sell the items. And the person who told me of the discovery said: "After all, if we give them up, what will happen? They'll stick to the paws of someone of slightly higher rank, and be sent home anyway!"

After that breakfast with the aspiring BTO, and the bland silence at the table, I didn't feel there was much I could say to that. But, feeling like an old fuddy-duddy, I suggested: "You might turn them in to the Korean National Museum."

"But we can't do that direct," my friend objected. "If we could just cart the things over to the museum and present them, I might feel a little worse about not doing it—but you know we'd have to go through channels."

"Channels." The word was a dank, clogged echo. I sighed, and dropped the subject.

On both sides, Korean and American, the disrupted economy created situations and practices which I am sure both sides have cause to be ashamed of and to regret. But on the whole, the black market struck me this way: There were Koreans, and there were Americans, and there were ideas of honesty peculiar to the history of the circumstances of each. There was the light-grey market patronized for necessities or small luxuries by the average Korean or American—and there was the black practice of the Big Time Operator.

Just why I should feel so much worse about the American who stripped the Buddhist temple than I do about the crafty Korean contractor who double-crossed us, I shall leave unelaborated—except to say that my sense of loss over what our officer did has little to do with the art or the gods of the temple.

Everybody Hates a Cop

One day I was discussing with Dr. Clarence Rhyee, Korean director of the Department of Public Information, the question of whether or not Korea is still a police state.

"Yes," said Dr. Rhyee emphatically. "Korean police are worse than the Japanese. They come to your home, knock on the door, and shout 'Open up!' just like Nazi storm troopers."

Now Dr. Rhyee, graduate of the Columbia University School of Journalism, was an extreme rightist, a Syngman Rhee man. If he would criticize the Korean police, who also were noted for their rightist tendency, how much more so would a leftist whom the police might question or jail for political reasons.

Under the Japanese it was well known that all phases of Korean cultural, political and economic life were controlled by a ruthlessly efficient police force. The police had charge of censoring the press, radio and films, suppressing all political activity, and dominating rationing and price controls. If a Korean was arrested on any charge, however trumped up, the police tried to wring out a confession by horrible forms of torture, notably the "water cure," drops of water falling monotonously on the forehead, and beatings with thin bamboo poles.

The Americans, when they arrived, found this police force some 25,000 strong, of whom about 5,000 were native Koreans. The big question was whether to retain these Koreans brought up to practice Japanese police methods, or to kick them out and build up a "democratic" police system from scratch.

Whether wisely or no, but largely to make matters of law enforcement easier for itself, Military Government decided to treat each Korean as an individual case, dismissing only those who proved unadaptable to democratic ideas.

The job of rebuilding this embryonic force to a full-fledged law enforcement body fell first on Colonel Arthur S. Champney, a rugged infantry veteran of two wars. He immediately began recruiting physically and mentally fit young men from the eight provinces of southern Korea for training in the National Police Academy taken over from the Japanese.

The Academy was found to be in sore need of equipment and repairs, for an investigation showed that the former Japanese faculty had been in the habit of dividing up the yearly appropriation among themselves. Furthermore, the four-week curriculum had to be reorganized down to its basic concepts and capable instructors had to be found from among available American and Korean personnel.

The recruitment program was immediately successful, for even though the police had been cordially hated by the Koreans, they had always enjoyed high prestige in the community. Furthermore, during the Japanese regime police work had been an extremely lucrative business, for extortion was practiced on a grand scale by almost every local cop. By the middle of November 1945, Korea had a native force of 15,000 with more recruits pouring in daily.

In trying to change the basic Korean concept of police methods, however, Military Government soon ran into formidable snags. In spite of training in modern criminology and "democratic" police practices, when the average policemen went out on the job he more often than not reverted to familiar brutality.

A certain American who had a room in the Bizenya Hotel overlooking Seoul Metropolitan Police Station told me: "No matter what people say, late at night after the American police advisor has gone home I can hear the bamboo slats coming down hard on bare backs, and later I see the battered and bloody victims being hustled off to jail."

Colonel William Maglin, a regular Army Military Police officer who placed Colonel Champney, himself said that he was continually forced to issue directives forbidding cruel and barbaric practices among the Korean police.

Colonel Maglin banished the short sword worn with the Japanese police uniform and replaced it with a large shield pinned to the left breast bearing the motto "Service and Order." These words were as unintelligible to the Korean as was all this American talk about a "democratic police force."

The lives of high Korean counterparts of American police officials were constantly in danger. Dr. Chough Pyeng Ok, Civilian Director of Police, against whom no charge of being pro-Japanese could possibly be brought, received innumerable anonymous threats; and Chang Taik Sang, head of the Metropolitan police in Seoul, several times narrowly escaped death when hand grenades were thrown into his limousine.

If the Korean police retained Japanese strong-arm methods of obtaining evidence and confessions, they also approximated Japanese efficiency. I remember one occasion when two blankets were stolen from a jeep parked in front of the WAC billet. We immediately notified the nearest police box—but with little hope of success, for no one had seen the thief and by this time he had no doubt lost himself in Seoul's human swarm.

Yet within the hour the culprit was kneeling on our kitchen floor, trussed up like a turkey in the yards of string Korean policemen use in place of handcuffs. Prodded by his captors he was offering us the ¥500 for which he had sold the blankets.

The yen, we explained, was of little use to us. Being accountable to the Army for the two blankets, we hardly expected a hardboiled supply sergeant to accept Korean money in their stead. Furthermore, we added, we were especially angry that he had let the blankets go so cheap! With violent hand motions indicating despair, we finally told his captors to take him away.

In directing traffic the Korean police were also surprisingly efficient. Every day on my way to work I passed the Korean traffic cop featured in Life Magazine. Gesticulating wildly, he somehow always untangled the jeeps, honey wagons and hand-drawn carts continuously converging at the Great South Gate.

So remarkable were these Korean traffic police that not a single accident occurred when the left-hand driving instituted by the Japanese was changed back to the right originally copied from the Americans. And so capable were they at handling crowds that not a single injury was reported when 100,000 persons paraded on the streets of Seoul *Sam Il* Day, March 1, 1946 in the first free commemoration of the Independence Movement.

Korean police showed their loyalty to the government during the angry demonstrations following the announcement of the Moscow Decision. Although urged by Kim Koo to desert and come over to him, they remained at their post, directing the parades in an orderly manner and keeping accidents to a minimum.

After this event, however, politics began creeping into the police force. Because the Communists had tried to divide them, the police ferreted out and expelled all Communists in their organization, thereafter recruiting only rightists.

The political unity of the police served Military Government well on more than one occasion, according to Captain Margaret Johnson, a WAC assigned to National Police headquarters in Seoul. The police tipped off the authorities to many a riot, demonstration, and plot to take over the government. The most notable attempted coup was in 1947—directed from Washington by Dr. Syngman Rhee, who was in our country with MG's blessing to plead Korea's cause! It was planned in three stages: first unrest and demonstrations, then riots and strikes, and finally the seizure of all government functions—on that memorable date, March 1. Fortunately the widespread intelligence network of the Korean police, equal to any the Japanese had devised, strangled Rhee's plot in its cradle.

However, the Korean police were no more free from avarice than their Japanese predecessors. An ex-WAC in charge of medical supply told me that any time of day or night she could reach into the pockets of the police supposed to be guarding her warehouse and find them stuffed with sulfa and other valuable drugs.

A bloody outbreak against police chicanery occurred in the city of Taegu in October 1946 when Korean peasants set fire to the police stations and mutilated or killed sixty policemen by dropping stones on their heads as the patrolmen passed the farmers' primitive ambushes. Although this riot was blamed on the Communists, from the citizens of this district came the almost unanimous accusation that the police had been appropriating the rice levies for their own uses.

Colonel Maglin admitted that the police may also have erred in arresting leftists en masse and letting strong-arm rightist youth organizations such as the MG-sponsored National Youth and the Dai Dong Youth assume too much control. He explained to me, however, that it seemed best to retain a national police force in Korea in preference to breaking it up into locally-controlled units as in this country—because of the political chaos in Korea, and especially because of the threat of communism.

One thing which greatly contributed to the power of the police was that until 1948 they were not required to issue a warrant before making an arrest. When MG first proposed this innovation the police protested bitterly that they would be stripped of their authority; so the proposal was laid aside for a year and a half. It was forced into effect only at the insistence of the UN Temporary Commission to Korea.

Just before I left Korea a group of intelligent, English-speaking Koreans assembled at the home of a newspaper correspondent to thresh out the virtues and vices of the National Police. Some remarks are worthy of record.

Herbert Kim, a young mining engineer working for the government, who had taken his training at the Colorado School of Mines, said:

"In March last year a mine manager was falsely accused of being a Communist and arrested. The police chief admitted he was not a Communist, but said the local people didn't like him, so to get rid of him they called him a Communist. This is a strong example that the police are ready to make unwarranted arrests and false accusations to please certain individuals."

Replied Mr. Shin, a University professor:

"Police are a necessary evil. I have no personal liking for the police, but when I think of the present situation in Korea and what is to be accomplished, I wonder what is the alternative if we disband what we have now. What group of people can we organize that will be more efficient and beneficial?

"Of course many are Jap-trained, but they themselves are Koreans with a Korean philosophy of life and social and religious background. We cannot expect that a man wearing a police uniform will be altogether different from other Koreans. When a policeman does something it may be because he is a policeman or it may be because he is a Korean.

"After August 15 (1945) the Jap-trained police disintegrated and feared for their lives. At that time anybody with strong biceps and weapons could become police, enforcing his own law. We've had to use the material at hand, and when we damn the police not damn everybody. They are poorly paid and hounded by members of the opposition. The lives of their families are in peril. Their homes are smashed and burned. Yet they try to enforce the law. The transition will have to be gradual and the bad ones weeded out gradually."

Danny Chai, an ex-detective who had the temerity to run against Dr. Syngman Rhee in the 1948 elections, dissented:

"During the Jap regime we called the Koreans in the Japanese police hunting dogs. The Japs used them to flush out Koreans so they could be shot down. Now the Japs have gone back to Japan but the hunting dogs remain.

"In Pyengyang I was police chief after liberation. I did not keep a single Jap-trained policeman, but I had order because the people were glad not to see Jap-trained dogs.

"I was kicked out of North Korea by the Russians, and I did not really want to get into the police force down here. But I found the police were trafficking in captured opium and behind all the opium deals.

"The police say they are hunting Communists, but they will hunt any one who does not give them money or food. When I am good to them I am not a Communist; when I am not, I am a Communist. They will make the accusation of 'red' to cover up anything.

"You are trying to put new wine in old bottles. Teach an old dog new tricks. You could train a new police force in one year. The Russians took laborers and students and now have a well trained force for their purposes."

An American who had lived many years in Korea was listening to the discussion. He summed up the police situation in South Korea this way:

"You can't have a democratic police force in an undemocratic society. In Korea there was strong anarchy under the Japanese, when anything the government did was automatically wrong. The police today have inherited this attitude. Inevitably, as democracy rises in Korea, the police will be relegated to their proper place in society instead of being the center of attention as they are today."

Is There Any Justice?

Once a Korean was arrested, what chance did he stand of a fair trial?

In old Korea before the advent of the Japanese the courts were in a sad state. It was generally admitted that the verdict in a trial would go to the side which showed the most money or could best intimidate the judge.

There were no lawyers in Korea so the suspected criminal had no one to conduct his defense and the witnesses no guarantee they would be questioned in a legal manner. In fact torturing both the accused and witnesses to obtain evidence was an accepted practice. Witnesses usually tried to discover what the judge wanted them to say so they would be spared the whip. No criminal was executed until he had been beaten almost to death. It was understood that before he died he must be made to confess his crime and acknowledge the justice of his sentence.

For this rough and ready legal system the Japanese substituted a civil code similar to the German—retaining, however, some oriental refinements such as torture and extortion.

From August 15, 1945, the time of Japanese surrender, until September 9, 1945, the time of the capitulation ceremony in Seoul, the Korean was as one observer put it "like a wild man turned loose from bondage . . . prison doors were flung open to release political and economic criminals . . . Prison walls were thronged by the families of other criminals. Guards were threatened and they opened the doors and the criminals flooded out."

To establish some semblance of order it was necessary for MG to require the Japanese police, upon threat of confinement, to arrest suspected criminals and send them to court for trial.

Next, of course, it was necessary to establish the courts. On September 17, 1945 although it was a Sunday the first Korean court was set up to try the first case in the Korean language after 40 years of Japanese domination. From then on progress was not easy. The appointments made seemed to please few people including the appointees, most of whom were desirous of higher positions. Personnel for local courts in distant provinces had to be chosen with little or no knowledge of their qualifications. Nevertheless by December 10, 1945 forty-one courts were somehow organized in South Korea.

What was the nature of these courts, and how did they operate? There was the Supreme Court of Korea in Seoul, two appellate courts located in Seoul and Taegu, nine district courts in the nine southern provinces, and twenty-nine branches of the district courts. In order to confuse the people as little as possible, MG decided to continue the civil code with which the Koreans were already familiar, with the elimination of course of those Japanese laws which were discriminatory against Koreans.

Under this system the prosecutor has greater powers than in Anglo-Saxon countries. He interviews the prisoner and the witnesses, takes written statements from both and presents these to the court. He actually makes a preliminary judgment on the case and recommendations as to the punishment that should be imposed. Although the court has the power to overthrow the prosecutor and to impose sentences other than those recommended, ordinarily it accepts the case as presented.

Such a system with its absence of a jury trial can easily be turned to the advantage of a dictator, especially with the connivance of the police—as we have seen happen in Germany, Japan and the State of Louisiana, the only state in the Union having a civil code. However such civil code republics as France and Switzerland have still managed to maintain their political freedom.

During the term of Military Government the civil code was augmented by various ordinances drawn up by the Department of Justice and signed by the Military Governor. Later the Interim Legislature was granted lawmaking powers with Military Government retaining only the right to veto.

Claims against the occupation troops were handled separately by a special claims officer of 24th Corps. The major in charge told me he was often amazed at Korean ingenuity in itemizing accounts to cut the most out of the occupation melon. Notice how in the following case a worthless girl child suddenly becomes a pearl of great price.

"2 September 1946

TO: 65th MG.

FROM: Mr. Lee In Dock, #109 Bon St,., Kongju, Gun, whose child was run over by GI Car.

APPLICATION

Cost of birth and education from her birth to present date.

Items:
1. When she was born, the money was paid as fee for doctor and medicine: ¥2,000.00
2. Cost which was paid to Midwife: ¥30.00
3. Cost of congratulate meeting to the first birthday: ¥1,000.00
4. Cost of mother's care of health during her child drink her mother's milk from Feb. 1940 to Feb. 1946: ¥1,500.00
5. The cost of education for child from March 1942 to 21 August 1946: 54 months. Clean Rice per month: 1 mull. Price of 1 mull clean rice: ¥170.00. Total cost of rice for 54 months: ¥9,180.00
6. Cost of Child's clothes from her birth to death: ¥2,700.00
7. Cost of medicine and fee for doctor consulted from birth to present: ¥2,000.00
TOTAL: ¥18,410.00

Cost of dead child's funeral:

1. Cloth – 3 pill: ¥2,400.00
2. Cotton cloth – 2 pill: ¥1,800.00
3. Fee for coffin: ¥750.00
4. Fee of employees: ¥800.00 – eight men
5. Fee for wine: a. ¥1,200.00 b. ¥250.00
6. Fee for vehicle rent: ¥226.00
7. Fee of rickshaw: ¥55.00
8. Tip for driver: ¥200.00
TOTAL: ¥7,681.00

Items:
1. After 49 days since the child was dead, the festivity will hold that will cost ¥10,000.00
2. Cost of every year's festivity in memory of child's death: We are going to buy 1,000 pyongs of rice fields in memory of child's death perpetually. ¥20,000.00

TOTAL: ¥30,000.00
SUB TOTAL: ¥56,091.00

I, as a dead Child's father, offer this application to get money in memory of her death. She is my fifth chld, whose name is Jong Ja."

Although in the above case Mr. Lee In Dock was certainly over-optimistic, we too were guilty of similar misjudgments. Sometimes our ordinances backfired through lack of understanding of existing conditions or Korean psychology. One such was Ordinance 72, which was a restatement and codification of previously existing regulations, generally aimed at sedition. It was attacked by the Koreans as being harshly phrased and General Lerch, recognizing the reaction, moved swiftly to suspend it. This open-minded attitude impressed many of the community, who were heard to say that a Japanese governor would have made his enforcement more rigorous if anyone had dared to criticize an ordinance enacted under him.

The law abolishing child labor also ran into difficulties. When I went through a silk-spinning factory at Chongju in October 1946 I saw twelve-year-old girls of the size, weight and strength of American eight-year-olds standing all day long on wet floors, dipping their hands into tubs of boiling water where bounced and jostled the white silk cocoons. Catching several threads they deftly twirled them together and attached them to spinning machines. Girls were used, I was told, because they were quicker and more adept than either boys or adults.

This visit sickened me with the exploitation of children in the Orient, based on Confucian ethics which regard children as the economic chattels of their fathers. All the political parties in South Korea were speaking pious platitudes on the abuse, but none dared come out with a vigorous attempt to uproot it.

Finally, when the Communist radio in Pyengyang proclaimed a child labor law had been enacted in the North and pointed at the unhappy contrast in the South, Military Government moved in to correct the situation. The ordinance forbade the employment of children under 14 and specified the hours and working conditions of minors under 18.

Some time after this ordinance was passed I met the Health and Welfare Officer from Chonju and asked how the law was affecting the textile mill.

"We are finding it almost impossible to enforce," he said. "Most of those little girls are the sole support of their families and if we throw them out of work the whole bunch will go on relief. We can't possibly take care of so many. And besides, there is no place for the girls to go. The schools are already so overcrowded they have to turn them away."

Everywhere it was the same story. Until the very end Military Government was still finding this law, which looked so splendid on the books, "almost impossible to enforce."

From the earliest days of our occupation there were loud outcries in the press concerning the incarceration of political prisoners in South Korea, an accusation which the Military Governor consistently denied. MG had insisted that all persons be arrested and tried for a crime in the statute books, such as inciting to riot or disturbing the public peace, and not for political beliefs. It is difficult to believe, however, that the rightist police body—combined with rightist prosecutors—universally obeyed this order. The fact that until 1948 no warrant was necessary to make an arrest and even after that no writ of habeas corpus could be issued gave the rightists almost free reign in the lower courts to vent their personal feelings against the left. On the other hand, rightists who themselves became entangled with the law were prone to escape with very light sentences.

Finally the Korean court outdid itself, pronouncing a maximum penalty of seven years imprisonment on one member of a rightist gang which had beaten two political opponents to death. Transferring the case from Korean to Military court, on December 1, 1947 the Military Governor served notice on the extreme right that he would tolerate no more such blatant miscarriages of justice.

One famous case involving both crime and politics was the discovery and arrest of a large Communist counterfeit ring, after a flood of skillfully made counterfeit 100-yen notes had inundated all of South Korea during the late spring and summer of 1946. The police brought evidence that the bills had been printed from stolen plates in an office building which housed both the Community Party headquarters and the printing presses of the *Hai Bang Ilbo*, official Communist Party newspaper. The counterfeiting was of definitely superior quality, with only two errors. The paper was slightly different from that used by the government, and the notes were not cut in exactly the same way.

Military Government proceeded with reserve—in order to be scrupulously fair to the Communist Party. Although all sixteen of the active agents of the counterfeit ring were Party members, no government agent declared what was perfectly obvious—that the counterfeit plot had been an act of the Party itself. No one was accused save those against whom there was overwhelming personal proof. Party headquarters was even permitted to continue operating in the buildings, though *Hai Bang Ilbo* was closed.

As was to be expected, there were screams of rage from the guilty. The Party issued a statement denying the whole thing in hollow tones: Two members of the ring who succeeded in evading arrest by flight, and who were executives of the Party, had nothing to do with the case; they had merely "left town for their health." The claim that the other fourteen were Communists was also false of course—they were in fact well known anti-communists, who were working on the official Communist paper merely by coincidence. The Party's official denial closed on the not-too-original note that the whole store was the effort of "political brokers" to damage the Party's good name.

The trial of the fourteen counterfeiters was extremely tense. Hearing that the Communists planned to stage a riot outside the Hall of Justice the day the counterfeiters were to be sentenced, another member of the Department of Public Information and I stationed ourselves in a jeep near the gate to watch the fireworks. A crowd of excited Koreans milled about us in the street, muttering, pushing, shouting. We crouched down, expecting at any moment to hear the bullets start whizzing over our heads.

The gates were suddenly flung open and out dashed two trucks filled with Korean Coast Guardsmen, rifles cocked and ready. As they whisked past us we barely caught a glimpse of white figures cowering in the center, baskets clamped firmly over their heads. Even a prisoner it seems has a right to his "face."

So the riot fizzled. But the counterfeiters got off with extremely light jail sentences considering the fact that counterfeiting was one of the three crimes punishable by a mandatory death sentence in ancient Korean law.

As long as we remained in control all death sentences were reviewed by the Military Government. It is interesting to note that at that time these consisted mainly of crimes of passion and the offenders were generally women. Here is the translation of a typical case upon which General Lerch was asked to pass approval for execution.

"OUTLINE OF CRIMINAL ACT
(Case of Choi Sook)

"Prisoner Choi Sook was married when she was 18 years old to Son Moo Suk. She was sentenced to 18 months on 7 March, 1936, in Taegu District Court, since she was convicted of attempted murder, as she resolved to kill him because there was discord. After finishing the sentence, she married again when she was 21 years old to Lee Sung Chul. Lee Sung Chul was not at home on about 15 January 1946. At that time she had intercourse with another Prisoner Kim Chang Soo, (aged 23 at that time) at her own house. After that they continued intercourse until about March 1946. Then they much loved more and more each other. So she does not liked her husband little by little.

"Kim Chang Soo after intercourse at 15 April 46, same place, taught to her that you may kill him with cyanide. And then she resolved to kill him. Lee Sung Chul, came back from outside at about 1:30 P.M. 28 April 1946. She gave him one cup of wine, which contained about 15 gms. cyanide. Lee Sung Chul (aged 39) died at about 2 o'clock P.M. the same day after drinking the wine."

After MG relinquished authority over Korea justice, its complexion changed considerably. In reply to the communistic threat the Rhee government openly stepped up the arrest of political offenders. By the time of the North Korean invasion some 14,000 had reportedly been thrown into South Korean jails—many being executed before the government fled the Capitol. Syngman Rhee was making good his promise to "crush the opposition," internally at least.

Youth Springs Eternal

Whenever we became particularly discouraged with our efforts to bring democracy to the older generation, we could look down at the round eager faces of the children running after our jeep as we passed through the villages and say to one another:

"There lies the hope of the new Korea."

One day I noticed sewn on the children's ragged jackets bits of cloth inked with Korean characters. In my "kitchen" Korean I asked what the writing meant. One boy, a little bigger than the rest, stepped forward and, pointing to his chest, proudly announced:

"These are our names. This means we go to school."

"Why aren't you in school now?" I asked, glancing at my watch and seeing it was the middle of the day.

"Some go in the morning, some in the afternoon," the boy said. "There are not enough schools for all."

In his simple way the boy had stated a tragic truth. Our hope for the new Korea might never be realized, because there were indeed not enough schools for all. These youngsters were fortunate to be able to attend even half a day, for in many districts there were no educational facilities whatever.

In accordance with their Confucian background, Koreans have always revered the teacher and scholar, but under the Japanese they were given very little opportunity to study. When we arrived, their illiteracy had reached the appalling high rate of 80%. Even those Korean children who were allowed to attend "common" or elementary school were forced to spend almost half their time learning the history, language and religion of the Japanese.

The Japanese school system was based on the German. To enter middle school, corresponding to our high school, the student had to pass a stiff examination. The Japanese preferred that the Koreans, upon graduation from common school, enter an industrial school specializing in agriculture, commerce or the trades. As for Seoul University, that was almost entirely given over to the Japanese, only one student in four being a Korean. All the professors in the University and almost all the middle school teachers were Japanese also.

Our first job was to get rid of the Japanese instructors and train Korean teachers to replace them. With the Japanese teachers also went the Japanese textbooks; but not a single text could be found written in the native script of *Hankul*.

Founded by the wise Korean King Se-jong in 1446 A.D., the Korean alphabet is simple and easy to read, consisting as it does of only 25 characters compared to the thousands of clumsy ideographs the Koreans borrowed from the Chinese. So deeply ingrained were the Chinese characters in the Korean mind, however, that the changeover to this vastly simplified writing was practically impossible at the time it was invented. The very thing that distinguished the upper classes from the lower was their ability to read and write the difficult Chinese ideographs. *Hankul* fell into disrepute, considered fit only for women.

Military Government now saw with the resurgence of Korean nationalism an excellent opportunity to re-introduce this alphabet and give it a standing it had never had among the people. This meant authors, translators—and most of all, paper. The Department of Education and Department of Public Information for three years carried on a friendly rivalry over who should receive the next shipment—and which was the more important anyway, propaganda or education.

The prestige of the Chinese ideographs cropped up even on the *Chukan Digest*. When I tactfully suggested that perhaps it would be better to print the *Digest* entirely in *Hankul*, I met with determined opposition.

"No," said Mr. Kim Tong Soo firmly. "This paper goes to city people. They will lose face. They want other people to know they can read Chinese." Only on the Farmer's Weekly could we use the native script throughout. The farmers, it seemed, didn't have so much "face" to lose. For the rest of the population, the only hope for the widespread use of *Hankul*, useful and democratic though it was, seemed to lie in educating an entire new generation.

Another "democratic" principle we found almost impossible to introduce was co-education.

"Are Koreans afraid that having girls in their classes will distract the boys?" I asked the advisor to the Department of Education.

"Oh, no," he replied. "That doesn't seem to matter at all. As I understand it, they fear that if a Korean girl sits in a class with a Korean boy she might outshine him scholastically—and that would never do. It would destroy forever the myth of male superiority. It's perfectly all right, of course, if she sits in another class where he doesn't have to see her and suffer from the comparison."

For girls the only higher education was at Ewha College, founded by missionaries in 1886. It was named "Pear Flower School" after the white royal flower and given royal blessing by the good Queen Min. At first Koreans refused to let their daughters attend this foreign institution, but finally two pupils came—a little servant girl whose mother could not afford to care for her and a high official's wife who wanted to learn English. After this humble beginning thousands of Korean girls broke through the shell of strict custom to enter Ewha's doors.

We found that all Koreans, high low and middle class, wanted to learn English. To them it was an open sesame to all things—a successful political career, a job with Military Government . . . or most hopefully of all, a trip to the United States. All MG officers were beseiged with requests to contribute to the fulfillment of these several desires, but very few had either the time or the inclination. The dependents, however, when they arrived had more of both—sometimes to their sorrow.

My mother was one who the first winter after her arrival succumbed to the blandishments of the principal of the largest boys' middle school in Seoul. They were desperately short of teachers; would she help them?

She arrived at a quarter to eight on the appointed morning, only to find that school did not commence till nine and the building was bleak, bare, and freezing cold. Since the school had formerly been Japanese, the Koreans had knocked out all the windows in the riotous days immediately following liberation and the zero temperature now literally whistled through the corridors.

Finally she came upon an old Korean janitor puttering about, who led her into the principal's office to warm her fingertips over a charcoal brazier. An hour later the principal arrived, accompanied by a shabby gentleman dressed in "foreign style" suit and flat-soled carpet slippers.

"I will be your guide," he of the carpet slippers announced importantly.

Slap-slap-slap, went the flat soles down the hall, up the stairs, down another hall, my mother trotting along obediently behind. At last, with a grandiose gesture, he flung open the door of a classroom.

"Stond oop!" commanded the field-marshall voice in the back row. Immediately forty figures in black uniforms left over from the Japanese regime snapped to attention.

"Bow," said the voice, pronouncing it as in "bow-knot"—and forty figures bent gravely from the waist.

"Set doon!" and the forty figures sat, folded their hands on their desks and looked up expectantly.

Brought up on the boisterous irreverence of California high schools, my mother was too stunned to speak.

The carpet-slippered gentleman touched her arm, breaking into her trance. "Now we go warm your body."

Slap-slap-slap—back down to the principal's office, to hold half-frozen fingers over the charcoal!

Three times in three classes this astonishing performance was repeated. In the last, the monitor became a little flustered.

"Set doon," said the voice when the door opened—and the boys promptly stood up.

"Bow." They bowed.

"Stond oop." And the boys sat down.

After this formal introduction, with intermissions for warming the body, she went back to teach the classes. But she was just barely recovered from a severe attack of pleurisy; and at the end of the day, realizing she could never take the sub-zero temperature of the classrooms, she regretfully resigned.

This middle school experience was not to be ended so easily, however, for out of it came Seo Cap Ken. Seo Cap Ken first made himself known to our household by letter—delivered to my father's office:

"The four school year's
In Yoang sang Middle School.

To My dear Teacher

It's a long time since I saw you
last. How are your health?

We are waiting My dear Teacher
to come our school.

Last Week, How fatigued you are!
My reverence teacher!

Mrs. Dana W Leek Teacher is pleasant
teacher than any other teacher.

I love teacher!

I am loving my teacher like my true Mother.

We were glad to learn With you.

I shall obey in your lead with
this simple mind.

I try to confess the true to the
teacher!

I am a boy Who came to Seoul
from North Korea.

My father died When I was early.

And I living with loving my
mother, my brother and pretty my
sister.

Our life was pitiful life

Now I was being to part from loving
My Mother and healthy my brother,
sweet my sister and under an
obligation to the almamater.

I came to Seoul for, to get personal-
freedom and liberty of Speech,
and Action.

I am a ardent patriotic spirit
of Korea.

Russian Army keep down all the
people in North Korea.

I was entered in prison in twice
for movement of personal freedom
and liberty of speech, action in
North Korea.

Russian Army harried Korean people
and personal house, shop and
every thing's in his weapons in
North Korea.

Russian people have no virtue in
his mind.

I was seeing own eye every state
of Russian Army.

Russian Army Keep down every Man
and every freedom, action.

But When I came in the Seoul,
I found that American people keep
order and moral and virtue

Of course I think that American
people have kind gentle it mind.
I like American people, So
Latter, I want tell you trival
circumstancs in North Korea.

If circumstances do admit my (me),
please take me your home Now!
The pardon Me!
at any rate

For; I make a plea for you to
correct my pronounce, and
I want that in go to your home for
know of American people life.

We have long holidays in winter.
And, As a matter of course I have
many spare.

And I want to teach you for Korean,
If circumstances do not admit my

  Tell me your address,

  I am very sorry, pardon Me!

  Your health;

    So long

Affectionately yours.

(Signed)
    Seo cap Ken."

This letter was followed by more letters, by gifts, and finally by Seo Cap Ken himself. In spite of his literary eloquence he proved to be almost completely tongue-tied. Whether this was due to a inability to catch the sound of English words or to an actual speech impediment my mother was never able to determine; and despite her efforts to help him, his English remained halting syllables painfully delivered, sounding as if his tongue must be twice the normal thickness.

At last one day he managed to sputter out the purpose of his campaign.

"I wish to be adopted noble American home."

Likeable as he was, Seo Cap Ken was one additional responsibility we felt we could not undertake at that time.

Other Koreans, in their efforts to get to America, were neither so sincere nor so subtle. America represented the Mecca for all who sought either fame or fortune. Once that golden land was reached, they felt sure all their troubles would be over. To realize this ambition two things were necessary. The Korean had to have a sponsor and he had to pass an examination in English. Of these two the English examination was often the greater hurdle, for there were various scholarships available to those who qualified.

A friend of mine became involved in the realm of higher learning when she consented to teach English at the graduate school of Seoul University. Thinking that an oriental university education was probably about two years behind the American standard, she worked out the equivalent of a college junior's foreign language course. This proved much too difficult, so she dropped to the freshman level. Still impossible. Her average university graduates, she finally decided, had a background equal to that of the average Ameican high school sophomore. When she gave her top fifty students an examination for entrance to American universities, two passed.

The day after the final examination a Korean woman beautifully dressed in brocaded silks appeared at the gate of my friend's home, where a sign said in Korean: TRADESPEOPLE GO TO REAR DOOR. OTHERS ADMITTED BY APPOINTMENT ONLY. The servants, however, overwhelmed by the magnificence of this lady, admitted her when she calmly announced that she was a friend of the family.

Frantically searching her mind in an effort to recognize this "friend," the teacher finally concluded she must be the wife of one of her husband's Korean officials. Then the visitor came to the business at hand.

"You teach my nephew Seoul University."

A bell rang. "Ah, yes," murmured the instructor.

"If my nephew pass, I make available to you most beautiful art object in Seoul," the visitor continued, unabashed.

In high dudgeon the American showed her Korean "friend" the door—furious at the attempted bribe, though recognizing it so well as an accepted oriental custom.

Disappointing as this incident was, it was better than what was happening to the thousands of youngsters who were not attending educational institutions. These long-haired individuals constantly traveled about the city in trucks, shouting and waving banners in support of some political organization or other.

There were over 100 such political young groups ranging from the Communists on the left to the Dai Dong Youth under the aegis of Dr. Rhee on the right. Of them all, the Dai Dong was the best organized—which meant it was the most vicious. Numerous complaints poured in from the provinces that this youth group was strong-arming its way into mines and factories, taking over the hiring and firing of personnel on the pretext that it was cleaning out the Communists.

In an attempt to corral so much misdirected youthful energy MG organized the National Youth, supposedly based on the Boy Scouts of America. Just as the Boy Scouts have always drawn inspiration from the simple virtues of hardy pioneers and from Indian lore, so the Korean National Youth looked to Tangun, the mythical founder of Korea. Tangun, it is said, came down from the great white mountain at Pak Tu San some 4,280 years ago and drew together the Koo-i tribes in one nation. He called his kingdom *Chosen*, meaning "morning brightness"—and made Pyengyang his capitol. Under his rule, according to tradition, the Koo-i developed just laws and useful social customs. They loved the earth that fed them and were honest and virtuous.

For these reasons the National Youth regarded the age of Tangun as the beginning of the true spirit of Korean chivalry and of the spirit of national consciousness and unity.

"After centuries of confused political thinking and foreign domination," said their handbook, "we again seek our own pure culture with its own unique philosophy of peace and progress."

Their leader was Lee Bum Suk who at the time of Japanese surrender was a lieutenant general in the Chinese Kwang Bok army.

Said General Lee: "The young people of Korea are interested in politics because to them it is the only way they can help achieve early independence for their country . . .

"Their patriotism, when not guided into constructive channels, results in political demonstrations and disturbances. When they join a political party in the hope of doing something for Korea, they are frequently betrayed by politicians seeking only their own selfish ends. A non-political movement such as Korean National Youth is the only answer."

The idea sounded fine to MG, but unfortunately there were many deterrants to its development. In the first place, "youth" included men from 18 to 30, too old to get a thrill out of the ordinary Boy Scout pursuits of hiking, camping, nature study and fire making; too old to stay out of politics. More and more the National Youth assumed the aspect of a political organization until by the time of the Korean election it registered as a political party and elected six representatives to the National Assembly.

More and more the military leadership of General Lee showed through the Boy Scout facade. As the National Youth marched through the streets of Seoul, 30,000 strong in snappy dark blue uniforms and Pershing-style caps, with shovels thrown across their shoulders, it took little imagination to exchange shovels for rifles. A private army, or at the very least another Hitler Youth, seemed in the making. In fact General Lee confided to Correspondent Mark Gayn that the youth leadership schools he was establishing would teach "methods of combatting strikes."

In just casually flexing their muscles the National Youth were so "helpful" to the police that the more sensient Military Government officers began to wonder at the Frankenstein they had created. After MG left, the National Youth became the Korean Youth Association with President Rhee as honorary leader, and in April 1949 it was renamed the Student National Guard.

Among the "intellectuals," the students in the high schools and universities, the Communists too had managed to do quite a bit of spade work. This was demonstrated in a student strike occurring in January and February 1947. The ostensible reason for the walk-out was a proposed merger of nine smaller colleges with Seoul University, but the strikers also carried on their banners demands for self-government rights and replacement of all Americans by Koreans. As an anti-MG shaft which rapidly assumed nationwide proportions, with thousands of students joining in who were not in the least affected by the "University Plan," the movement was found to be guided by instructions coming down from Communist Headquarters.

The students were particularly receptive, said the older and wiser Koreans with a twinkle in their eye, because it was examination time and students are no different the world over.

Fortunately, there was a brighter side to this picture of Korean education. The rehabilitation of the elementary schools, training of teachers and printing of textbooks progressed so favorably that by the end of 1947 Military Government could announce compulsory education for the first and second grades. Pitifully inadequate as this seems to us, for Korea it was a great step forward, as it insured at least the rudiments of *Hankul* for the next generation.

Most startling of all was the success of the "folk schools," adult education classes established under the auspices of the Department of Education. Reaching down into the smallest and most isolated villages, these groups encouraged illiterate farmers to learn their native script, which could easily be mastered by a Korean-speaking adult in about six weeks. So successful was this grass-root movement that by the end of Military Government in 1948, illiteracy had been cut from 80 to 25% – perhaps the most worthwhile of all our accomplishments in Korea.

One Pace to the Left and Three Behind

Some years ago Mrs. Pak In Duk, notable as the first Korean woman to obtain a divorce, created a pun. While lecturing in America she said: "Here in your country I have learned that a party for men only is known as a stag party. In Korea we have been operating a nation for men only for so many centuries that it has become a stag-nation!"

My father tells me that when he first came to Korea the better class woman was seldom seen on the streets—never without her face covered. The covering, of which I have seen a few, was unlike that worn anywhere else in the world. It was really a cloak with the armholes sewed shut. The wearer threw the cloak over her head, crossed the sleeves in front of her face, leaving a small triangular opening for her eyes.

According to one Korean whom I questioned concerning this strange custom, it originated when women tried to conceal their faces from the insults and prying eyes of the Chinese soldiers of Yun Shi Kai. Another story is that once during a seige of the city of Seoul when the men at the walls were hard pressed, the women rushed to their aid, throwing their cloaks over their heads in their haste. With the help of the women the city was saved and the Emperor decreed this unusual manner of wearing the cloak as a badge of honor. As with many outmoded customs, as time passed its honorable significance was forgotten and it became instead a symbol of Korean women's subservience.

In the old days I am told for one hour at dusk men were ordered off the streets so women could stroll about uncovered, freely visiting with one another. At all other times they were supposed to remain in the woman's quarters in the rear of the house, cooking the food and rearing the children of their lords and masters. They were merely a functional appendage to the male, caring for all his physical needs but none of his social or intellectual ones.

For several centuries until the coming of the Japanese only the farmer's wife and the *keesang* or dancing girl in Korea enjoyed relative freedom. The former because she had to work in the fields, where she exposed not only her face but her breasts as well from under a jacket cut short for expediency. The *keesang* was considered a fallen woman in any event, since her *raison d'etre* was the entertainment of men.

Over a period of years before the war I watched Korean women gradually emerge somewhat from their seclusion. The majority still ate apart from their husbands, took no part in entertaining his guests, and kept their eyes lowered when speaking to any man. But they appeared on the streets more and more—although the proper ones always walked one pace to the left and three behind their mates, as does a dutiful Japanese wife.

Concubinage continued to exist, as it has for centuries. Attempts on the part of well-meaning Occidentals to do away with it sometimes met with surprising results. An early missionary once told me this story.

He had discovered that a recent convert had two wives. The one he had married as a young man was now old and toothless; the other he had just acquired was a good-looking girl in her teens.

The missionary called upon his new disciple and laid down the ultimatum that as a Christian he must now get rid of one wife.

The old man pondered a while, then asked: "Which one?"

The missionary had an answer for that, too.

"Your new wife, of course. The first one has served you faithfully many years. How do you suppose she feels, having her place taken by another woman just because she is young and beautiful?"

The old man went away, shaking his head at this strange new religion.

A few days later the missionary had a tearful visit from the first wife of his parishioner.

"For first time my life," she said, "I no work so hard. I have strong young girl to cook meals, wash clothes and look after husband. I have someone make talk all day. Then you make bad talk my husband and he send new wife away. What kind of religion this, make everybody unhappy?"

Concubinage has been largely misunderstood by the Western world. There are three main reasons for it: if a man has no son by his first wife, if the wife is an invalid, cripple or old, or if the man is a libertine.

Even if one or all of the above conditions exist, the man still may not be able to take a concubine. It depends on his financial circumstances. If he is of the upper class he must be able to support each in a separate establishment, the number of such establishments being a symbol to the world of his prosperity. Among the common people, however, the wife and the concubine often occupy the same house, as in the case of the Christian convert mentioned above.

A man may have a dozen sons by a concubine, yet not one of these may call him father or sacrifice to him after his death. If he has no legitimate heir to do these things, he will adopt a son from a distant branch of the family, for Koreans lay great stress on the purity of the family strain.

Five years of American indoctrination, public and private, have done their work. Many Korean women now seem convinced that concubinage will have to go. In the summer of 1949 three thousand embittered females marched on the National Assembly chambers to demand a purge of all government officials who kept concubines in addition to their legal wives.

Korean men gathered on the curb to watch them go by did not seem to share their enthusiasm. "There's getting to be too much democracy in this country," muttered one bearded male.

The one spectacular exception to the establishment order is the island of Cheju Do off the coast of southern Korea, where one of the few authentic matriarchies survives to this day. According to legend there was a time when men were allowed on the island only once a year to perform their service in the propagation of the race. Although today they are allowed to remain, they are still subservient to the female.

Women have always controlled the economy of this insular community, as women divers bring up out of the deep coastal waters the seaweed and rare shell fish for which the island is noted. I first visited Cheju Do with some American officers who were making a special trip to view these "mermaids." They were comically disappointed at finding only the plainest, huskiest Korean women they had yet seen! These Amazonian creatures do all the heavy farming and carrying of burdens, while the "weaker sex" stays home to keep house and mind the children.

As they did everywhere in the world, the GI's upset Korean custom by bringing the "gum and candy-bar circuit" to the women. Taxi-dance halls and other places of entertainment soon sprang up in all the larger cities.

In the early days of the occupation before they were closed by government order, I was invited to one such establishment in Seoul called "The Moon Palace." To my surprise it was crowded with svelte creatures in evening dress, marcelled and heavily made up, dancing the latest steps with their GI partners to two swing orchestras alternately beating it out at either end of the floor. One GI remarked he would rather dance with them than any American girl—they had so much more rhythm!

Some of these girls worked in offices or restaurants in the daytime. Although still considered part of the demi-monde, they were the first truly emancipated females of South Korea—the Korean counterpart of the *mōdern gurū* I had seen emerging in Japan just before the war. It seemed hardly possible they were in the same world with their sisters outside, "one pace to the left and three behind."

Korean men, alarmed at what was happening to their women, could only flail out in anger and frustration. Many times on returning home late from a date my car would be waved to the side of the road by Korean police who peered through the glass to see if any Korean girls were inside. They would undoubtedly have been dragged out and beaten on the spot.

Typical Korean male reaction was shown in an anonymous handbill circulated in Seoul early in October 1945. Entitled "The 'Bomb' Declaration to Womanhood," it asserted:

> "We could not overlook you, womanhood, when you feel around with Westerners in just showing your vanity and worldly desire, which is nothing but scandalous, while you should put all your strength in establishing the state of New Korea.

"From now on, anyone who shows the following scandalous actions, be aware that you will be insulted right in front of the public.

1. Those women who are quite animated, in riding automobiles with Westerners.
2. Those women who wink at Westerners in saying 'Hello, gum?' and 'My home?' and such short words.
3. Those women who chew the gum and stroll all over the town.
4. Those women who are whispering to the Westerners in the night.
5. Those women who go to the dance hall just because they are crazy about coffee and chocolate."

Even American officers were not immune to Korean feminine charms. The Officers Club, which opened in Seoul in December 1945, was soon overflowing with the most advanced and pulchritudinous members of the sex. On one occasion I was considerably uncomfortable at finding myself the only American woman present during the entire evening.

Most of these Korean girls were pick-ups, one officer told me confidentally, who would hang around the steps of the club every night waiting to be invited inside. Such behavior was a great shock to the more respectable Korean women. When an UNRRA official invited the famous educator, Dr. Helen Kim, to the club, she refused on grounds that she would be associating with *keesangs* and harlots.

The officers' wives have often wondered how the club managed to get ride of these "liberated" females before their arrival. Actually, it was very simple. Two weeks before the first boatload of dependents was due, a new ruling required an officer to put a request in writing twenty-four hours ahead if he wished to bring a Korean girl to the club. Nobody's name appeared on the list. The problem was solved, and the wives took care that it never arose again.

While most American men were considering Korean women merely playthings—if they considered them at all, the Communists were already beginning to realize their possibilities as a hitherto untapped source of political influence. Several of the political parties formed auxiliary women's organizations, but the Communist-inspired Central Women's Union was the largest and best organized.

I attended their tremendous nation-wide conference held in the gymnasium of a Seoul elementary school on December 22-23, 1945. The speakers at the meeting were all men, who seemed to be haranguing the women to support the Party cause.

Not being interested in the man's point of view, I asked to be introduced to the famous Korean woman Communist who was reputedly the mainspring of Central Women's Union.

Like all women zealots everywhere, she was brusque and businesslike. Her hair was short, her clothes severe, her eyes alight with the fire of purpose.

In fair English she told me that her father was a physician in North Korea and she had received her education before the war in Shanghai and Moscow. She advocated an immediate program of reform for Korean women, including equal property rights, equal pay for equal work, and government-paid maternity care.

Gently I pointed out that even in America, where women were considered quite advanced, we had not managed all these reforms as yet. I suggested that perhaps such an ambitious program might take a little while in a country where women were just finding their way out of the dark ages.

Then I asked the sixty-four dollar question. "Does your group support the Communist Party?"

"We will support any party that will support our interests," she replied. "So far the Communists are the only ones who have."

Soon, however, others among the Korean women were actively at work for the advancement of their backward sisters. Following are excerpts from a petition presented to the Department of Public Information early in February 1946, to license the first women's magazine in Korea. In spite of its awkward and sometimes ludicrous language, it indicates the trend in feminine thinking following liberation.

"It is the greatest task of the present time for all the Korean women, how they absorb their liberated 'Today' which contains the all chances of reformation, of sexual equalization and of women suffrage, and how to use it—'Today'—in the most effectual and positive way . . .

"We believe that the women's power can be the important element in constructing a new nation, encouraging the major part of the men who are wandering and straying like the sleep walkers as they have not distinguished yet on the order of their propulsions besides have no any knowledge concerning the principles of spring-up . . .

"Now! At the great turning point of the whole world, we anxiously hope that all Korean women show their real figures, displaying completely their entire abilities and energies.

"The 'Boo Nyu Shinmoon' (Ladies' Journal) is planned to be published to sweep out the Japanese imperialistic idea of life out of our daily life, and enlighten the people in a democratic way, having self-confidence that we could be the representative organization of the whole Korean women and liberate them completely . . .

"In conclusion, we hope heartily that you will kindly lead and stimulate us, having right recognition on our purports and works, and advice us without any reserve at the beginning of our publication."

Major Mildred Lucka, who worked with the Korean nurses, represents Military Government's first concrete help to Korean women. Prior to her arrival nurses had been the scrubwomen and orderlies about the hospitals with no professional standing of any kind. Their pay was one tenth that of an ordinary day laborer.

Major Lucka and her Army nurse assistant set up a professional two-year training period for nurses with a third year added for obstetrics. Before long trained women were seen in all hospitals in Korea in the capacity of midwives, graduate nurses or administrators. For her strenuous two-year service with its notable results, Major Lucka was the only woman in Korea to receive the Army's highest non-combatant award, the Legion of Merit.

Meanwhile in the spring of 1946 the Communists in North Korea came out with a startling declaration: "Whereas the emancipation of women has been effected, and whereas men and women are now equal, therefore be it enacted that adultery is prohibited." Although it is doubtful that this magnificent *non sequitur* could be effected by legislation, it, followed by the formation of a Women's Bureau in North Korea, made quite an impression on the Koreans.

Not to be outdone, Military Government the following summer established a Women's Bureau of its own as well as a women's division in the national police. To head these two organizations MG chose two Korean sisters who, like the Soong sisters of China, had led lives so off-pattern as to be virtually unique.

Born of Korea's first Christian wedding nearly half a century ago, they had already established an outstanding record among their own people in the fields of social work, medicine, education and music.

Their father, Myung U. Koh, was a doctor and a good one, whom my father credits with having once saved his life when he fell ill at an isolated mining camp with a severe infection.

Unlike most Korean gentlemen, this remarkable man believed that his daughters should have an education rather than marry at an early age and produce innumerable grandsons. Gladys Koh, the elder daughter, studied at the Wesleyan Conservatory of Music in Macon, Georgia, while Evelyn Koh earned a Ph.D. at the University of Michigan. A third daughter Nan got her M.D. from Tokyo Women's Medical College and became a gynecologist with MG's Department of Public Health and Welfare.

Physically there is a strong family resemblance between the three, accentuated when they appear in Korean dress. They are all short, stocky and bespectacled. Temperamentally they are as different as sisters could possibly be. Gladys is the wit of the trio, voluble, eager to make friends. Evelyn is the crusader, sincere, earnest, pleading her cause to all who will listen. Nan is the baby, studious soft-spoken, reserved.

After they returned to Korea from America Gladys and Evelyn decided to open the first welfare settlement for women that their country had ever known. They established it in a little village on the outskirts of Seoul, and named it "Chamaiwon," meaning "Sisters' Garden."

"The villagers couldn't understand at first why well-educated people would bother with them," says Dr. Evelyn, "but soon the whole village became part of our family."

Some of the services they brought to their countrymen were a well-baby clinic, pre-natal care and general medical service, a club where girls of marriageable age could learn home making, a recreation program for older women, and an orphanage.

The war interrupted all activities except the baby clinic and kindergarten.

Warned that in all probability Seoul would be bombed by the United States in August 1945, the two social workers packed up nine of their orphan babies, and with five trucks of equipment moved to a town north of the 38th parallel. After the surrender they sneaked back over the border to place the babies in a Catholic orphanage. Not until the barrier is removed can they hope to retrieve their personal property and funds.

These were the two sisters Military Government asked to be the Frances Willard and Mary Agnes Sullivan of the new Korea. Evelyn Koh became chief of the Women's Bureau, where she joined Helen Nixon, an ex-American Red Cross worker, in trying to improve the lot of Korean women. Gladys Koh became the first head of the Korean Women's Police.

When time came for the Korean elections, Korean men did not want to give women the vote, for which the Women's Bureau had conscientiously worked. The men I talked with murmured stock phrases like "It's too soon" and "They aren't ready." But the election law granted female suffrage nevertheless, partly under American pressure and partly because anything less would have been grist for the Communist propaganda mill up north. If communism served no other good purpose in South Korea, it was a sharp goad toward certain types of progress.

Four women were appointed by General Hodge to the South Korean Interim Legislative Assembly, but none were elected to the National Assembly in the Korean elections of May 9, 1948. Some of the more cynical among the Americans believe that the vote, women's police and perhaps even the Women's Bureau will not survive our withdrawal. Some backsliding was already evident in a clipping I received from Seoul in January 1949. A government spokesman told the United Press that the number of imported American movies would have to be severely cut down, because they tended to give Korean women "a mistaken impression of their equality with men." Even so, Korean men will find that they are trying to close a Pandora's box. Once a woman has been released, I feel sure no force on earth can stuff her back into the secluded women's quarters of half a century ago.

Ladies' Night
In a House of Repute

One oriental delight most MG officers resolved to savor for themselves was the geisha, or *keesang* as she is known in Korea. When back in Military Government school I compared the geisha to a night-club entertainer, they snorted incredulously. When I further commented that I myself had visited many geisha houses before the war, they insisted I must have known a strictly expurgated version.

As a matter of fact, the true geisha has spent many years attaining perfection in the graceful arts of dancing, playing musical instruments and conducting sprightly intellectual conversation. She looks down on the *modern guru* as an amateur upstart who is cutting in on her earnings without putting in the necessary training.

In a country where wives are no more than chattels, the geisha is an essential member of society. She gives the oriental man the female companionship and light-hearted entertainment which he does not find in his own home. She may have her own special patron, usually a wealthy manufacturer, but she is definitely not a prostitute.

Unfortunately, since the war the geisha has degenerated. The American soldier did not appreciate her languid classical dances and her twanging on the *samasen*. Since most of her former patrons are either dead or destitute, she has often had to turn to more sordid pursuits.

I was aware of this. Also that the *keesang* has always been of a notoriously lower order than the Japanese geisha. So in spite of my brave words I was slightly dubious when another WAC and I accepted an invitation from two American officers to visit a *keesang* house in Seoul.

We left our shoes at the door and were conducted down several drafty corridors to a long room with sliding panels. The party was being given for one of our escorts by a wealthy Korean, who had already arrived and was seated with his companions at a low table that extended the length of the room.

We settled ourselves on cushions in the place of honor, squirming to get comfortable on the floor in the cross-legged Korean fashion. Suddenly the doors slid back and the *keesangs* scurried in, gracefully settling themselves down beside us. There was one apiece, even for the WACs.

The girls at our elbows busied themselves keeping our plates filled with such delicacies as octopus tentacle and crisp fried grasshopper, and our thimble-like cups brimming with Korean rice wine.

Some of the Korean dishes I actually enjoyed, such as *sun sin lo*, or "food of the gods," which is a mixture of meat and vegetables cooked at the table in a brass charcoal-burning brazier. It is sometimes called the Korean *sukiyaki*, although I fail to find any resemblance.

As the meal drew to a close one of the girls began to beat out a weird rhythm on an hourglass-shaped Korean drum, while another went through the slow, hesitant motions of a Korean dance. I knew it was supposed to represent some old folk tale, but none of the Koreans at the table knew enough English to explain it.

By this time the Korean men were getting puffy-eyed and a few had already sprawled out on their cushions. They had been engaging in a lively game of *gambai* or "down the hatch" with the American officers, but an American can always drink an Oriental under the table.

The girls were still chattering brightly, and I began to notice that my WAC friend and I were acquiring quite an audience. Even the men still awake were deserted as the girls crowded around us to ask about our lipstick, perfume and face powder. Men in a *keesang* house were old hat, but a woman was quite a novelty and therefore much more intriguing.

Promptly at ten o'clock a bell rang to tell us it was time to go home. As we all stood up and loudly sang the Korean national anthem to the tune of *Auld Lang Syne*, my WAC friend and I had a *keesang* on each arm. Then the *keesangs* went their way and the rest of us went ours as the house closed down for the night.

When *keesangs* are called in to supplement entertainment in private homes, their behavior is not always so circumspect, I have heard. One officer told me of his shock and surprise upon dining with a prominent Korean, to find that the two winsome Korean dinner partners whom the host had introduced as friends of the family were meant to be companions for the night as well.

Quite apart from the *keesangs* there was a large prostitute population when we arrived in South Korea. Licensed prostitution, say the Koreans, was one of the evils the Japanese brought to Korea with their conquering armies. The red light districts were immediately put off limits to GI's, but according to one newspaper account they continued to carry on a flourishing native trade, taking in up to ¥1,000,000 a night.

An official investigation revealed that about 44% were following their profession because of poverty, 25% because of abduction, 20% due to the death of parents, and 10% had been sold for money. An early MG ordinance forbade the buying and selling of "females"; but since this would apply to horses, cows and hens as well, it caused a great deal of confusion all around and had to be amended.

The unabashed manner in which Koreans deal in these matters is shown by the fact that they founded an organization called The Public Whore-Monger Association which formally petitioned Military Government on sundry matters relative to its "industry."

Finally in February 1948 although the whoremongers passed out a bribe of ¥7,000,000 the South Korean Interim Legislature pushed through a bill abolishing legalized prostitution and releasing the girls from their intolerable slavery. The girls, however, refused to budge. They staged an unanimous sit-down strike, claiming that the rooms and furniture were their own and demanding equally profitable employment.

A certain Miss Chai, Sun Choo stated when interviewed by a newspaper reporter:

"This building belongs to enemy property and I have a good right to remain here in this room. The mirrors and beds which we have used are all ours. Most of us have no place to depend on, and we have to remain here until we find a place to move."

One generous whore-monger replied:

"All citizens blame us for having black hearts who are holding the white slave market, but we have considered this our business. The removal of the licensed prostitution is proper, but when we think of our individual interests, we feel somewhat sad. I'll consider the prostitutes my own daughters, so giving them beds and all others."

Other whore-mongers not being so liberal, the struggle between the girls and their former employers continued. Thirteen days later the *Min Joon Ilbo* reported:

"Even now, when more than ten days have passed already since the abolition of the public prostitution, the prostitutes are remaining still in their rooms, sneering at the attitude of the authorities. But the Seoul City authorities decided to make 200 of them work at restaurants at Seoul and got the approvement from the businessmen. And the city authorities are negotiating with those concerned to make the rest of the 300 work at the bus or streetcar companies. But on the other hand, the prostitutes are not accepting these recommendations, saying that they have had the income of ¥10,000 a month up to now."

The tense problem of the ungrateful prostitutes gradually eased. With the help of various church and government agencies some of the recalcitrants found congenial employment. Others no doubt drifted off, lost themselves among the nameless masses, and continued to practice the oldest profession without government blessing.

Old Korea

I
From the album of the author's father Dana Winston Leeke

Tile roof construction South Korea

Temple at Mitsuyo South Korea

Three bronze Buddhas temple in Diamond Mountains

Su-Won temples wall and gate

A Chinese temple across Yalu River

Pleasure Palace, South Gate Su-Won

Survey office site, Tul Michung

Mrs. J. S. Collbran (wife of mine owner-partner), Morachi Creek

Korean river boat

Chinese junks on the Yalu

Gensan Coast

Korean ferry boat crossing rapids

Seine fishing, South Korea

Pole and line fishing, South Korea

Native cloth weaving

Earthen ware street market

Kimchii jar

Pipe and cloth market, village street

Hat maker

'Sool' Still, wine distilled from rice or Kaffir corn

Korean blacksmith, forge and anvil

Frozen well, Tul Michung Korea

Grinding millett, Nam Nori Korea

Natives, Coolie class

Author's mother, Mabel Brown Leeke

Staff Seoul Mining Company, Tulmi Chung, August 1918: Fifth from right in the back row, Dana Winston Leeke

Author's parents at Tul Mi Chung's Seoul Mining Company

II

From postcard collection of the author's maternal grandmother Ada Cary Wright Brown who lived the year of 1915 with the Leekes

These postcards are captioned at times in quaint idiom. Evidently GETTING OUT OF WOMEN is a fusion of our GET-UP and OUTFIT!

(イ196) A FIREWOOD CARRYER　薪材ノ搬運　（朝鮮風俗）

From Mrs. Brown's record: 'The most conspicuous animal in Korea is the magnificent bullock. Every road in Korea is made picturesque by long lines of bullocks carrying on their backs huge loads of fuel in the shape of grass, faggots of wood – or else fat bags of rice and barley . . .'

(イ73) HARVESTING.　打麥　（朝鮮風俗）

(イ148)　A Nobleman going out on the Palanquin. 轎乘ノ官大舊(俗風鮮朝)

(イ222)　FILLED UP CAKES IN THE CERIMONEY OF CONGRATURATION 物盛ノ戲(俗風鮮朝)

（ソ）13 AN APPEARANCE OF GENTLEMAN. 士 紳（俗 風 鮮 朝）

（イ25） PALAJQUIN OF HIGH CLASS OFFICER IN THE FORMETLY 輿ノ官大 （俗風鮮朝）

The intent of 'Formetly' for the high class officer's ride is lost in time!

(京81) THE STONE IMAGE OF BUDDHA 京城ξ漢山麓ノ石佛 (朝鮮名所)

(京125) The Pagoda park, Seoul. 京城パゴダ公園音楽堂ト塔 (朝鮮名所)

(京122) THE PAGODA PARK SEOUL 京城パゴダ公園音樂堂ト佛塔 （朝鮮名所）

(京123) The Pagoda-park, Seoul. 京城パゴダ公園大圓覺寺龜ノ碑

CITY GATES

Population of Seoul in 1914 was 300,550

(1309) GETING OUT OF WOMEN 出外ノ人婦 (朝鮮風俗)

High caste

(1574) FULL DRESSES KEE-SAN 盛装ノ妓官 (朝鮮風俗)

Dancing girl

(1572) Mother & her child. 子親 (朝鮮風俗)

(京142) THE PLACE WHERE LATE KOREAN EMPRESS BIN WAS KILLED　景福宮閔妃御扇舊蹟　（朝鮮名所）

(京144) THE SEERYORI STREET, SEOUL　京城東大門外淸凉里道　（朝鮮名所）

(イ376) DOMESTIC FOWL VENDOR 賣 鶏 （朝鮮風俗）

(イ401) A laborer. （シタミ）夫運荷 （朝鮮風俗）

(イ364) ON THE WAY HOME FROM MARKET 松葉賣ノ歸路 （朝鮮風俗）

(イ443) THE WATBR-MEL LON SELLER 甜瓜賣 (朝鮮風俗)

(イ411) DRAWING OF COUNTRY 田舎ノ水汲 (朝鮮風俗)

(イ317) Riding on Ass. 驢馬 (朝鮮風俗)

'DRAWING OF COUNTRY' seems to be fractured construction for rural water carriers.

What the well dressed man will wear before noon?

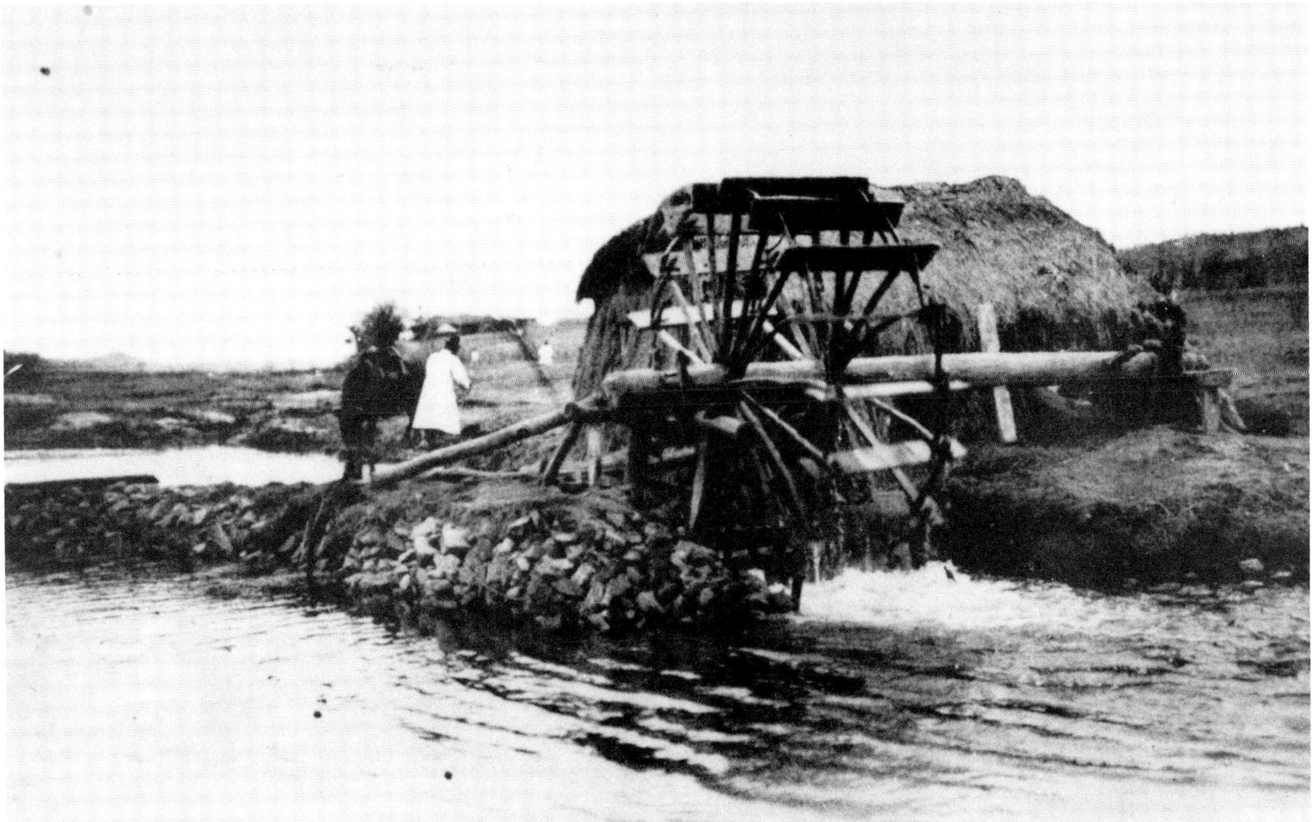

(イ59) WATER WHEEL. 水車 (朝鮮風俗)

(イ194) A FERRY BOAT. 渡船 (朝鮮風俗)

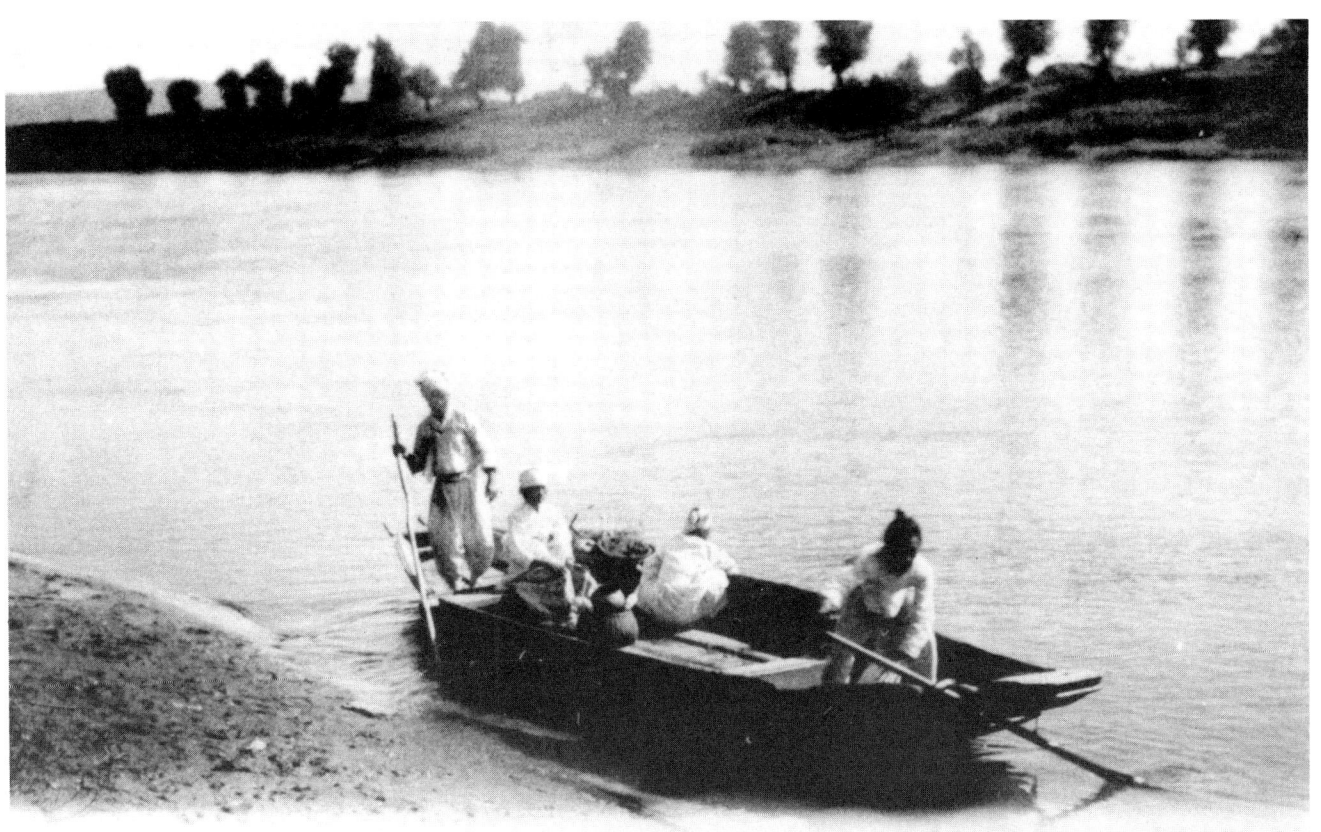

(313) Hulling of Rice. 搗米 (朝鮮風俗)

(458) A Carrier of timber on the Back. 搬運木材 (朝鮮風俗)

Chosen Hotel whose grounds were formerly part of the Old South Palace precincts whose Temple of Heaven (right) still stands

Pyeng Yang

Brass candlesticks and Korean chest in Leeke home 1915

Kilroy's Father Was Here

Although few Americans realized it at the time, our earlier contacts with the Korean people hardly presented us in a favorable light as their first democratic mentors.

When I came into Seoul in 1945 I felt a glow of pride that we used electricity which had been installed by American engineers.

And water from a water-works constructed by an American company.

And rolling stock of American make.

But these marvels failed to assuage my sense of guilt as I relived in my unquiet mind America's former diplomatic relations with the Hermit Kingdom.

Koreans would remind me gently that Americans had let them down three times in the past—and imply we might do it again.

The first time, they pointed out, was when we failed to live up to the Treaty of 1882, completely ignoring the frantic appeal of the Korean King whose throne was threatened and in immediate danger of overthrow by the arrogant Japanese adventurers who were over-running The Land of the Morning Calm.

Few Americans ever heard of the Treaty of 1882, although at one time the United States lost quite a number of American seamen trying to obtain it.

The history books tell how in 1853 Admiral Perry sailed into Tokyo Bay and under the menacing shadow of his long guns opened up Japan to foreign trade. Not many add that thirteen years later the United States Navy tried the same tactics on Korea, with disastrous results.

In September of 1866 we might have seen the American gunboat GENERAL SHERMAN sailing up the Taedong River in the direction of Pyengyang, the second largest city in Korea and now the capital of the Russian zone. When the governor of Pyengyang sent a message asking the reason for this 'invasion' the captain replied that he desired to open trade with Korea.

In spite of warning that the river farther up was not navigable, the GENERAL SHERMAN sailed on and on, taking advantage of exceptionally high tides and the drain-off from summer rains. When she had almost reached the city of Pyengyang the river suddenly receded and the gunboat was hopelessly grounded.

The Koreans at first treated the crew courteously, furnishing them with food but at the same time refusing to trade. The Americans retaliated by seizing the governor's adjutant when he came aboard to bring official messages. For an entire day the mayor of Pyengyang pleaded vainly at the ship's side for his release.

After the crew had consumed the provisions the Koreans had brought them, they went ashore to get more—killing five Koreans and wounding seven in their plundering. The Taiwunkun then gave an order to attack the ship unless it departed immediately—which of course it was helpless to do.

At first the ship's guns were far superior to the futilely inadequate Korean arrows, but soon the defenders conceived the idea of trying to set the ship on fire. They fastened three scows together, piled them with brushwood sprinkled with saltpetre and sulphur, torched them ablaze, and floated them downriver, aiming at the American vessel. The first two of these crude and unwieldy fire-torpedoes missed but the third try was successful, causing the officers and crew to jump in the river or be burned to death. Those who jumped were killed when they reached shore, and the GENERAL SHERMAN's anchor chains were triumphantly hung as a victory festoon over the gates of Pyengyang.

After this first devastating disenchanting contact with the West, the Hermit Kingdom retreated even farther into its shell.

On the Island of Kangwha at the mouth of the Han River I have seen the monument which marks the United States' second attempt to pierce that shell: it has stood over the grave of an American naval lieutenant since 1871.

In that year Minister Frederick F. Low in Peking received instructions to conclude a treaty with Korea for the treatment of shipwrecked seamen. Arriving with a flotilla of five vessels near the present site of Inchon, the port where American ECA supplies are pouring in today, Low dispatched an envoy to the capitol to arrange terms. The Taiwunkun, however, suspecting the mission had something to do with the SHERMAN massacre, decided to act accordingly.

While the American flotilla waited for an answer, its commander sent two small vessels to investigate the estuary of the Han River between Kangwha Island and the mainland. The island opened fire. After returning a few shots, the American boats withdrew to report.

To uphold the honor of the United States flag, the American commander sent a large force against the Korean fort on the island. Although the Koreans fought with desperate valiance, even throwing gravel in their attackers' faces when ammunition gave out, the fort was stormed and taken. One American naval officer lost his life in the attack and was buried on the island.

Our flag having been defended, the American forces withdrew, satisfied that it was indeed impossible to conclude any kind of agreement with Korea at this time.

Now we come to the Treaty of 1882. In spite of our shamefully inauspicious beginning the United States actually was the first Western power to come to diplomatic terms with Korea.

In the fall of 1878 Commodore Robert Shufeldt, sailing around the world on the USS TICONDEROGA, was instructed to "visit some part of Korea with the endeavor to open up by peaceful means negotiations with the government."

It was four years before the compact was concluded. The actual negotiations took place at Tientsin between Commodore Shufeldt and a Chinese envoy, since at the time China still held Korea as a vassal state. The Treaty of 1882 permitted American citizens to trade at open ports, to erect residences and warehouses in these cities; and it contained a mutual aid clause which the United States was to casually ignore.

Protected by this treaty, a few enterprising American businessmen and engineers ventured into the country and on concession from the Korean King started various developments. Had it not been for the Treaty of 1882 it is very possible my father would not have gone to Korea, my mother could not have joined him at his work site, and I would not have been born there.

The Treaty of Portsmouth, which brought the Russo-Japanese to a close, was the United States' next official contact with the Land of the Top Knots. It was arranged by President Theodore Roosevelt, who received the Nobel Peace Prize for his efforts. It granted Japan paramount political, military and economic interest in Korea, but at the same time guaranteed "Korean independence." This treaty too was important to us at the mines, because it protected the sanctity of all concessions granted by the Korean King. Faced with it and with American force behind it, the Japanese did not dare interfere with nor violate American interests in Korea by other than "legal" means.

But the treaty did not prevent the Japanese from taking over the Korean postal and telegraph system, controlling all political activity, and on various pretexts seizing lands. In 1906 the Korean Emperor dispatched a letter to the President of the United States calling attention to these evils and asking American help as promised in the Treaty of 1882. Professor Homer G. Hulbert, an American in the employ of the Korean government, was chosen to hand-carry the message, since the Korean Foreign Office was already "in the sleeve" of Japan.

The Japanese in Seoul set about forestalling the effect of the Emperor's plea. Marquis Ito was sent to Korea with definite instructions that the country was to be induced to sign away her independence voluntarily. By a series of ruses, including the confinement of the Korean King and the Prime Minister and the addition of a clause stating that when Korea was ready her independence would be returned, a majority of the Korean cabinet was persuaded to sign the paper. Then the Japanese authorities in Washington announced that Korea had voluntarily entered into an agreement granting Japan a protectorate over the country.

Apparently without consulting Korea as to the truth of the matter, our American government recognized Japan's claim, withdrew its legation from Seoul, and informed the Korean representative in Washington that all diplomatic business would henceforth be conducted through Tokyo. When Professor Hulbert arrived with his message from the Emperor he was faced with a *fait accompli*. The Korean sun had set and Japan's was in the ascendancy.

In his classic book *The Passing of Korea*, so hated and feared by the Japanese it was confiscated whenever found, Professor Hulbert writes a terrible indictment of American indifference at this time.*

". . . Even while the whole Korean people were convulsed by the high-handed act of Japan, and some of the very highest Korean officials were seeking oblivion of their country's wrongs in suicide, the American Minister in Seoul was feasting the Japanese who had compassed the destruction of Korean nationality. Can it be wondered at that the feeling of confidence which Korea reposed in the friendship of America should have experienced a sharp and sudden reaction. Americans of every class had been telling Korea for a quarter of a century that the American flag stood for fairness and honesty, that we had no purely selfish interests to serve, but stood for right, whether that right was accompanied by might or not; but when the pinch came we were the first to desert her, and that in the most contemptuous way, without even saying goodbye."

Current history has it that World War II in the Pacific started with the Manchurian Incident of 1931. I believe it started in Korea in 1906. Who knows but that if the United States had lived up to her commitments at this time, Pearl Harbor and the entire Asiatic conflict could have been averted. For Japan's march through Asia followed step by step in logical progression once she had this first taste of power.

The next time we failed Korea was as already stated when we took no cognizance of the revolution inspired by President Wilson's own doctrine.

The third and most recent betrayal occurred in 1945 when we allowed Korea to be divided at the 38th parallel, thereby tearing apart a people ethnologically united, setting brother against brother, and sowing the seeds of civil war.

Is it any wonder that an American in Korea confronted with this damaging array of evidence is sometimes at a loss? For the Koreans have for generations remembered what most Americans never knew.

Yet where our national policy failed, certain individuals succeeded. American missionaries arrived in Korea in 1884, the first being a physician, Dr. H. N. Allen, later American Minister to Korea. Dr. Allen saved the life of one of the Korean princes, became physician to the King, and with the King's full consent and blessing established the first modern hospital in Korea.

Dr. Horace G. Underwood, Sr. and Dr. Henry Appenseller arrived the next year and opened the first modern schools where education was available to girls as well as boys. The missionaries and their Korean helpers translated the Bible and other books into the vernacular phonetic script. Their insistence that converts should learn to read and write this script did more to popularize it in a generation than had been done in the five hundred years since its invention.

Through the help and influence of American missionaries many Koreans went to the United States to study and brought back American ideas and methods. Although many of these proteges disappointed their sponsors by becoming "pro-Japanese collaborators and national traitors" or by acting as if a college degree set them a notch above their countrymen, others were leaders in the resistance movement and later of great assistance to us in Military Government.

American business and commerical interests also played an important part in the opening of Korea. The first Korean railway, a twenty-mile standard-gauge stretch between Inchon and Seoul, was built by the Colbran-Bostwick Development Company on concession from the old Korean Emperor. Because of American construction Korean railways today have a standard-gauge track and utilize American pullmans, while Japan's are narrow gauge and employ the European compartment-style car.

Arthur Colbran, son of one of the partners in the railroad company, discovered gold near the town of Suan by sampling Korean workings and he obtained from the Emperor a concession to work the property. My father, as a young Colorado School of Mines graduate, was offered his first engineering position at this mine when Korea was no more to him than an indefinite spot on a new map. Here I was born and lived until I was five years old, when the mine closed down for lack of ore.

In 1930 my father returned to Korea to work at another American concession, the Oriental Consolidated Mines in the northernmost province of the country. The five mines in this group were opened in 1894 by hardy American engineers who treked north on foot and horseback the 500 miles from Seoul. These mines were flourishing until in 1940 the Japanese put an embargo on gold and refused to pay the standard world price at the Japanese Mint. After making it impossible for the

---

*Hulbert, Homer B., *The Passing of Korea*, Doubleday, Page & Co. 1906, p. 223

Americans to operate at a profit the Japanese came along with an attractive offer and the company sold out. The last payment on the mines was deposited in a New York bank just a few months before Pearl Harbor. After the war, Korean refugees from the north reported to us that the Russians did start up operations at one of the mines but shipped the machinery from all the rest back to Russia.

In 1898 the Korean Emperor issued an edict: no more concessions would be granted to foreigners. However in this same year Colbran and Bostwick organized the Seoul Electric Company to construct the first tramway and electrical plant for Seoul, and another American firm began work on the city's first modern water system.

Koreans were all agog at the miracle of electricity. One engineer, Mr. Henry English who wired the emperor's palace, told me how the Koreans would swarm around him, poking their wide-eyed heads into every aspect of his work. Deciding to have some fun, he announced that he would now kill all the frogs in the palace pond, and then bring them back to life again.

Passing a wire through the water, he turned on the current. All the frogs rose to the surface, stiff and glassy-eyed. He switched off the current and they stretched themselves and calmly paddled away.

The Koreans bowed down in unison, chanting breathlessly: "Ai-go, Aigo," an expression of tremulous astonishment and awe. Such tricks as this one earned for Mr. English the title of "Taigum" or "Great One."

The Seoul Electric Company had an arduous time of it in trying to educate Koreans in the proper way of riding its street cars. The populace who automatically left its shoes at the doors, was bewildered that these should be missing when it disembarked. It also butted its skulls through the windows which like a disoriented bird it failed to see in time, until all the panes were shattered and its heads bloody if not bowed.

When Military Government came to Seoul after World War II we were grateful indeed for American-installed drinking water, electricity and the railway's rolling stock, but we never found a military use for the Korean street cars. With paneless windows, with swarms of human beings clinging to every hand-and-toe-hold on the outside like robber bees to a honey comb, with additional throngs densely packed within, they were more an object of wonder than utility. I rather often overheard my fellow Americans brag they were actually going to ride in a Korean trolley before their days in the country were done, but as far as I know nobody every got up the courage.

I Meet the Russians Again

On June 25, 1947 representatives of all shades of Korean political thought from black to white sat down peaceably together in the Capitol Building for the first time since liberation. This momentous occasion was an open session of the reconvened United States-Soviet Union Joint Commission.

For more than a month preliminary meetings between the two great powers had already been taking place in the Duk Soo Palace, the Commission's official residence. In these historic grounds not only did we meet the Russians but the new Korea met the old architecturally, formal modern structures erected by the Japanese almost touching the weathered tile-roofed oriental living quarters which had been home to the last of the Korean kings.

Now from the press gallery we watched an eager, optimistic assemblage filling the Capitol's Assembly Hall, which a short time before had been built in a vast empty marble foyer for the sessions of the South Korean Interim Legislature. Today these representatives of South Korea's political parties and social organizations were foregathering in the bright hope of being consulted on the formation of a Provisional Government for all Korea.

The basis for the reconvening of the Commission, after nearly a year of diplomatic wrangling, was laid at the very top—in a series of letters between Secretary of State Marshall and Foreign Minister Molotov. The agreement stated that the Commission would now consult with all parties who signed the Declaration proposed by General Hodge in 1946, confirming their intention of upholding the Moscow Decision. Furthermore the Commission could by mutual agreement exclude from consultation any individuals or organizations which after having signed the Communique did "foment or instigate active opposition to the work of the Joint Commission or either of the Allied Powers or to the fulfillment of the Moscow Decision."

The opening session began with full-dress fanfare. Promptly at one-thirty in the afternoon the members of the Commission filed into the new Legislative Hall to the music of the Lee Household musicians, a court orchestra attached to the remnants of the last Korean Dynasty. Dressed in red robes and old-fashioned horsehair hats, they sat with their antiquated native instruments in an alcove above the rostrum. Bulbs flashed and movie cameras ground. Major General Albert E. Brown and Colonel General Terenty F. Shtikov, Chiefs of the American and Soviet Delegations, seated themselves under the Korean flag in the center of the stage, while members of the various subcommissions ranged along the wall. The presiding officer for this meeting, General Shtikov—a rotund figure in a blue uniform—rose and declared the session officially open, whereupon the Lee Household musicians struck up the Korean National Anthem, the Star Spangled Banner and the Red Song.

At General Shtikov's invitation General Brown, tall, grey-haired and noted among his troops as a strict disciplinarian, addressed the assembly on the aims, procedure, and order of consultation.

"It is certain that the political parties represented here today with have a divergence of opinions," he said, "but you all agree on one thing—a desire for independence."

He told them that in an effort to learn and to understand their ideas about the future government of Korea the Commission had compiled a questionnaire, and he urged all representatives of these various groups to fill this out with care and in their thinking about it to put the welfare of the Korean nation and its people above partisan interests. He came to a close in which freedom rang:

"It is your proud responsibility to participate in the rebirth of your nation."

The high note sounded in this opening meeting was not to be sustained for long, however. It began to trail away when the American Delegation journeyed north to Pyengyang to consult with North Korean political leaders.

This American Delegation, with its retinue of nearly one hundred, arrived in Pyengyang on June 30. It was the first time this many Americans had any opportunity to find their answer to the question most frequently asked in the South: "What is North Korea really like?"

North Korea proved to have two faces, one of which was deliberately and specifically put on for our benefit. Streets had been cleared and stores along the main thoroughfare from the railroad station to the hotel were closed and boarded up. Although Americans were given permission to travel at will throughout the city, the privilege was a dubious one, for they were constantly followed — from General Brown on down to the privates. Some of the camera-happy GIs took pictures of these "tails," only to find themselves threatened with arrest. One actually did go to the police station — to take another picture.

Americans were especially interested in a store in Pyengyang which had an almost exclusive stock of US Army and P.X. goods. When a soldier tried to photograph this, he was forcibly prevented by a North Korean policeman. The next day the store reopened with a complete new stock, all American items having been withdrawn.

Our Delegation discovered that the day before their arrival great quantities of polished rice had been released to the market for the first time in more than seven months, causing a big price drop. Soviet women in coarse inferior clothing were shopping for this sudden bargain right along with the Koreans. In fact there seemed to be very little distinction between the Soviet citizens and the natives, no areas nor compounds having been set aside for Russian occupancy. This was a point in Russia's favor as far as most Koreans were concerned, for they almost universally resented the superiority implied by American aloofness and segregation in the South.

By chance several Americans with their Korean interpreters stumbled upon the "People's Private Children Technical School" for Japanese boys and girls. The assistant director told them that there were 67 pupils in the school, and that all classes were conducted in the Japanese language. This confirmed information previously received through the Korean "whispering grass" intelligence, that the Soviets were retaining Japanese technicians to operate mills and factories, and flatly contradicted the statement of the Soviet Commissioner in Seoul that there were no longer any Japanese living in North Korea.

The effect of anti-American propaganda was nicely highlighted by this, overheard on the street by an American fluent in the Russian language:

Two small Soviet girls were arguing loudly.

"You act exactly like a German girl," one finally said spitefully.

The other retorted with what was obviously considered even stronger approbrium: "And *you* are behaving like an American!"

On the day of their arrival the American Delegation were treated to a parade and demonstration, Soviet style. From a balcony overlooking a public square they watched for nearly three hours some 50,000 spirited North Korean citizens, mostly young, waving an ocean-sea of Soviet and Korean flags, holding up huge pictures of Joseph Stalin and Kim Il Sung, and carrying banners which eulogized the North Korean People's Committee and "democracy" as correctly practiced only in their promised land. Photographers took pictures from all angles of General Brown shaking hands with Kim Il Sung, the North Korean puppet leader — a forced ceremony which lasted through some ten awkward and uncomfortable slow-motion minutes.

Next speeches by prominent North Koreans nominated Kim Il Sung for future presidency of all Korea, demanded that the People's Committee be accepted/adopted as the authority and form of the new government, and praised the many democratic reforms in the North. Blunt condemnations of all leading rightists in South Korea were vigorously enunciated, and a firm insistence that these specific men — a list including some fence sitters — be barred from consultation with the Joint Commission. Not a single speaker had a word of even faint praise, nor any expressed friendship, for the Americans. Following these orations, in column formation the crowd of banner carriers and flag wavers marched in review, several groups attempting a "goose step" as they passed the balcony.

In a brave effort to see around and behind the Russian window-dressing, General Brown and another senior member of the American Delegation asked official permission to interview Cho Man Sik, formerly the outstanding political leader in North Korea. Cho for the last 18 months, ever since a tangle with his Russian masters on practical interpretation of trusteeship, had been under house arrest at the Koryu Hotel in the city. Cut off completely from the changed political scene,

Cho was not able to give a detailed estimate or opinion of the Communist control over the populace. He did state that with the exception of Communist Party members, who constituted not more that 15%, the people did not like the present regime. He revealed to us that his dearth of information extended even to his own Chosen Democratic Party, whose leadership had been usurped by a group calling themselves the Enthusiastic Faction Conference!

At a luncheon held after this interview Cho spoke of the urgent necessity of implementing a land reform program *before* an election was held. The farmers, he said, would never be happy and productive as the new nation would need them to be, until they owned the land they were working. He did agree with the 15-year sale program we outlined to him, including its provision for compensation to Korean landlords.

The farmers our delegates questioned in the outskirts of Pyengyang were generally sharply discontented with their lot. Most of them said very frankly that they considered conditions to be worse than under the Japanese; but this was a complaint we heard also, and all too often, in the South. The principal specific northern complaints were: (1) Far more than the official 25% of total production was being collected from them in taxes; (2) the high taxes applied to all farmers whether they had formerly owned their farms, or had only just claimed them under the land redistribution program; and (3) control of the farms was actually vested in the local People's Committee rather than in the individual farmers themselves.

Personal observation and study in Pyengyang and vicinity convinced the American delegates that the Soviets were making an all-out effort to Sovietize the economy of North Korea and that they would be unlikely to agree to any unification plan not rigged on their own terms.

Factory production remained at less than 20% of capacity although posters throughout Pyengyang graphically presented high production goals for the current year and exhorted workers to build a strong People's State. Prices were found to be generally lower than those in the South (except for rice) but this appeared to stem more from want of purchasing power and from rigid government control over profiteering than from improvement and increase in production.

Before the Delegation left Pyengyang one enterprising GI, in a defiant gesture repudiating all Russian stage effects, scrawled at the base of a monument commemorating the liberation of Korea by the Glorious Red Army: KILROY WAS HERE.

Soon after its return to Seoul on July 4 the Commission began to come apart at the seams. The actual consultation with Korean political parties and social organizations which had been scheduled to begin July 5, never took place.

In response to General Brown's invitation to fill out the Commission questionnaire, 425 from the American zone and 38 from the Soviet zone had complied. All organizations from the North Korea list were members of the People's Front and affiliated with the North Korea People's Committee. The groups replying from southern Korea represented a wide divergency of political opinion: more than two thirds of respondents were of the right, moderate or moderate left; fewer than 25% were members of the People's Front.

Claimed membership of all 463 organizations was 68 million, even though at the last estimate there were only some 30 million people in all Korea. This ludicrous discrepancy was caused by hopeful and/or willful overestimation in large part, but also by multiple overlap and duplication. For example, membership was counted for individual political parties, and at the same time for any and all coalitions of these same groups. One large youth organization was discovered to have registered under three different names and to have been counted and re-counted that way. After all this was sorted out and pared down to actual living size, the political persuasion of South Korea was calculated at 58% right and moderate, 42% left.

Such a state of affairs was unacceptable to the Soviets. They began their attack by quibbling over the definition of the southern word "social," contending that it would be beneath their dignity to consult with such social organizations as the Merchant's Association for the Dae Dong Moon Market, the Kyonggi Province Mid-Wives Association and the Korean Young Men's Esperanto League. The United States Delegation insisted that since the Moscow Decision did not define the word "social" and since every attempt to do so jointly prior to the distribution of questionnaires had met with Soviet opposition, the Commission should stick to the dictionary terminology.

Then the Soviets drew up a list of parties and organizations with a claimed membership of over 10,000 with whom they were willing to consult, but pointedly excluded 24 major rightist groups who they said were members of an Anti-Trusteeship Association.

An anti-trusteeship demonstration led by Syngman Rhee and Kim Koo had been held outside Duk Soo Palace on June 23. This, the Soviets claimed, represented *de facto* opposition to the work of the Joint Commission. Acceptance of the Soviet stand would tip the balance of power heavily to the left and insure Communist domination of a unified Korean Provisional Government.

While by day the Commission was drawing closer and closer to deadlock and disintegration, I was watching by night well-fed Russian officers in natty blue and grey uniforms trimmed in red as they whirled our American civilian office workers around the dance floors of the various officers clubs in Seoul. In broken English they chatted with us, flattered us, and played the exaggerated gallant. One of the girls, probably entranced with the bizarre novelty of the situation, even chose a Russian as a steady boy friend. On our higher echelons as well, wine flowed and music played and entertainment was lavish. The Delegation had been given P.X. privileges and Russian women who had accompanied their husbands to Seoul daily haunted the counters and carried out huge baskets of candy, cosmetics and canned goods — perhaps for resale in the "Branch P.X." in Pyengyang.

All this unofficial fraternization and good will could not prevent the joint discussions in Duk Soo Palace from slowing down to a standstill. On August 26 General Marshall again communicated with Foreign Minister Molotov pointing to the deplorable stalemate and suggesting that the four Pacific Powers — Britain, China, the USSR and the United States — meet in Washington on September 8 to consider the impasse in Seoul. At the same time he proposed that the Commission draft a joint report on the reasons for its inability to function.

Molotov agreed to the later proposal, but sharply criticized Marshall for his "unilateral act" in seeking to involve China and Britain, protesting that the Joint Commission was far from exhausting all its possibilities and potential. Nevertheless when the request for a report was referred to the delegates in Seoul they found themselves mutually and jointly unable to agree even on why they had been unable to agree.

The basic rocks and shoals for this Second Commission were exactly the same as had wrecked the First: only "democracy" as defined and practiced under the idealogy of the United Soviet Socialist Republics would ever be acceptable to the Russians as a basis for the reunification of Korea: only a People's Government on the Communist pattern, with all dissenters controlled or stifled.

This was our final attempt to do business with the Russians. We had finally to accept the fact that bilaterally we could accomplish nothing.

The United Nations in Korea

Koreans bundled up in overcoats or their heavily padded native garments braved the icy January wind en masse, flanking the road in one solid line from Kimpo airfield to Seoul. It was the same road I had taken more than two years before but a better road now, having been graded and oiled by our occupation troops. Today fresh arches appeared overhead in Seoul, with a new greeting: WELCOME TO THE U.N. COMMISSION ON KOREA. The Koreans, ever hopeful, had turned out in unprecedented numbers to hail this new attempt to unify their beloved country.

The previous fall when it became obvious that the Second Joint Commission was doomed, Secretary of State Marshall in an address to the United Nations General Assembly September 17, 1947 asked that the problem of Korea reunification and independence be included on their agenda. The Russians countered this with a proposal that Soviet and American troops be withdrawn simultaneously and the trusteeship system be dropped.

The U.N. decision which followed was a telling blow for the Soviets. The Assembly voted 73-0 with six (the Soviet bloc) abstaining, for the establishment of a United Nations Temporary Commission on Korea, and defeated the Soviet proposals 34-7. The U.N. resolution further recommended that elections be held in Korea not later than March 31, 1948 and that immediately upon the establishment of a National Government the Commission should arrange with Russia and America for the withdrawal of their armed forces from Korea—"if possible within 90 days."

Early in January 1948 the United Nations Temporary Commission on Korea, or UNTOK as it came to be called, arrived in Seoul to see that the Assembly's instructions were carried out. Eight countries were represented: Australia, Canada, China, El Salvador, Syria, France, India and the Philippine Republic. The ninth appointed member, the Soviet Ukraine, boycotted the Commission from its inception at Lake Success.

The representatives with their secretaries, assistants and interpreters made such a large delegation that two hotels had to be fitted out for their accommodation. One was the Tanaka house, an old WAC billet which had seen considerable wear and tear since the early days of the occupation but now was so magificently refitted and refurbished that we hardly recognized it.

Once again the ash trays were set out and the chairs placed around the green-baize conference tables in Duk Soo Palace. On the flag pole where the Stars and Stripes and the Hammer and Sickle had formerly flown, the United Nations banner was raised—olive branches surrounding "one world," white on a blue field.

At the opening session Dr. K. P. S. Menon of India was named chairman. Menon promised that the Commission, mainly Asian and small-power in composition, would review and view the Korean problem "with utmost sympathy and realism and without fear or favor."

He added that in his own country India, independence was barely six months old and "its bitter sweet taste is still fresh in our mouths."

UNTOK discovered before many days had passed something that almost anyone in Korea could have told them: Russia was not going to have anything to do with the Commission nor allow its members to enter the Northern zone, not even for a courtesy call upon the Soviet commander.

Stymied as to how it might legally proceed, in February UNTOK referred the question back to the Interim or "Little" Assembly, which recommended by a vote of 31-2 that the Commission proceed with the elections anyway, in defiance of the Soviet boycott. In accordance with the American-proposed plan which the Little Assembly adopted, the balloting would begin in the South and work northward. If Russia continued to refuse entry into the Northern zone balloting would have to stop at the 38th parallel. A National Assembly would then be set up with representatives elected from the Southern zone occupying two-thirds of the seats. The other one-third belonging to the North would remain open.

The Canadian and Australian representatives on UNTOK opposed the American plan on the ground that the Little Assembly had no legal authority to make such a recommendation. Nevertheless when put to a vote the plan was passed 4-2, with two abstaining. The election date was moved up to May 9, which was later changed to May 10 out of respect for an old Korean superstition that events which fell on the same day as an eclipse of the sun were star-crossed by evil omen.

One abstention was that of Syria whose delegate explained that an election under the American plan, of only the southern two-thirds of a legislature "would be an endorsement of the cleavage of Korea and the dangers are clear. The Arab world, of which Syria is a part is a victim of this kind of division and will not support division at any time." It must be remembered that on the other side of the world another Commission was simultaneously hard at work on the highly flammable questions and answers surrounding the partition of Palestine.

The UNTOK Commissioners proceeded to spread out on tours of South Korea, to see for themselves whether the elections could be conducted in "a free atmosphere" as the Little Assembly had directed. In his first report to the Assembly Dr. Menon declared that South Korea was a "police state," a condition which made him apprehensive that anywhere from 10,000 to 50,000 citizens could be arrested without cause by police who feared their votes. In reply General Hodge made a public statement guaranteeing civil liberties and we in Military Government were pledged to do everything in our power to avert or correct abuses. At UNTOK's insistence an ordinance was quickly drafted requiring a warrant to be issued before the police could make an arrest. Also of its own volition MG reviewed the cases of about 6,000 prisoners languishing in Korean jails and released 3,140 of them—without admitting however, that they might have been incarcerated for political reasons.

UNTOK gave the strong impression that it was not going to be awed by American power and prestige, nor take as gospel anything MG proclaimed just because MG said it was so. The attitude was neither critical nor suspicious; it was simply and entirely objective and, as such, a healthy life-giving breath of fresh air in a stale situation which for far too long had been utterly subjective on all sides.

I remember one evening being rocked back on my heels by seeing that the rosy altruistic light in which we were inclined to view our own actions and motives was not always visible to others. I had been invited to dinner at the home of Herbert Kim, the same Korean who had a few things to say about the police. Herbert had a mining degree from Nevada School of Mines, was married to a Jewish American. Among the guests this evening was Mr. Wang, a member of the Chinese delegation to UNTOK. As the conversation wound around to contemplation of Russian's obstructionism and inordinate use of the veto, Mr. Wang addressed this very calmly to me:

"You know, don't you, that in San Francisco in 1945 when the UN Charter was drawn up, it was you Americans and not Soviet Russia who insisted upon the veto. I was there, acting for my country. You did not wish to surrender your sovereignty. You wanted to reserve the right to say whether your troops should be sent overseas to act for the United Nations."

Sovereignty like charity must solidly begin at home and our further discussions at table this evening indicated that there was in Korean political circles everything but solidarity—something I had known all along and which would be evident to any analyst from the proliferation of political parties alone. The coming elections were loudly opposed by leaders of the left, who marched in signal demonstrations by day and then lighted bonfires atop Seoul's surrounding hills by night. On the right, leadership was split wide in two camps, Dr. Rhee and his followers asserting that the elections were the only rational and practical means of setting up a national government.

"Let us have our government first and then if we want to fight, let us fight it out," was the stance of Rhee and Pak Sar.

Kim Koo and Kimm Kiu Sic on the other side were equally as vociferous. Before a gathering of Dr. Rhee's Nationalist Society for the Rapid Realization of Korean Independence, Kim Koo declared (in a speech read by proxy—a wise precaution of the Old Assassin's):

"The election simply encourages the slaughter of our own people and does not live up to the spirit of the United Nations. In order to cover up these ugly things they want to conduct a general election in one half of the country and then set up a central government for South Korea. Let us not be deceived—we may regret it later."

Kimm Kiu Sic resigned as president of the South Korean Interim Legislature in protest and took about thirty of his followers with him. From this time on, the influence of the Legislature waned rapidly, members feeling that the life of this body would be short and its legislation ultimately be discarded by the new Korean government anyway.

The Soviet-controlled authorities in North Korea, seeing this dissension, reacted by tossing one last monkey wrench into the United Nations machinery.

Through Radio Pyengyang there was broadcast to all political leaders in South Korea an invitation to come to a Joint meeting on Korean unification in the Northern capitol on April 14. Kim Koo and Kimm Kiu Sic accepted. For his stand in opposing the election, Kim Koo had been dropped from the Communist list of "traitors and reactionaires scheduled for liquidation."

Both these rightist leaders, one of whom had been handpicked by our Military Government for leadership in the South, were completely carried away by what they saw in the North.

In a speech at a dinner party given in Pyengyang by North Korean leader Kim Il Sung, Kimm Kiu Sic had this to say:

"In North Korea everything is based on the principle of self-support; whereas in South Korea factories are idle, there is no production and everything is dependent on American loans [he should have said *gifts*] . . . We have to dance according to our own music . . . The coalition movement taking place in South Korea is perhaps dancing to American music. Hereafter the best thing is to dance according to our own music."

Since even the Koreans seemed not to agree on just which of their music to play, the United Nations and our Military Government and the Korean rightists who danced to the tune of Dr. Rhee did proceed with the election plans.

On the eve of the elections Military Government stepped in and took the number-one political plum, land, out from under the thumbs of right and left alike. A drastic land reform, long overdue, was put into effect by executive order of Major General William F. Dean, the new Military Governor. The New Korea Company was dissolved and some 630,000 acres of former Japanese lands were put on public sale, with farmers actually then tilling the soil having priority of purchase. The price was three years full production of their principal crop, to be paid over a period of fifteen years at the rate of 20% of the crop per year—less than the farmer had formerly paid in rent.

The rightist press universally labeled this an abuse of power, saying the disposition of the land should have been deferred for decision by the future Korean government. But the land-hungry peasants flocked to the National Land Administration offices in droves, some 5,000 a day, building up a solid bulwark of private ownership to confront the Communist promises of "a better life" under Marxist doctrine.

Korean Elder Statesman

When the United Nations decided to go ahead with the South Korean election, one man saw a lifelong dream come true.

"I came back to Korea at General Hodge's invitation," said 81-year-old Dr. Philip Jaisohn when I interviewed him for the FARMER'S WEEKLY as "an historical character."

His grey head shook slightly and his eyes took on a dim faraway look as he recalled for me his 60-year struggle to help bring his people out of the dark ages into the light. As Suh Jai Pil, one of Korea's first progressives, he had seen the need for democratic reforms in the country as far back as 1882 when Commodore Shufeldt concluded the American treaty with the Korean King.

Born of an aristocratic or Yang Ban family, he was educated in the Chinese classics at the school for young patricians in Seoul. Early he came to realize that his own class, the Yang Bans, were ruining the country, keeping the common people ground down in total ignorance and abject poverty. As they swept through the dust and filth of the city in silk-covered sedan chairs, dainty silk handkerchiefs held to their noble noses, they were the personification of palace arrogance and corruption. They didn't even really see the poor peasants who scattered in fright at their coming—the people who paid the exorbitant taxes which paid for the high wide and handsome life these ignoble aristocrats were living.

Suh Jai Pil and a growing number of other young palace reformers could see that the only hope for the rebirth of their nation lay in training for progressive leadership. At that time Japan, which had so eagerly taken to Western ways, seemed to offer new hope and resurgent vitality to all who rebelled against Oriental decadence and lethargy.

With 46 other aristocratic gentlemen Suh journeyed to Japan in 1882 to study agriculture, commerce, law, medicine, silk culture and military science, Suh himself specializing in the last. When he returned to Seoul two years later he was appointed "Principal of the Military Training School," but there was in fact no such school and nothing was done to put the training program into effect.

Sick and tired of such all-pervasive lassitude and exasperated with chronic delays and half-measures at every level, the young Progressives staged the "Palace Revolution of 1884," capturing the King and holding him prisoner for four days during which they drafted an edict changing the government from an absolute to a limited monarchy. Under duress he did sign this. But the revolutionaries were swiftly put down by Chinese troops stationed in the city, led by the powerful Yuan Shin Kai. The King was released, three of the Progressives were killed, and the rest—Suh Jai Pil among them—made a forced march through a snowstorm to the Port of Inchon whence they escaped the country.

In May 1885 Suh arrived in San Francisco aboard the American ship *China*. Between 1885 and 1895 he earned two academic degrees, one a Doctor of Medicine from George Washington University. During this period he coined an Anglicized name, reversing the syllables of his Korean name and making a slight adjustment for euphony. Thus did Suh Jai Pil become Dr. Phillip Jaisohn, who was invited in 1895 to return to his homeland as advisor to the King.

"I arrived back in Seoul," Dr. Jaisohn told me "to find the Korean government being manipulated by the Japanese. I asked if I could publish a free, untrammeled newspaper for the benefit of the common people. Getting the government's consent, I started publication in May 1896 in an office building opposite the American consulate. This was the first newspaper published in Korea. I called it the *Independent*."

"I have seen copies of the *Independent*," I said "which have been very carefully preserved. They were published in English. Did you do that, too?"

"Yes," he answered slowly. "I wanted a foreign edition that would tell the world about our Korean situation. The paper was very popular."

"What finally became of it?" I asked.

"Well," Dr. Jaisohn was shaking his head sadly "it became quite influential among the Koreans. So much so that we made powerful enemies. The Japanese and the Russians didn't like the *Independent* because it was pro-Korean. I'm sorry to say that Americans at that time were not much interested in Korea. Single-handed I could accomplish very little to combat the opposition. The authorities found all kinds of ways to prevent delivery, even to letting copies of the paper pile up in our post offices. Finally someone sent me a fake telegram that said my wife's mother was dying, so I dropped everything and hurried back to the United States."

While in America Dr. Jaisohn had married Muriel Armstrong, daughter of Colonel George B. Armstrong of Chicago, founder and first superintendent of the Railway Mail Service of the United States Post Office. I had recently met Dr. Jaisohn's youngest daughter Muriel, who returned to Korea with him.

"The *Independent* wasn't my only way of trying to educate our people," Dr. Jaisohn continued. "One thing I did was to organize the Independent Debating Society outside Seoul's West Gate. This was a public forum for discussing problems of the day—something entirely new in Korea. Here for the first time Korean citizens were able to hear an explanation of the political theory of democracy, including its first principle that a government must obey the majority will of the governed. Of course at that time they hardly dared hope they would ever be able to exercise that right themselves."

During this period Dr. Jaisohn was also lecturing on democracy and international affairs at Pai Jai High school, where the young Syngman Rhee was one of his pupils.

"Finally," he told me sadly "through the machinations of the high officials in our palace cliques and in certain foreign delegations—that is, both the Russian Minister de Speyer and his officers and the unduly influential representatives of Japan—my mass education work was sabotaged and the freedom of speech and assembly which we had enjoyed were curbed."

So all that remained of Dr. Jaisohn's work was a symbol: Independence Arch which by popular subscription he had caused to be erected at the beginning of Peking road to celebrate Korea's emancipation from China following the Sino-Japanese War. Along this road the Korean emmissaries had formerly borne their country's annual tribute to the Dragon Court of the Manchus.

Much later, during the Independence Movement of 1919 the Japanese were to awake one morning and find this arch bore the Korean flag in brilliant colors, painted they thought by an artist unknown. But the people were gathered around the monument talking about the "miracle." How otherwise could the flag have been painted so high in the air, without the raising of a scaffold? Calling the fire brigade, the infuriated Japanese police directed that Independence Arch be sprayed and the accursed paint washed off. But the red only turned a brighter hue. The stain remains to this day, a token not only of courage and freedom but also of Japan's era of tyrany.

When Dr. Jaisohn was forced to leave Korea for the second time, he served with the rank of Captain in our Spanish-American War. He was a contract surgeon under Dr. Walter Reed. In recognition of his distinguished services the Congress of the United States made him a special grant of American citizenship—a most unusual gesture, especially toward an Oriental.

In 1919 Dr. Jaisohn was active and prominent in the Korean fight for independence. He organized the Korean Congress, composed of Koreans from all over the United States, to broadcast the facts of Japanese atrocities and make known the efforts of those inside Korea to free their country from Japanese rule. He also was one of the delegation who presented to the Armaments Limitations Conference in Washington (1922-1923) an appeal for justice to the suffering Korean people.

Now that at long last Dr. Jaisohn was back in his own country and seeing the realization of one of his earliest dreams, I asked him whether he had any advice for his people.

"Tell them through your paper," he replied "that this is the first time they have had a chance to express themselves—the first time in history a foreign nation has acknowledged and upheld their right to choose their own rulers. If they utilize the responsibility, it will be the making of a new nation. If not, the future will be dark indeed."

He advised the voters to select candidates who were honest, not those who were looking for a job and temporary advantage. In order to do this, he said they must learn as much as they could about the background of those running for office—know not only what they had done in the past but also what they advocated and what they were qualified to help accomplish in the future.

"Even though South Korea is the best the United Nations can give us now, half a loaf is definitely better than none at all," he added. "We have here the nucleus of a Korean nation."

Off the record Dr. Jaisohn admitted he felt Korea was still a police state. There were too many Japanese-trained policemen remaining. Tortures, hidden threats, and the detention of people in jail without explanation were all too prevalent.

In his conclusion at last I felt I had an honest answer, neither flattering nor slanted by Communist propaganda, to a question which had plagued me since the first days of our occupation: Just what do the Koreans think of us? Dr. Jaisohn, an American citizen who was also one of Korea's pioneer progressives, certainly ought to know:

"Koreans don't seem to understand the real intentions of the Americans. One reason is, the interpreters you have to use may in translation give an entirely different meaning from the one you intend. On the whole, a Korean when asked what he thinks of the Americans and Military Government will say they are just a little better than the Japanese."

First Election in 4,000 Years

"Have there been any riots?"

"How many people have been killed?"

These were the questions foreign news correspondents asked in the Capitol pressroom where I was busy tabulating election returns phoned in to us from the provinces. No one particularly cared which party was leading in this race, for the very good reason that although some fourteen parties had their names on the charts hung around our walls, to all practical intents and purposes there was only one political way the election could go—to the right. The Communists had early broadcast their intention of boycotting the polls and with the exception of a few left-wing splinter groups, were making good their threat.

Even though no political issue was involved, there was a question of gravest import: would there be ballots, or bullets? Would the people who wanted to vote be allowed to go to the polls at all?

A tide of opposition rose formidably in early February, when the issue of whether to go ahead with the election in South Korea was still before the Little Assembly. On February 8 General Hodge received a letter announcing a three-day general strike and proposing a list of demands which included withdrawal of the United Nations Commission as well as all American occupation forces. This letter was signed by the "General Strike Committee of South Korea."

There ensued a wave of violence and sabotage in which forty-seven people were killed and several hundred injured. Communists disabled some 50 locomotives and cut power and communication lines in an effort to cripple the economy of South Korea.

Although the strike failed to enlist popular support, fewer than 200 persons actually leaving their jobs, the disruption and disturbances were played up by the press and radio of North Korea as a "great popular movement of the masses in opposition to the United Nations Commission, the tool of American imperialism whose purpose is the enslavement of Korea."

While the violence and sabotage were in progress a huge military demonstration was being staged in Pyengyang. In sub-freezing weather Russian puppet Kim Il Sung reviewed the Soviet-supplied North Korean People's Army, now 200,000 strong. Tanks, mortars and field guns rolled by, while overhead droned fighter planes—and the citizens along the route of the bristling parade cried *Mansei! Mansei!*

Kim Il Sung proclaimed: "The People's Army is not for the purpose of staging internecine civil war, as certain reactionaries maliciously publicize. It will move to check in advance any attempts on the part of reactionaries to divide and kill the people."

Two American liaison officers in Pyengyang were badly mauled when they attempted to watch the parade. As they stood at a vantage point near the official reviewing stand they were approached by six Korean civilians and a Korean lieutenant colonel from the People's Army. The colonel protested that the officers were "on Korean soil and the United States has no business here."

Immediately afterward a mixed group of Korean civilians, officers and police tried to drag the two Americans to a nearby police box. When the Americans proved too much for them, the Koreans surrounded the American officers and attempted to block their view of the parade. In the ensuing scuffle one officer's camera was snatched away by an unidentified Korean.

When the Americans protested to the Soviets, they were met with the reply "Sorry, we have no authority."

These military liaison teams had been set up in each zone by mutual agreement at the beginning of the joint occupation, to keep their respective commands informed on matters of import. In the South we were accustomed to seeing a jeep flying a miniature Red flag and bearing two grey-caracul-capped Red officers tearing freely about the city of Seoul photographing parades or anything else they pleased.

Through our liaison in the north we knew that the Russians had been rushing to complete a North Korean government before the Little Assembly could finish its debate over what to do in the American zone. A week following the "inauguration" and parade of the People's Army the text of a constitution for a People's Republic was broadcast over Pyengyang Radio, to be voted upon by a special session of the North Korean People's Council in March.

"Sovereignty rests with the people through the People's Committee," the constitution said, and its preamble proclaimed "the new type of government the people established upon their liberation August 15, 1945."

The constitution throughout was identical with those adopted by other Soviet satellite countries. The flag of the Republic was described as having a red star in the center with crossed hammers above and crossed sickles below.

Meanwhile in the south the United Nations Commission was resolutely going about its election business. In April at U.N. request an intensive publicity campaign was launched, sparked by Military Government's Department of Public Information. Now that order was restored we sought to inform and reassure the people and bring all eligible voters to the registration booths.

We very nearly succeeded, attracting the amazingly high turnout of 92%.

In accordance with the franchise law originally drawn up by the South Korean Interim Legislature and adopted with some modification, eligibility to vote was granted to all over 23 years of age regardless of sex, education, or property ownership. The high age limit had been insisted upon by the rightists who feared strong leftist tendencies among the youth.

In view of the high rate of illiteracy it would take ingenuity to devise a ballot which could be readily understood, and both the UN and MG knew this was vital to gaining full representation. A system was finally arrived at: pictures of the candidates were matched with the hashmarks, I, II, III, IIII – up to the number running in any given district. In his campaign a candidate was encouraged to impress upon the illiterate the number of strokes which matched his name and face, and in every voting booth all pictures would be posted.

Two hundred election districts with a total of 13,800 polling places were established in the nine South Korean provinces and the island of Cheju Do. To become a candidate for election an aspirant had to present to his local election committee a petition bearing the signatures of at least 200 eligible voters. On the eve of the election some 920 candidates had duly qualified and were vying for the 200 seats in the National Assembly.

On the weekend before the voters went to the polls anti-election violence burst forth in renewed fury. On Saturday morning the business manager of the rightist Kyongsang-Ilbo plant appeared in my office and announced with his usual cheerful smile:

"Last night Communists come, burn our plant."

Fortunately the arsonists forgot about an auxiliary plant a few blocks down the street, so the Farmer's Weekly came out with the election news on schedule. This was only one of three newspapers attacked in Seoul, and at least 22 locomotives were damaged or wrecked over the weekend.

As I sat in the Capitol pressroom on May 10, peacefully taking down the returns which came over the phone, I found it difficult to reconcile the serenity of my immediate surroundings with threats of violence and terror in the land. Yet the very air was electric with the tensity of the situation. All Military Government men who could be spared had been drafted to spread out through the provinces to assist the nine United Nations teams in maintaining a free atmosphere at the polls. This presence and surveillance consisted of everything from seeing that the voters were not intimidated to keeping the ballot boxes from being stuffed, stolen or burned.

Newspaper correspondents who drifted into our pressroom late in the afternoon reported the voting was proceeding satisfactorily, with long lines of voters waiting to write down their hash marks—at least half of them women with babies tied to their backs. To prevent interference thousands of Korean police and American MP's had set up virtual road blocks at every intersection, and guards stood at the mouth of every one of the narrow dirty alleys that twisted between the native hovels. When the polls closed, trucks bristling with guns transferred the locked ballot boxes to local election committees for counting. It was a strictly enforced rule, however, that no armed person, policeman or otherwise, was to enter the polling place.

All these precautions might have seemed ridiculous were it not for the fact that in the capitol alone there were some 15 attacks on the polls and two election officials were killed. In the provinces things were considerably worse, centering around the island of Cheju Do where Communists landed with guns and sharpened bamboo spears so terrifying the voters that more than half of them stayed away and many of the election officials resigned.

Altogether when the dust cleared away and the score was added up, over a hundred lay dead and many more were injured in the fight over Korea's first election in 4,000 years.

A few days later an exhausted Mr. Schmitt of Military Government's Coal Mining Section told me the story of his three days and nights without sleep as an election inspector in the province of Cholla Namdo. During this whole time he was driving from place to place in a jeep, checking on the voting and counting.

"When the villagers came out with guns and spears and wouldn't let me pass, I didn't argue," was his simple understatement.

Warned by the Governor of the province to watch himself at a certain spot where a high stone overhung the road, he approached it nervously, fearing a possible ambush. The first time he got by the rock without incident, but as he passed it again at night he heard a shot in the dark.

"I got the hell out of there but I didn't think too much about it," he said "until I reached my destination. Then I found a bullet had pierced the locked ballot box which was sitting beside me in the jeep. The ballots were all churned up and about 60 of them ruined.

"To make matters worse," he added with a grin "after it was all over and I was dead for sleep, the Korean election officials insisted on an all-night party. I fell asleep in the middle of it from the wine, the food and sheer exhaustion; but when I woke up several hours later they were still going strong, eating and drinking and talking. I don't see how they do it."

In spite of the reign of terror and the sabotage in the provinces 90.6% of the eligible voters did go to the polls and make their marks, a higher percentage by far than has ever turned out for an election in the United States. But the question remained: Was the election really free?

From simple country folk such as our servants I gathered that the ever-zealous neighborhood associations had been extremely active in rounding up voters and even in telling them how they should vote.

"I hope I remember right picture," our amah worried.

The large turnout then was probably a response to mild coercion, and the strong rightist vote to some form of suggestion. But there were no armed police standing at the polls, there were no black and white ballot boxes to "choose" from as in the Russian zone, there was no mere ratification of one man—all of which are part of a controlled election. Once the voter did enter the voting booth he was on his own and his ballot was secret. No one would ever be able to check up on whether or not he had followed either subtle or unsubtle "advice." The United Nations after considerable debate decided to accept the returns and declared "a free and unfettered election."

The result was largely as expected with Syngman Rhee's Nationalist Society for the Rapid Realization of Independence taking 57 seats, the Korean Democratic Party 29, the Dai Dong Youth 13, National Youth 6, and ten minor parties 1 seat each. The one surprise was that 85 candidates rode in on no-party tickets, offering some hope of breaking up extreme-right domination of the Korean National Assembly.

One unsolved election mystery was the case of Danny Chai versus Dr. Rhee. Danny Chai, it will be remembered, was the former detective who resigned in a huff to become an outspoken critic of the National Police.

In the elections he was so ill-advised as to attempt to run against Dr. Rhee in the Master's own East Gate district. At the last moment, after the returns had already started coming in, we were ordered without explanation to scratch Danny Chai off our charts. He had been disqualified.

Later I made every effort to run down the story behind Danny's downfall, only to find there were two stories. One high source said that he had circulated a false petition which people had signed, then torn off the top, inserted his own name and fraudulently used these signatures to register his candidacy. Another source told me that forty strong-arm rightist youths had waylaid Chai's secretary and snatched the briefcase containing his registration papers. On whichever side the truth was told the result remained the same: Dr. Rhee rode in to the National Assembly triumphant and unopposed.

Actually the election proved nothing except what everybody already knew anyway: that through fear, propaganda, or sheer weight of authority South

Korea went the way of its political masters—even as North Korea had gone the way of its.

The election solved nothing either. A government south of the 38th parallel had been set up to oppose that in the north. Each proclaimed itself "the government for all Korea." Each was fired/inspired with a sacred mission: to unify the country— its way.

Ashes of an Era

Immediately following the South Korean election the Russians turned off the power supply to the southern zone: the lights which Americans had installed in Seoul in 1898 were put out in 1948 because Americans failed to pay an electricity bill to the Soviets.

The controversy was complicated in the extreme, but I learned these essential points from a member of the National Economic Board who sat in on the hearings.

We had made a deal with the Russians. They would continue to furnish South Korea with about 85% of its power from the big hydroelectric plants in the north, as was done under the Japanese. In return we agreed to supply the Northern zone with a long list of electrical items which they said were necessary for the repair and upkeep of the North Korean equipment. Unfortunately the Americans who negotiated the original agreement did not know that about one fourth of the material they promised to procure for the Russians was extremely critical even in the United States and was therefore not available for export.

At the time the switch was thrown we had already sent to North Korea 25% of the items requested and 40% was on its way from the States. General Hodge had been trying for some time to arrange with the Russian command some mutually acceptable way of settling the balance of the bill. We were prepared either to supply alternate or substitute items upon request or to pay about five million dollars in gold.

The Russian command, however, persistently refused to discuss any compromise, saying that we must make arrangements with the People's committee, as the matter had been turned over to them. Since this would be tantamount to recognizing the People's Committee as the legitimate government of North Korea, this General Hodge as persistently refused to do. In retaliation, the middle of May the Russians shut off our electricity.

It was a literally dark time for South Korea. In most places there were no lights after nightfall. We had either to go to bed with the chickens, sit up in the dark, or try to read by flickering candle or Coleman lantern. Factories in Seoul ground almost to a standstill, power being allocated to various parts of the city for only two hours a day.

With typical American resourcefulness and ability to rise to a crisis, the military command moved to remedy the situation. Standby plants which had been readied for emergency started humming and the output of hydraulic plants already in operation was stepped up. The Army brought in two large electric power barges and anchored one off Inchon near Seoul and the other at Pusan on the southern tip of the peninsula. Within a few months the impossible had been achieved: the power supply was nearly back to normal in South Korea.

About this time I received an invitation from Mabel MacFarlane, who was now attached to the Canadian delegation of the United Nations Commission, to attend a long-delayed memorial service for her father at the foreign cemetery near Seoul. It was Mrs. MacFarlane's wish that the ashes of her husband be laid to rest among the other "foreign nationals" who had died in Korea.

The small group which gathered at the foreign cemetery to pay their respects that day were all the "old Korea hands" who had come back to the country during or after the war. My mother and father were the former mining people in Korea, Dr. and Mrs. Underwood and a few of their colleagues the missionaries, and Bill Taylor the former Chevrolet representative.

On the tombstones all surrounding, I read the names of many others who had taken part in the building of the Korea I had known. Among those I remembered with special feeling was Christine Collbran, whose father had been prominent in the construction of the first rail system. Christine had died at the age of only 21, shortly after finishing a small book on the Far East.

As the small urn which held Mr. MacFarlane's ashes was slowly lowered to his grave I was thinking that we too, who were standing on its edge, represented the ashes of an era. That era had its good, as well as its inherent evils. It was in some ways a bright day of vast colonial empires, a day of business as individual enterprise when a man or group of men carved great fortunes out of the rock in the backward countries of East Asia, or grew them in the jungle plantations. In return these men had brought to the primitive communities railroads, electric lights, and the gospel—even as we had brought these things to Korea. It had been a fabled era in the Kipling meaning: his *White Man's Burden* had been its creed.

> Take up the White Man's burden—
> Send forth the best ye breed—
> Go bind your sons to exile
>   To serve your captives' need;
> To wait in heavy harness,
>   On fluttered folk and wild—
> Your new-caught, sullen peoples,
>   Half-devil and half-child . . .

With the national resurgence of suppressed Asiatic peoples following World War II, the passing of this dramatic era of exploitation was inevitable. We said we had fought the war to uphold the four freedoms, and the natives of India, Indonesia, Indo China and Korea took us at our word. They quite naturally felt those freedoms belonged in equal measure to them. Inexorably this spirit moved them. Gradually and often most reluctantly the Empire builders of the nineteenth and early twentieth century were seeing their empires disintegrate as the natives in uprisings liberated/redeemed what was theirs, toppling one protectorate after another. Even we ourselves were affected: under pressure we granted the Philippines complete independence before our leaders were convinced they were ready for it, and we gave up many and various commercial and industrial enterprises in the Far East.

When I returned late in 1948 to the United States I was astonished to learn that Mr. Henry Wallace and Senator Taylor had during their election campaign accused our occupation and foreign aid programs of being used to build up American cartels, open markets for American business men, or dump surplus commodities. I can recall having seen only two American businesses represented in Seoul during my last three years there. One was the Singer Sewing Machine Company whose representative came over from Shanghai to inspect the company's former offices. Because of the lack of foreign exchange he decided they were not worth opening up, even though Koreans were crying for parts to repair the old broken-down sewing machines one found in every village. The other was Standard Oil whose personnel set up the Petroleum Distribution Agency, strictly under the control of Military Government. Their goods and services were eminently necessary not only to fuel our MG vehicles but also to help the Koreans get going with their delapidated trucks and automobiles which had been reconverted from Japanese coalburners.

I did hear that an American importer was in residence for two days at the Chosen Hotel while he tried to find suitable Korean baskets and lacquer ware for the American market, but that he had gone away again without finding anything he thought Americans would buy.

As for the accusation that we were dumping war surplus, it was the consensus overseas that most of our surplus commodities left in the Pacific were not worth shipping home because it would in the long run be more economical to replace them with new. But these aging jeeps, trucks, bulldozers, and one hundred and one other items, were certainly a boon to the bankrupt Korean economy. We even wrote off as a gift in September 1948 the $250,000,000 loan we had orginally provided Korea for the purchase of these commodities at 20% of cost.

Yes, we had definitely laid down the White Man's Burden. No longer did we send forth the best we bred to reap vast rewards in colonial wealth and international prestige. In China, Korea, and throughout Asia our prestige was at nadir, and our wealth all flowing in the other direction.

We had laid down the White Man's burden, but we had taken up another. We had not simply withdrawn and left the liberated peoples of Asia alone to work out their destinies in their own way. Today there were thousands more Americans and millions more American dollars in the Far East than there ever had been in all the centuries past—with the jobs of relief, rehabilitation, and ultimately of defending these liberated Asiatics from Communism (this without actually knowing whether Communism might not be just what they needed or wanted). I stood there in the foreign cemetery that day wondering whether our new objectives were any more altruistic than the old, and where it was all going to end.

As the ashes of the old era were laid to their rest, a new one was rising—bright and frail as the new spring grass under my feet. Looking about me at the little colony of tombstones which marked the end of so many earlier dreams, I had to feel grateful and glad to have been a part of both.

MacArthur's Korea

I agree with those who believe that General of the Army Douglas MacArthur is one of the greatest as well as most criticized figures in our national history. I personally admire not only the General's incomparable record, but MacArthur the man. His flair for the dramatic, as I see it, stems not from a coldly calculated sense of showmanship but from a warm and deep spiritual conviction which moves the man himself every bit as much as it moves the millions of Americans who hang on his every word. Greatness is, in so large a measure, just simple homely sincerity carried to the nth power by the dedication of a penetrating mind to a cause the conscience can accept and the spirit move forward. MacArthur's greatness lies partly in the fact that after fifty-two years of service, he is just exactly what he thinks he is: ". . . an old soldier who tried to do his duty as God gave him the light to see that duty."

I feel that I shall not be misunderstood even by the General himself if I venture an honest estimate of my own: that Korea in the early days of his command represented an area where the light failed him. I am not quite sure why this was so. It could very well have been our complete lack of official planning for Korea that accounted for the General's inattention to us and his utter failure to see this little country as a separate problem. It could, on the other hand, have been due to inattention to duty on the part of some who served him. God after all does leave a lot to the competence and integrity of junior officers in this matter of lighting the way for any general, even the greatest.

In any case the result was an unhappy one, and our complaints about it I am afraid even more unfortunate.

It is MacArthur who said that the peoples of Asia are not interested in issues and ideologies but in more or better clothes on their backs and a firmer roof over their heads. When we who served in Military Government began to feel so sadly neglected we were exactly the same as the peoples of Asia. We complained not about the dangers inherent in the problems which were arising in Korea, not about Korea's proximity to alien ideologies even then stirring to violence, not about the impression our troops with their shabby morale and loose morals were making upon the people they were supposed to be protecting; instead we complained that there was not a single snack bar in Korea and Japan was full of them, that we never got vegetables but they were being served at every meal in SCAP headquarters, and so on and on!

Actually the complaints we did make were fully justified—and as the General's remark about the Asiatics indicates, of profound fundamental human importance. But never shall I forget that we, even as the least privileged, thought first of food and quarters, and *then* of burning issues.

MacArthur never visited Korea. But then he never "visited" in Japan either: he stayed in the Dai Ichi Building and did his work. If he had come to see us in Seoul, his presence and a few words from him might have done much to make sense to us of what we were doing—provided of course that he himself had made sense of it. But I seriously doubt that he would have been permitted to detect the inexplicable discrepancies between our way of life in MG and the way his command was treating the troops and the staff members stationed in Japan. For wonders can be accomplished when hitherto disinterested parties hear that a General is about to inspect. One of our complaints as I have said, was that we never had any lettuce nor any other fresh vegetable. If MacArthur had made an official inspection, "they" would somewhere have found a head of lettuce for the General's table—and have pulled weeds if necessary, to garnish our plates. When finally we did get some attention—a Congressional Committee coming to investigate the supply and quarters situation because of complaints from constituents who were personnel serving in Korea—snack bars sprang up like

Japanese water flowers, barracks were refurbished right and left, and during the stay of these distinguished visitors our meals were excellent. The congressmen must have left wondering what it was all about; and certainly they left us wondering too.

This particular aspect of neglect was only a symptom of a far greater ill. The same unequal treatment that had caused such hardship in supply and quarters prevailed and plagued us in our efforts and in our requests on behalf of the struggling Korean government. If anyone at SCAP, MacArthur's headquarters in Tokyo, ever thought Korea was the least bit important, I never heard about it nor personally saw any evidence. My work was made a nightmare by our inability to get indispensible materials which were readily available in Japan. A prime example is paper. I finally decided to violate GI standard operating procedure and take some initiative over no-matter-how-many heads, even if mine rolled. I was desperate. We had to have newsprint if our publications in Seoul were to survive. I personally went to Japan to get as many of these giant rolls of paper as they could possibly spare.

I haven't a doubt in the world that had I gone to MacArthur the man I would not have had the trouble with this brave new procurement system that I did. But naturally and rightly MacArthur the General was so protected by rank that a mere first lieutenant could never have gotten to him with the word that things were not as they should be. In a way this was part of the problem: the lower ranks and ratings who are doing all the hardest work and/or fighting at the operational level *should* be seen and heard.

Before I left, I did see MacArthur the man.

His headquarters the Dai Ichi Building is the large grey stone pile across the moat from the Imperial Palace. Every day at two o'clock the General left his offices to return for lunch to his home in the former American Embassy. Also every day at two o'clock, the steps of the Dai Ichi were crowded with throngs of Japanese craning their necks to catch a glimpse of the General before he stepped into his waiting staff car.

Citizens of Tokyo were generally shoddy and unkempt then, the glaze of defeat still in their eyes. One wondered why they waited here so patiently for so many hours at a time. Was it the idle curiosity of the hopeless? Or were they really building up a new Emperor worship for MacArthur Taisho, as their newspapers feared? I was standing among them mulling over these questions when there was a stir in the crowd. It surged forward, pushing me to the rear. I recovered my balance just in time to see a cloud of dust as MacArthur's vehicle whirled away.

Resolved to beat the Japanese at their own game, next day *I* surged through the press of them at the entrance and sat down to wait inside the Dai Ichi building where sightseers were not allowed. Promptly at two o'clock the elevator descended, the doors slid open, and out stepped General of the Army Douglas MacArthur himself.

I had to look twice to distinguish him from his aides, for he was not nearly so tall as he looked at the angle used by newsreel cameras.

"Hello! How are you?" He was smiling, and he seemed to be looking straight at me.

"F-fine, sir," I stammered—embarrassed that I had been caught staring, too flustered even to remember to stand up.

He nodded and passed with his entourage into the waiting crowd.

This little incident left me with the very strong feeling that a five-star general who could be kindly amused by the stares and the sloppy, civilian behavior of a WAC lieutenant was hardly the cold aloof personage his public relations officers had made him out to be—that he was, in spirit, far taller than the press angle had been making him look. This legend of austerity was undoubtedly valuable in his dealings with the Oriental traditionalists, who are conditioned to believe that the more inaccessible the person is, the more important. But I remember thinking then, how unfortunate that it could not have been dropped with his own troops who, being Americans, were all too prone to mistake reserve for arrogance.

I doubt very much that our most important complaints from Korea to SCAP headquarters in Tokyo, the protests that did seek remedy for "burning issues," ever reached the General. His staff did almost nothing about them, and no one ever told us why.

General MacArthur finally did visit Korea on August 15, 1948—on the occasion of Syngman Rhee's inauguration as president of the South Korean Republic. It was far too late then for anyone even on the highest level, to mend the failures we had made because of lack of support from his command—the failures this history of our Military Government has shown you.

The General had been in Korea just once before. In 1905 First Lieutenant Douglas MacArthur went there as aide to his father, Major General Arthur

MacArthur, Jr., who was observing Japanese conduct of the Russo-Japanese War. Many things in the country had drastically changed since then, but also Douglas MacArthur's knowledge of the entire Far East had steadily grown along with his rank. I find it difficult to understand why a man with his grasp of Asian affairs and their growing importance to our own, could have failed to see that Korea was a vital spot—and dangerous.

Our Military Government supply-support problem of which I have made example was, I am told, traceable to our Congressional system of allocations. The allocations for Japan were large. The allocations for Korea were small. And that was that. Only the most scrupulous attention to consideration and cooperation between our American commands in the two countries could have created a workable balance and as I have said, the Americans in Japan were as indifferent to Korea as the government in Washington.

Few Americans anywhere seemed to think Korea was important. In our own command in Seoul were very few who would have understood even if Congress had shown the foresight to do what history now is full testimony it ought to have done: send to Korea all that could possibly be spared of everything we asked for, when we first asked for it. I am no longer talking about snack bars and lettuce. I mean all the personnel and material and everything else we would need to work with to do a supremely good job of Military Government, as good a job as MacArthur's staff were doing for Japan—a job which not incidentally they were doing in close compliance with guidelines direct from our nation's Joint Chiefs of Staff.

The thing I am wondering is whether, in his dealings with the Joint Chiefs, our forthright General ever did speak out for Korea. It certainly is possible that he did. But if so, if he addressed to his Chiefs any questions at all concerning this aspect of his command. these were never published.

Those of us who served under him in Korea are still waiting for our answers.

COLLABORATOR'S NOTE:

Following her retirement from San Diego Mesa College in 1979, Ada Leeke tutored Asian graduate students at University of California San Diego and reviewed books professionally. In 1981 she did this double critique:

Hirohito, Emperor of Japan, by Leonard Mosely
    Prentice-Hall, Inc. 371 pp., 1966
American Caesar, Douglas MacArthur
    1880-1964, by William Manchester
    Little, Brown and Company, 793
    pp., 1978

This excerpt from her review supplements Leeke's chapter on MAC ARTHUR'S KOREA by offering you some of the answers she and her colleagues in Military Government were waiting for:

Korea of all places proved to be MacArthur's blind spot. We were the end of the line, receiving what was left over from Japan in supplies and creature comforts. He seemed to think Korea was outside his parameter of defense or interest, even though it was technically under his command. Just five weeks before the North Korean invasion MacArthur said such a thing was unlikely, because world opinion would never permit it. As Manchester puts it, "He was dead wrong."

We all know of the early humiliating defeats when the United Nations forces were almost pushed off the end of the peninsula, of the subsequent long stalemates which MacArthur broke by his brilliant end run around opposing forces and his surprise landing at Inchon, followed by his swift and sustained drive north to the banks of the Yalu River which divides North Korea and Manchuria.

When the Chinese, feeling their homeland threatened, poured thousands of volunteers across the river (another threat which MacArthur completely and inexplicably failed to anticipate) the fateful confrontation between the General and President Truman had its onset. It will probably always be debated as to who was right.

MacArthur advocated bombing the bridges across the Yalu and the enemy sanctuaries in Manchuria. When Truman objected on the grounds it might widen the war and invite Soviet intervention, MacArthur was furious. He called the decision "the most indefensible and ill-conceived order ever forced on a field commander in our nation's history." In his view, once an enemy was engaged there was no substitute for complete and total victory. He retaliated in typical high-handed MacArthur fashion, going over Truman's head by giving interviews to the press and writing to various members of the Congress—something Truman could not forgive—until the President and Commander in Chief finally muzzled him. Manchester compares General MacArthur at this point to the tragic heroes of Greek plays who were figures of massive integrity and powerful will, struggling nobly but vainly against fate and who were ultimately brought down by a fatal defect in their own characters:

> "So it was with Douglas MacArthur. Brave, brilliant and majestic, he was a colossus bestriding Korea until the nemesis of his *hubris* (Greek for excessive pride) overtook him. He simply could not bear to have his career end in a checkmate. In his view it would be a betrayal of his mission. Now, as he saw it, his enemies everywhere were threatening his last crusade."

As Truman saw it, given his character and convictions, this was insubordination and there was but one thing to do. If he would not cross the Yalu he would cross the Rubicon and he did so on April 10, 1951 by drafting a gruff and abrupt presidential order relieving General of the Army Douglas MacArthur of his command.

But as Manchester reports, MacArthur was to have the last word in his memorable address to the joint session of Congress:

> "Why, my soldiers asked of me, surrender military advantage to the enemy in the field?" He then paused theatrically and his voice dropped to a whisper. "I had no answer." He ended with words few will forget. "The world has turned over many times since I took the oath on the plains at West Point, and the hopes and dreams have long since vanished. But I can still remember the refrain of one of the most popular barrack ballads of that day which proclaimed most proudly that 'Old soldiers never die. They just fade away.' And like the old soldier of the ballad, I now close my military career and just fade away—an old soldier who tried to do his duty as God gave him the light to see that duty. Goodbye."

However, MacArthur did not just fade away. He ran unsuccessfully for President on the GOP ticket, served as chairman of the Remington Rand Corporation, and with great prescience (as well as anguished hindsight) on his deathbed in Walter Reed Hospital in April 1964 he begged President Lyndon Johnson to stay out of Vietnam.

Manchester sums up his opinion of MacArthur in these words:

> "No more bafflingly exasperating soldier ever wore uniform. Yet he was endowed with great personal charm, a will of iron, and a soaring intellect. Unquestionably he was the most gifted man of arms this nation has produced."

Paved with Good Intentions

We failed in what we set out to do for Korea after World War II. We failed for the same reason a teacher does, if she expects perfection from her students. We failed for the same reason a parent does, who may not be a divinely good example but who is as strict a human as if he were. We failed because we did not understand and were not in the least prepared to cope with the powerful opposing forces already lined up against us. We failed because we tried to bring to Korea a theoretical state of democracy which we never have had at home—which probably never existed anywhere, outside the covers of a political science textbook.

Some people say our occupation of Korea was part of a new foreign policy. We have no real foreign policy. Not yet. Ever since my lower division work in political science at Chaffey College I have been advocating that we take foreign service out of the political arena and make of it the profession which it is: my first step were I responsible, would be the founding of a foreign service academy.

This country so far, in foreign affairs, is like the amoeba. What the amoeba needs to sustain itself it engulfs; whatever its undeveloped sensory capacity for irritation tells it is bad medicine, it tries to avoid. Now there is nothing malicious about the amoeba. Nothing expansively capitalistic or imperialistic: nothing acquisitive nor aggressive in its naturally harmless existence among other entities. But certain things it must engulf—for survival—and certain other things escape.

The only thing at all definitive so far is our quest for a direction toward a concerted policy. This quest both past and present has lain in the too-often dis-concerted efforts of our countrymen who have represented us abroad—as in Korea. I want then, to tell you who were not in Korea something about the Americans who were. For these people, far more than any immediate objective or any theoretical policy, were the reason why our occupation of Korea was what it turned out to be—a thing in all ways human, and incomplete. It was brave, idealistic, well-intended—sometimes remarkable for its clumsiness, at other times inspired. It was, as I have said, not a success. But of such human adventures will our foreign policy, when at last it does emerge in a vertebrate body, be born. And it will then be not the Secretary of State's foreign policy, nor the President's. It will be neither the work of gifted statesmen nor the fault of political bunglers elected through unsavory influence. It will be what we the people did, in unison and in parts, wherever we went to represent our country. And why we were sent will not in the long run, even in matters of a firm policy, prove nearly so important as the fact that we the people were there.

Even as private citizens, we represent the United States in whatever we do, wherever we go. This is inevitable and always has been. Whatever their ideology, people are people everywhere, and everywhere they think the same: as you are, so must your country be. They feel this way particularly, of course, about persons in uniform.

During my last three years in Korea as a Military Government officer I found that my colleagues and I represented to the Koreans all of our past failures as a country, as well as our current commitments.

Thus far, individual American enterprise in the Far East had earned for us along with the money—even among liberals of our own country—the name of exploiter.

As a mining family, the Leekes lived as "exploiters" in Korea for many years. I would like to point out a fact that meant nothing to the natives, whose own lives were even more primitive for the most part: Nearly all the Americans who came to Korea lived as we did—without benefit of radio, plumbing or adequate diet. And they did not deliberately come to exploit but rather to earn a living at their profession or trade. Engineers, missionaries, business men or whatever, they worked there precisely as people do here, because that was where the work was.

So very many, like us, were fervently thankful to go back home when their jobs were finally done—where they could turn on a faucet that would work, or listen to the radio, or have their teeth fixed. We preferred the wordless vacuum cleaner, the amiable honest automatic range and the miraculous washing machine to that "army of servants" our Stateside friends so envied.

So very few of these Americans ever made their fortunes—and so many fled with only a single suitcase before the flood tide of our latest failure in Korea, in June of 1950.

In the United Nations last-ditch effort to see that the bath was drained with the baby still upright in the tub, Secretary General Trygve Lie characterized South Korea as a foster child placed on the UN's doorstep because its natural parents had quarreled.

The unhappy fact was that one of the parents was refusing to acknowledge the child at all, contending that it was illegitimate and the North's own bouncing republic the sole and true heir. And to all practical intents and purposes it mattered little that the infant was nominally on somebody else's doorstep: the single parent in the South was still giving its all in child support.

The three-month period of May, June and July 1948 saw the dissolution of Military Government in preparation for the inauguration of the foundling Republic of South Korea on August 15, the third anniversary of Japan's surrender—in token of the Koreans' keen appreciation of the nicities of timing.

As the last survivor of the Department of Public Information I was assigned to write a history of our activities to be combined with those innumerable other histories the Army keeps tucked away in its archives. Sitting alone in the large room which had once accommodated nearly 50 Americans, trying to piece together what was left of the files after our many peregrinations, I was given more than enough time and cause for thought.

"To What Extent Have Our Major Objectives Been Achieved?' was one of the outline topics I was supposed to fill in—in the customary cautious and stuffy military language . . . Well, to what extent had we succeeded—not just in the Department of Public Information and in the Publications Section of which I was Chief, but in all the rest of United States Military Government in Korea as well?

There were those who said we had failed utterly and entirely—that personally we were superior and arrogant, that we blundered in, changed age-old habits and customs the Koreans didn't want changed, insisted that the American way and sometimes "the Army way" was the only right one—and that in all our busy officiousness we had served only to confuse the ignorant and alienate the educated.

This cynical attitude was best expressed in a lengthy doggerel by an unknown wag, ODE TO USAMGIK. Its first and last verses:

The Army they say in Korea reigned:
for three long years they there remained.
Civilians and soldiers and generals too,
strutting and swaggering—my God, what a crew.
There were doctors and lawyers and bakers and bums,
there were drunkards and psychos and all sorts of crumbs.
From the ends of the earth misfits came on the run,
Hodge raised his baton and the whole farce was begun . . .

. . . The Koreans—poor devils—at first were delighted
for they felt that their wrongs all now would be righted.
They laughed and they cheered and they shouted hooray,
but slowly their joy has turned into dismay.
Their faces show pain though with Far East applomb:
what they have learned is, our worst threat is not the A bomb!

Unfortuantely even those of us less cynical than "Author Unknown" must face the fact that Some Of The Above is all too true. Americans did not turn out to be nearly as wonderful as Koreans had first thought. And as always, the reputation of the many suffered for the actions of the few.

A small but telling proportion of our countrymen behaved outrageously. A few of them, from black market activities and just plain loot, *had* "gone home rich" as Kimm Kiu Sic declared. There was one famous case which did not come to light until after the outbreak of the Korean War, of an American colonel's living with a Korean woman and having a son by her. This in itself would not have been notorious cause for consternation, but the lady turned out to be a Korean Mata Hari, collecting information, weapons and even jeeps from her paramour to pass on to her Communist boy friends in the north.

Others in Military Government ordered Korean officials around as if they were domestic instead of public servants, and called them "gooks," the disparaging GI term for natives everywhere. Ironically the authentic Korean name for Americans is *Migook*—*gook* standing for people and *Mi* for American in the Korean language.

Even among the many conscientious and well meaning MG officers the turnover had been abysmally high. Everybody wanted to go home as soon as his time was up, and the bewildered Koreans no sooner got to know one American officer than he was replaced by another—usually with different ideas. Also, American and especially Army red tape was only one degree less annoying and destructive than Japanese red tape, and the delays and confusion it caused were often damaging and sometimes tragic.

Koreans blamed us, and rightly so, for the division of their country at the 38th parallel—which one State Department spokesman had admitted "was picked up by a tired meeting on a hot night in Potsdam." The Koreans further felt that the line had been indelibly drawn by our ideological conflict with the Russians, and that left to themselves from the beginning they could have erased it in a matter of weeks. Now after three years of occupation propaganda a nation that should have been one was artificially divided in two, and the only way they saw to put the pieces back together again was civil war.

On the material side no one could deny that in our three years we had greatly benefited the Koreans. The hated word "trusteeship" had been changed to the more euphemistic "aid and assistance program." Under this program in the first year, between May 1946 and March 1947, Korea received items valued at $91,000,000—including clothing, grains, petroleum, fertilizers, medical supplies, vehicles, locomotives and heavy equipment. We had greatly reduced illiteracy, rehabilitated the transportation and communications systems, stepped up agricultural production by the importation of chemical fertilizers, repatriated and fed and clothed and housed over two million refugees—the list could go on ad infinitum. Not surprisingly, the Korean people were not particularly grateful for any of this, seeming to take it all for granted as a child takes for granted the food and clothing and general comfort provided by its parents.

I remember how surprised I was to find that even Mr. Kim Tong Soo shared the common Korean philosophy on this point. One day as he and I were putting the paper to bed down at Kyongsong Ilbo, he laid an accusing index finger on a report of the arrival of the most recent shipment of UNRRA clothing.

"That story make me mad," he said.

"Why in the world should it, Mr. Kim?" I asked, amazed.

"*I* not get any clothes," he muttered.

It did little good to explain to him that UNRRA clothing was only for the destitute. When largess is being passed around, everybody wants his share.

What was not being passed around, only too many were trying to take by stealth. The stealing and pilfering which began as a mere trickle down the drain in early days of occupation, at last swelled to a gully wash that threatened to sweep everything before it. This was a private as well as public affair: every dependent house however modest was a bristling arsenal of home-made booby traps and assorted odd-looking weapons. In our own area, the Army's Seventh Division, every home on the block save our own had been broken into at least once, leading us to believe that most of the robberies were inside jobs. We felt certain we were spared only because of our faithful and formidable old *amah* who had fought her way back down from North Korea to be with us again.

Worst of all, between pilfering on the docks and in the warehouses, less than half the staggering volume of supplies coming in from the States to rehabilitate and relieve the Korean economy were reaching their proper destination. Koreans simply seemed to feel that we Americans were so rich, both individually and as a nation, that anything they took would never be missed.

Some of the neater jobs showed a morning-calm cunning and ingenuity that raised our grudging admiration. One instance was the gang who dug a hole into the rear of the Post Exchange through which they placer-mined a ceiling-high wall of cigaret cartons until, when the theft was discovered it was nothing but a tottering honeycomb of empty boxes. Also on our list of legends was the contractor who, having won on his bid to build us a Commissary warehouse, sublet another contract to lay a tunnel up through the floor—so he could remove the supplies he helped to store. If all this energy and ingenuity could only be put to some constructive honest use, Korea could be another Switzerland.

As I sat typing away at the history of D.P.I., I was thinking nostalgically of the old-time Koreans I had known. Of their wonderful simplicity, their native honesy and virtue. How few of these we had seen in the past three years—among the city slickers, the politicians, the entrepreneurs, the thieves and the repatriated dregs and sweeps who had accompanied the Japanese armies. But they were still there, I hoped and prayed—out in the country, watching over their rice paddies in the little valleys between the dragon tooth mountains. I had recently heard the story of an old farmer who waited half a day by the side of the road to return a wallet which had bounced out of a passing jeep; but incidents like this seemed to be growing fewer, and Koreans like those I had known were becoming harder to find. Was this moral deterioration all we had to show for the money and materials we had poured into the country? Here too, had Uncle Sam become Uncle Sugar whom nobody loved nor even liked except for what he had in his pockets?

At the end of July 1948 I finished my report, turned it in, closed up the American side of Department of Public Information and packed my trunk for the States.

The Korean Director of Department of Public Information Dr. Clarence Rhyee, being a good Syngman Rhee man, was retained by the new government. Some time later he came out with a pamphlet entitled "Korea Reborn," printed in English for the edification of the Americans still left in his country. My mother sent it to me with "Hunt for a word of thanks!" penned in the margin.

I did. The only mention of the United States was this:

> *Welcoming the American and Russian Armies of Liberation, the Korean people were stunned to find that a secret agreement had drawn a line through the middle of their land, separating families, violating a unity centuries old, and dividing their industrial north from their agricultural south. Strangled by an Iron Curtain, and ruled by foreign armies of occupation, their dream of freedom collapsed in bitter disillusionment.*

This then, out of the mouth of my own Department, is how they felt about us all along. We were just one more of the "foreign armies of occupation," a talking, sitting anathema. Such a thing would be no less galling to us, no matter what assistance or improvement the occupation were to bring. Perhaps the worst of our failure was this spiritual one: a complete lack of understanding of Korea's need so like our own, for a proud and sustaining and unified nationalism.

So, *hunt for a word of thanks* . . .

Perhaps in taking final stock we should be completely honest with ourselves—not simply honest about the Koreans. What we did in Korea we did not do for them but for ourselves. Korea had existed for 4,000 years, with few in our two-century-old republic ever having paid her any attention. Not until we suddenly felt threatened by the Asian influence of an alien ideology did we feel called upon to bestow on this ancient Land of the Morning Calm the blessings of democracy. And they should thank us for something as alien to them as communism is to us?

As for the gifts we came bearing, I am remembering the words of dying St. Vincent de Paul to his youngest novice, on the eve of her first work of charity: "Love them, my child. Only for your love will they forgive you the bread you bring."

That perhaps was our most grievous fault. We did not love the Koreans, and they knew it.

I left Korea on August 3, 1948 after a month's leave in China, but my parents stayed on with the Economic Cooperation Administration, thus leaving me a window open on this second phase of our democratic experiment.

I regretted just having missed the inauguration of the Sovereign Republic State of Korea and of its president Dr. Syngman Rhee. I could however vividly imagine these historic ceremonies and their pageantry . . . the Capitol steps hung with banners and flags as they had been on Sam Il Day and so many other occasions . . . the Korean officials dressed in frock coats and striped pants which the Japanese had taught them were proper formal wear and which they somehow contrived to come wearing . . . the streets lined with uniformed Korean police, rifles at rest, clear down Pennsylvania Avenue which was the broad thoroughfare leading from the Capitol all the way out to Kimpo airport where General MacArthur was landing in his first visit to Korea . . . the snow-headed Dr. Rhee, raising his hand to take the oath of office—seeing at last the realization of his lifelong ambition.

It was inevitable that Dr. Rhee, first president of the 1919 Provisional Government, should be elected to lead the new state by an overwhelming majority of the National Assembly (180-6). Doubly inevitable, since all his formidable rivals were now dead.

There are those who call Dr. Rhee a Fascist, this despite the fact that he studied under Suh Jai Pil and under Woodrow Wilson at Princeton. Others contend that his political cast and feelings belong to an age in which the concept of fascism was totally unknown: they maintain that he is in fact one of the last authentic living Bourbons, and they cite in evidence a remark he once made in talking back to an American Army officer: "You need not tell me the great value of political unity," Dr. Rhee said testily. "There is no one in Korea who understands it better than I do. As you will observe from my speeches, I have frequently said that I want all Koreans without exception to follow me."

Soon after taking over, President Rhee began to negotiate for the withdrawal of American troops, contending that their presence violated the rights of a sovereign state: foreign troops stationed on its soil gave too much the appearance and the feeling of continued occupation. This very strong feeling on the part of all Koreans was understandable in the light of the innumerable military occupations they had suffered way back to the time of Genghis Khan; but viewed in the light of future events it was to prove unfortunate to say the least.

The Russians as usual beat us to the draw: they announced complete evacuation of all their forces at the end of December 1948. Accordingly the United States made arrangements to follow suit by the end of June 1949.

Although the Koreans of the South emphatically did not want us, they just as emphatically did want our weapons. All during the month of June long parades halted traffic in the busy streets of Seoul while the participants carried, waved or wore banners reading

AMERICAN ARMY
COMPLETE YOUR DEFENSE MISSION
GIVE US ARMS PRIOR TO EVACUATION
PROTECT DEMOCRATIC SOUTH KOREA!

In response to these pleas the occupation troops left $110,000,000 worth of equipment when they departed—including 14 tanks, 2,000 bazookas, 4,900 vehicles, 100,000 rifles—and an uninventoried but very large number of 37- and 57-millimeter anti-tank guns, howitzers and mortars fully supplied with ammunition.

With this material we left behind 500 officers and men to form the Korean Military Advisory Group under the command of Brigadier General W. L. Roberts. Its mission was to make an efficient fighting force of the Korean Constabulary, which along with the Korean Coast Guard had been established in the early days of our Military Government occupation.

Clad in GI helmets and U.S.-style uniforms the new South Korean Army looked like a snappy outfit as it paraded along Pennsylvania Avenue or went through its field maneuvers. So pleased was General Roberts that before he left for home in June 1950 he called it "the best damned shooting army outside the United States." Why then did it not stand up better under the initial Communist drive into South Korea?

Dr. Rhee has accused our military aid of being "too little and too late." It is true that of $10,000,000 appropriated by Congress for arms and equipment for South Korea, only $200 was spent and this single item was all that arrived in the country after we left: 56,000 feet of communications wire! The failure to use the congressional appropriation has been blamed by officials involved as one "largely due to procurement red tape."

General Roberts has since stated that the Koreans were not given more tanks, heavy artillery or combat planes in the first place because the United States was afraid the South Koreans would attack the North. It is a fear which was not unfounded. Even back in our Military Government days an advisor in the Department of National Defense had told me that his Constabulary officers boasted, "Just you give us the guns and the tanks, and we'll take care of those North Koreans."

The carrying out of this threat would have left our country in a most embarrassing position: we would either have to back up our obstreperous child in an aggressive war, or disown it—abandon it to face alone the certain death of punishment at the hands of the Communists.

Meanwhile the "aid and assistance" program was going on apace. On February 10, 1949 Congress appropriated $60,000,000 under the E.C.A. program for Korea. On that same day, ironically, sentences ranging up to 12 years were demanded in the trial of 13 members of the Korean National Assembly accused of dealings with the Communists. Some, it seemed, didn't know on which side their bread was better buttered.

The following June another $150,000,000 was appropriated at the personal request of President Truman. This brought our total military and economic aid since 1948 to an approximate total of half a billion dollars.

Under the Economic Cooperation Administration the American advisors became "Consultants" and the Korean heads of departments were exalted to the status of Minister. There was more intermingling of ideas, more social contact between the two groups. Koreans usually presided now at meetings. The officers clubs from which they had formerly been barred were open to Korean guests, and even the ban on dating Korean girls was lifted. On the surface things were radically different from the old Military Government days.

Our Military Government people who stayed to serve in E.C.A. reported tremendous superficial progress. The city of Seoul was cleaned up. Traffic control improved. Railroads ran on time. In most of the major industries production increased from 25 to 200 percent, largely due to American technological help and supplies. A firm word in the ear of Dr. Rhee which he passed on to the Korean police even put a stop to most of the thievery.

On a living everyday individual scale however, the slow pace of the Orient was still doggedly declining to turn itself into the hustle and bustle of the West. American technical consultants still found most Koreans only partly emerged from the age of the bull cart, in matters mechanical inept and without the dimmest grasp of western ideas of order and efficiency. My father tells me that in the coal mines the workers dug only about half a ton per day per man as compared to the four tons produced on average by American miners. The Koreans, he said, would rather sit and hold conferences than get their hands dirty—with the result that there were on most jobs he was observing, too few indians and a lot too many chiefs. He saw little hope of immediate change, and reminded me of the sage truth of that timeworn epitaph which says HERE LIES AN OCCIDENTAL WHO TRIED TO HURRY OR CHANGE AN ORIENTAL.

Just emerging as they were from the handcraft state, Koreans were also in technical and mechanical affairs unwise. They wanted beautiful up-to-date equipment, such as the expensive xray machines which they saw in the catalog, but they did not have the faintest idea how to operate or take care of them. And during all of this period they were when left to themselves failing to oil, do parts replacement, or otherwise do proper maintenance on the equipment they already had.

Of 200 new trucks my father at great effort had procured from Japan to haul urgently needed coal from the mines at Samchok to Seoul, he saw at least 20 broken down and abandoned by the side of the road within two weeks.

All these general and specific comments and cases add up to a dim promise for a far future. As everywhere else in the world, there were some good and competent exceptions—but in the eyes and the opinion of our American Consultants, not enough to make a team. Most Koreans with their new modern machines were behaving like children with new toys: they played with them, broke them up, and threw them away.

Deterioration of the roads is another thing hindering modernization and mechanization. Only the bull can stolidly plod along through the ruts, mud and chuck holes which make up the rural Korean roads during most of the year. Many Consultants felt that unless the Koreans could show more enterprise and pride in improvement and upkeep of these roads, the whole Korean economy would sink back into the bullcart age from which it was still trying to emerge.

When asked why his countrymen had so much national pride and so little civic or personal ambition one Korean replied: "The Japs took it all out of us, those 40 years." So Japan was still the favorite whipping boy.

In the ideological realm too, we failed to win the hearts and the minds of the Korean people. A major aspect of this failure is that we had been put in the unfavorable light of having "backed" the Rhee government, although this was not strictly true. That Dr. Rhee's regime was growing in unpopularity was shown by the second election held at our insistence in May of 1950. Incumbents and party regulars were beaten soundly, while non-partisans took the majority of the seats. In conformity with the Korean Constitution, however, Rhee held his own position as head of state.

No conceivable claim can be made that the Rhee government is a democracy in the civics-book sense. It remains largely a police state shot through with corruption and graft. Only one instance of the latter is The Case of Miss Louise Yim.

For services rendered to Dr. Rhee while in the United States unofficially representing Korea to the United Nations, Miss Yim was named, incongruously enough, Minister of the Department of Commerce and Industry. In April 1949 the government's Special Investigating Committee, entrusted with unearthing illegal activities among government officials, charged Miss Yim with receiving more than 20,000,000 yen (or *won* as it was now called) from prominent Korean businessmen for her election campaign. The report of the Committee implied that she had in return passed out favors from her high position to those who had chipped in. Dr. Rhee's defense of his protégé was more staunch than convincing.

Given all the problems briefly summarized here, the future looks bleak enough with no help from the worst of our own mistakes: having allowed the cutting in two of this little country. The two parts of Korea can no more be permanently divided than the two charges of a magnetic pole. Our best contribution to the future of Korea would be to march up to the Manchurian border and erase forever a line which we should never have allowed to be drawn in the first place.

Failing this—and I do agree in principle with President Truman's restraint in this highly volatile matter—we must apply ourselves assiduously to the way that things are. There will be a tremendous job of rehabilitation and extended training, for which we cannot shirk our fair share of responsibility. But rather than go it alone, as we have done in the past, I suggest that we step down and allow the United Nations to take full charge of the raising of its foster child. A new UN Commission largely Asiatic in character would spike the favorite propaganda thrusts of the Communists: AMERICAN WALL STREET IMPERIALISM and WAR OF THE WHITE RACES AGAINST THE YELLOW.

No one should for a moment expect that the north and the south Koreans are going to settle down immediately and live in peace side by side after all the upheaval and grief they have been through. However, an election for all Korea supervised by the United Nations and protected by the UN police force (which if possible should be expanded to include many more countries, but preferably neither Russia nor the United States) would be an important first step. Such an election would determine as far as is humanly possible just what kind of government the Koreans actually do want—rather than what kind they may have been forced or propagandized into accepting.

There is no doubt that during this election and afterward, there would be more cracking of heads and more subversive activity. United Nations supervision backed up by controlled force would have to remain for some time to come—until the Koreans both north and south of the 38th parallel have learned in living everyday terms that their future lies in working together.

What I am proposing is an ideal. But it is a practical and realistic textbook solution which if it could be brought into being, could not only redeem us as well as the Koreans, but also could stand before the whole world as a first shining example of our new United Nations' power for justice and peace.